T0261482

A Customer-oriented Manager for B2B Services

Series Editor
Régine Teulier

A Customer-oriented Manager for B2B Services

Principles and Implementation

Valérie Mathieu

WILEY

First published 2022 in Great Britain and the United States by ISTE Ltd and John Wiley & Sons, Inc.

ISTE Ltd
27-37 St George's Road
London SW19 4EU
UK

www.iste.co.uk

John Wiley & Sons, Inc.
111 River Street
Hoboken, NJ 07030
USA

www.wiley.com

Library of Congress Control Number: 2021949549

British Library Cataloguing-in-Publication Data
A CIP record for this book is available from the British Library
ISBN 978-1-78630-757-6

Contents

Foreword

I am very honored that Valérie Mathieu has asked me to write the Foreword to her book. I am even more honored because the CMA CGM Group, with its customer-oriented approach, is a perfect example of how the dynamic relationship between a company and its markets can create value for both the customers and the service provider. The organization of our group, a world leader in maritime shipping and logistics, shows how a company in the B2B sector can create value by giving an important role to its managers. It is, therefore, a great source of pride to contribute to this book, which will be read by students and professionals alike, as our group works, as part of its employer brand strategy, to showcase the variety of jobs in the transport and logistics sector, an emblematic B2B sector.

Relationship with the customer at the heart of value creation

CMA CGM has always placed the customer at the center of its concerns and priorities. This may sound like a banal statement for a company, but in reality, we have to know how to organize ourselves to listen to their needs, and even try to anticipate them, in order to design and deploy efficient services, and establish processes around customer satisfaction.

The core service we have historically offered – transporting goods in maritime containers – can very easily be done by one of our competitors. Hence, for several years, we have witnessed a "commoditization" of our industry. Faced with a plethora of choices, our customers chose their shipping line based on price alone. The industry engaged in an intense price war, which each of the players hoped to compensate with volumes. This logic led to overcapacity and serious difficulties for the sector in 2009 after the subprime crisis. It was at this point that the group completely rethought its approach, seeking to answer the question of how we could get a client to choose our services, even if we were more expensive than the competition.

This was a long-term process that required constant dialogue with our customers and partners. We had to understand what their problems were, what their challenges were and what they expected from their shipping company.

And contrary to what we thought, price was not necessarily the determining factor in their choice. One example of this is the premium service we have implemented on the *Transpacific*, which has been a huge success. This service makes it possible for an exporter or importer to have guaranteed space on a vessel and offers faster availability thanks to a Fast Lane upon arrival in Los Angeles.

Paradoxically, we know today that the peripheral services related to maritime transport are our best assets to develop customer loyalty and relationships.

An evolving relationship

And we are evolving with them: with the acquisition of CEVA Logistics, the CMA CGM group has changed its nature and is now able to offer end-to-end services, anywhere in the world. We can support our customers throughout their supply chain, with air transport solutions for shipments that do not suffer any delay, or warehousing and storage solutions to delay the pace of imports according to their specific needs.

The group has also started a major digitalization movement, in order to give our customers more autonomy in managing their supply chain.

Finally, we have taken the relationship to the extreme, since, thanks to our global presence and the customer portfolio we have developed over the past 40 years, we have become a true "business provider" for our customers who would like to expand internationally and are looking for reliable suppliers or partners.

We are now seeing that the future of our competitiveness is being played out in areas that were still weak signals in our industry 10 years ago. For example, our group launched studies on the use of liquefied natural gas as a fuel for our container ships, and today, ships capable of carrying 23,000 containers are operating service using this cleaner source of propulsion. In the meantime, environmental issues have become absolutely crucial for our largest customers, who now require their carriers to have a committed environmental approach.

The manager: essential interface for a win–win customer–supplier relationship

In maritime transport, it is absolutely crucial to know how to foresee. This is true for the crews on our ships. It is also true for our employees who are in the field every day, in contact with our customers. At CMA CGM, we have developed a very decentralized organization, where the managers of the agencies in the countries where the group is present (160 worldwide) occupy a central position. They are the ones who can inform the lines about changes in their region, about development projects, about companies that are setting up internationally or that, on the contrary, have growing import needs. Hence, we pay particular attention to their training. We have a training program specially dedicated to them, so that they have all the necessary assets to listen to our customers. It is on the initiative of these field managers that we develop new lines, new offers and new services. It is thanks to them and the special relationship they have with their customers in the field that we can set up pilots that can then be extended to our range of services. This requires them to be in a constant position of observing and actively listening to their clients and to maintain an ongoing dialogue with managers and department heads at headquarters so that they can study, design and deploy tailored and adapted solutions. This requires true teamwork, with each party working hand in hand to create value.

The experience and organization of our group resonate with the book we are holding in our hands. It offers an excellent opportunity to question, learn and progress for B2B companies like the CMA CGM Group that I represent.

Thierry BILLION
General Secretary
CMA CGM Group
November 2021

Preface

On August 19, 2019, 181 presidents of the largest companies in the United States, from Apple's Tim Cook to Amazon's Jeffrey P. Bezos to Dennis A. Muilenburg of Boeing, gathered at the influential Business Roundtable and signed a manifesto that redefines the mission of business[1]. Believing that maximizing shareholder value should no longer be the company's primary focus and sole priority, the signatories put stakeholders, first and foremost the customer, at the heart of corporate responsibility: "delivering value to the customer", "investing in employees", "dealing fairly and ethically with suppliers", "supporting the communities in which the company works", "protecting the environment" and "generating long-term shareholder value".

Although the most skeptical commentators see it as an obligatory and principled response to the injunctions of investors[2] and the most enthusiastic as a revolution, the manifesto nevertheless brings to light principles that are widely debated in management. Stakeholder theory and customer orientation, long discussed in the academic literature and applied to corporate practices, clearly resonate with this new definition of the company.

Since the 1990s, customer orientation has been recognized as a major alternative approach to positioning on price, product or business, in order to

1 www.businessroundtable.org/business-roundtable-redefines-the-purpose-of-a-corporation-to-promote-an-economy-that-serves-all-americans.

2 Laurence Fink, CEO of Blackrock, the world's largest asset manager, in his January 2019 annual letter asked business leaders to think about their purpose and get involved in societal issues. www.businessinsider.fr/us/larry-finks-annual-letter-2019-1-2019.

better face competitive challenges and keep the company focused on its markets. This customer orientation is seen as a strategic orientation of the company, validated by the general management, and put in priority in the hands of the senior executives of the C-suite such as CMO (Chief Marketing Officer), CCO (Chief Customer Officer) or CXO (Chief Customer Experience Officer). So how do we get this customer orientation down to the field? How can we find the intention of the leaders in the practices, behaviors and interactions, especially with customers, and more broadly with all the stakeholders of the company? How can we also free up energy at all levels of the company, so that customer orientation can be enriched on a daily basis? The key lies in the involvement of managers and field staff in the implementation of customer orientation and in their strong adherence to its principles and values. A customer-oriented manager becomes, on the one hand, the intermediary between an ambition and its realization, and on the other hand, the activator of a continuous renewal of this orientation as close as possible to the market.

B2B[3] service is a legitimate, necessary and urgent field of application for customer orientation. First, it is legitimate to focus on it specifically because of its economic dynamism. In an economy dominated by services, business services account for nearly half of the value added of market services and concentrate exports[4]. While the field of services is widely covered by a large body of academic and managerial literature, it is essentially focused on B2C. It is, therefore, necessary to deepen our knowledge of B2B services, beyond a simple superposition of the specificities of the service offer on the one hand, and the B2B market on the other hand. As markets inevitably mature, the challenges of increased competition and commoditization of the offer will sooner or later make customer orientation particularly urgent for service providers. A technical or business orientation, in which customers are insufficiently understood in their complexity and taken into account in their needs and expectations, is still dominant. While managers in charge of developing and launching offers are in a strong and lasting relationship with customers, observation of practices too often leads us to the findings that, at best, the players are not aware of their role in this customer orientation, and that, at worst, they reproduce approaches and behaviors that are in conflict

---

3 B2B stands for business-to-business, that is, a service offered to a private or public company or to a professional, as opposed to B2C, business-to-customer, a service offered to consumers.
4 www.insee.fr/fr/statistiques/4255850?sommaire=4256020.

with the balance between customer satisfaction and the profitability of their company.

The aim of the book is to provide managers with the skills that will enable them to launch customer orientation in their area. More precisely, the objective is to provide managers with the knowledge and tools necessary to implement this customer orientation by themselves, while involving their extended team. With this in mind, the book develops a structuring approach in four steps: *Understanding the fundamentals of customer orientation in B2B services* (Part 1), *Knowing the customer* (Part 2), *Making the most of the offer* (Part 3) and *Delivering the service* (Part 4).

While this new managerial skill may seem burdensome at first, both in its acquisition and implementation, the resulting benefits should encourage the manager to go beyond this apparent difficulty of the task. Managers will benefit in three ways: as collaborators, they will be recognized for having implemented a strategic intention and vision; as leaders, by consolidating the performance of their perimeter, their legitimacy will be reinforced and as a person, the pleasure of building a relationship of trust with their clients and their extended team will give their actions the meaning so often sought after.

This book is not about management, but for managers, whether they are active or aspiring. Regardless of the size and stakes of their perimeter, whether they are accompanied by functional teams or in autonomy and whether they are employees or entrepreneurs, managers will be able to easily adapt the roadmap proposed here to their specific context. Engineering students, most of whom will sooner or later be called upon to take on managerial responsibilities, will be made aware of this customer orientation issue as soon as they start their studies. Finally, and more broadly, students in management schools will find in the book a complement to their courses in management and marketing of services, which are increasingly common in training, as well as to courses dedicated to B2B, which are rarer. In view of the numerous internships and work-study programs offered to these students by B2B service providers, this supplement should enable them to more quickly grasp the specificities of their missions.

November 2021

Understanding the Fundamentals of Customer Orientation in B2B Services

Introduction to Part 1

This first part presents the three fields at the intersection of which this book is positioned: customer orientation, service and B2B.

Customer orientation is debated in a dense literature that focuses on defining and justifying its benefits and also questions how it can be implemented in the company. This customer orientation is a direct result of the marketing culture. Translated into a managerial skill, customer orientation allows for the diffusion of a marketing culture within the organization as a whole.

The interest in the service sector in particular is justified by its economic weight and also indicates the need for a specific approach in order to implement customer orientation in a relevant and effective way. It is, thus, necessary to understand the reality, the stakes and the specificities of the service sector in order to introduce an adapted customer orientation.

As for the focus on B2B, it implies a significant distinction between B2B and B2C in terms of customer orientation. One often resorts to endless lists to justify what distinguishes B2B from B2C. Two specificities are in fact essential to understand, the first one is related to the market and the second one to the relationship. While the first one, involving the notions of channel and derived demand, is specific and exclusive to B2B markets, the second one, which defends the importance of the relationship between customers and their providers, is also at the heart of B2C. Nevertheless, the B2B relationship, because of its strength, depth and duration, is becoming a major managerial challenge.

Customer Orientation

1.1. Outlines and challenges of customer orientation

Customer orientation is an old hand in the young management literature. The concept appeared a little more than 30 years ago[1] and has been attracting the attention of researchers, consultants and managers ever since.

1.1.1. *Customer orientation framework*

1.1.1.1. *Customer and market orientation*

The notion of market orientation was first proposed in the academic literature, whereas a more managerial literature would later more easily refer to the term customer orientation. Market orientation has historically been defined on the basis of three pillars: customer focus, broad involvement of different departments in the company and profitability (Kohli and Jaworski 1990, p. 3).

Here the preferred term "customer orientation" seems to be more anchored in reality and pragmatic. While the invisible hand of the market does not need to be tightened, on the other hand, many customers will judge one by one's handshake! Nevertheless, a full and true customer orientation must also integrate competitive issues and more broadly a set of stakeholders that will be presented throughout the book.

---

1 More precisely, it is the term market orientation that first appeared in 1990, in the title of an academic article (Kohli and Jaworski 1990).

1.1.1.2. *Customer orientation between cultural and behavioral approaches*

The literature on customer orientation has been built around two approaches that are more complementary than truly opposed: the cultural approach and the behavioral approach. The cultural approach speaks of a state of mind, values, beliefs and attitudes, rituals and even a philosophy, centered on the customer in order to create maximum satisfaction and achieve the ultimate goal of long-term profitability[2]. The behavioral approach is more operational and focuses on understanding the conditions for implementing this orientation. It questions the organizational behaviors to be implemented, the organizational and managerial structure to be put in place and the actions to be taken to make this orientation effective[3]. More specifically, we are looking at the conditions that will enable the organization to understand the market, to anticipate its changes and to respond favorably. Information is at the heart of this behavioral approach: the collection of information, its dissemination and its translation into strategies, decisions and actions.

Today, we find these two questions in the company: how to spread an actual customer culture within the organization and also how to implement strategies, actions and behaviors that are truly customer oriented.

1.1.2. *Benefits of customer orientation*

Customer orientation is an investment for the company. Specific resources will be mobilized to implement this new orientation. Disseminating a strong culture within the company, listening to the customer, collecting and analyzing information, relaying it and building offers that take this information into account are all direct or indirect investments for the company. The question of return on investment is legitimate. Does customer orientation have a positive impact on the company's performance? Will this investment in customer orientation really be profitable? Will it allow the company to really build a sustainable competitive advantage? Will it be a means of differentiation from the competition? These are all questions that can be asked at the overall level of

---

2 The cultural approach is defended in particular by authors such as Webster (1988), Narver and Slater (1990), Deshpandé *et al.* (1993) and Day (1994).

3 Authors such as Kohli and Jaworski (1990) and Matsuno and Mentzer (2000) have taken a more behavioral approach to market orientation.

the company to validate a customer orientation, as well as for managers who wish to implement this orientation in their area.

1.1.2.1. *Customer orientation and company performance*

The impact of customer orientation on factors such as return on investment (ROI), sales volume, market share and sales growth was quickly identified. Studies based on different methodologies have validated the link between customer orientation and performance, including:

– **a meta-analysis of 114 empirical studies** (Kirka *et al.* 2005): the results of 114 empirical studies on the effects of market and customer orientation on performance were analyzed. The results show that market and customer orientation have an impact of 20% on a company's ability to innovate, 10% on its market share and 7% on its profits and sales;

– **a longitudinal study over three periods** (Kumar *et al.* 2011): the observation of the same sample of companies, in 1997, 2001 and 2005, showed that the first companies to have adopted a market orientation benefited from an impact that was twice as strong on their sales and profits, compared to companies that adopted this orientation later;

– **an analysis based on a sample of 7,500 French companies** (Pekovic and Rolland 2012): the relationship between customer orientation and EBITDA per employee was highlighted. The relationship appears to be stronger the more the company operates in a competitive, growing and uncertain market.

If we consider the strategic dimension of company performance, it is widely accepted that market and customer orientation have an important impact on building a sustainable[4] competitive advantage. It is by keeping abreast of what customers expect, how their preferences evolve and change, and by disseminating this information widely internally, that the company and its members can identify the resources needed to build the value expected by the markets, and thus maintain a sustainable competitive advantage. By going beyond the simple observation of current customer expectations, and by asking questions about the evolution of these expectations, the company puts itself in a position to capture latent market

---

4 This benefit was put forward by Narver and Slater in 1990 (Narver and Slater 1990) and reaffirmed in 2000 by Slater and Narver (Slater and Narver 2000).

expectations more quickly than its competitors and thus to strengthen its competitive position over time (Narver *et al.* 2004).

1.1.2.2. *Customer orientation and its impact on the customer*

Customer orientation can be expected to trigger positive attitudes and behaviors from the customer. Customer satisfaction is of course the most important consequence of customer orientation. As a corollary to this satisfaction, the customer's positive word of mouth is more active and thus has an impact on the company's reputation. Customer loyalty is also easier to build from a stronger customer relationship (Mullins *et al.* 2014). Knowledge of markets, consideration of customer expectations and preferences makes it possible for the company to develop and perform better services (Hartline *et al.* 2000).

The employee, immersed in a customer-oriented culture, should more naturally engage in building strong and lasting relationships with the customer. It is the values, attitudes and behavior of the customer-oriented employee that will increase the customer's trust and encourage the latter to behave cooperatively with the service provider (Poujol and Siadou-Martin 2012). It is, therefore, not surprising that customer orientation is an approach that is now in demand in the sales context (Julienne and Banikema 2017).

1.1.2.3. *Customer orientation and its impact on the employee*

From a more social perspective, a number of empirical studies have sought to establish a relationship between a company's customer orientation and the work attitudes of its employees. These studies have focused on variables such as job satisfaction, organizational commitment and involvement. Strong links between customer orientation and these variables have been consistently shown. Customer orientation would build *esprit de corps* among employees, greater job satisfaction as well as greater commitment[5].

1.1.3. *Implementing customer orientation*

While it is clear that customer orientation is a relevant strategic approach, the challenge is to implement it within the company. A gap may exist

5 Several studies, some of them based on empirical validation, elaborate on these different links (Kohli and Jaworski 1990; Piercy *et al.* 2002; Esslimani 2012; Zablah *et al.* 2012; Sousa and Coelho 2013).

between what the company says about its customer orientation and what its customers say about it.

When it comes to customer orientation, it is not so much what the company says, but what the customer perceives. Cap Gemini Consulting, in a 2014 research report, highlighted this potential divergence: "56% of companies claim to be customer oriented. Only 12% of their customers approve!"[6]

1.1.3.1. *Commitment of top management*

Top managers must have a strong and clear message about their commitment to customer orientation. The discourse must transmit a vision centered on this orientation, be able to mobilize energies by carrying a deep meaning beyond the conventional and act on the cognitive and affective organizational systems[7]. The speech must be concrete, illustrated with real examples, stories and real-life experiences and animated by symbols in order to be as mobilizing as possible. The speech must be followed by strong and clear decisions about the organization, its structure and the chosen strategy. To be effective, customer orientation must be based on more fluid decision-making processes and more cross-functional collaboration between teams and departments. New organizational and management methods, like the agile method, which puts the customer at the heart of the process and encourages team autonomy and accountability, are likely to be effective in supporting the implementation of customer orientation.

Guillaume Faury, successively CEO of Airbus Helicopter, then of the civil aviation branch of Airbus and finally of the Airbus Group, has always put the customer first in his speeches:

> We are starting the year under a new brand, Airbus Helicopters, which is for us much more than a new name, it touches the

---

6 This is a CCO Council source taken from Cap Gemini Consulting: Cap Gemini Consulting (2014). L'expérience client à tout prix. *Journal of Marketing Revolution*, no. 2, p. 13 [Online]. Available at: www.capgemini.com/consulting-fr/wp-content/uploads/sites/31/2014/02/journal_ of_marketing_revolution_2_capgemini_consulting.pdf [Accessed 31 August 2019].

7 This commitment from the highest managerial levels is emphasized by Weick (1995), Kennedy *et al.* (2003) and Bonin and Jean (2010).

DNA of Airbus, it touches ambitions like customer satisfaction, quality, safety, industrial efficiency.[8]

The first challenge for Airbus is obvious. It's about serving our customers and ramping up production.[9]

We need to prepare the Airbus of tomorrow in order to better serve our customers, increase our competitiveness and grow in a sustainable way.[10]

1.1.3.2. *Manager's adhesion*

The quality of management, and especially middle management, is widely considered to be the essential foundation for implementing customer orientation (Hartline *et al.* 2000). This is all the more true in a service environment where proximity to the field, the market and the customer is strong. The managerial challenge is twofold: managers must be personally involved in a customer orientation and must also lead their team in the direction of a customer orientation. They must set an example, be a reference in terms of behavior and attitude for their team. Their decisions and arbitrations must clearly show the priority given to the customer. They will also have to be attentive to the way in which their team lives this customer orientation. Customer relations and customer satisfaction are not always easy realities for employees. They must also encourage collaboration between teams, functions and departments. It is up to managers to allow their teams to break out of their strictly defined perimeters. There cannot be customer orientation without autonomy and risk-taking. Expected managerial skills are, therefore, inevitably enriched. While traditional skills, like technical skills for an engineer, remain essential, they are no longer sufficient to effectively implement customer orientation. This customer orientation becomes particularly sensitive in the context of the implementation of entrepreneurial projects with high technical content.

---

8 www.youtube.com/watch?v=rOo42TBYF4k&t=3s.

9 Grasland, E., Bauer, A., Trévidic, B. (2018). Interview de Guillaume Faury : "Avec Airbus le CSeries a tout pour devenir un succès commercial majeur". *Les Echos*, June 1 [Online]. Available from: www.lesechos.fr/2018/06/guillaume-faury-with-airbus-the-cseries-has-everything-to-be-a-major-commercial-success-991647 [Accessed 12 September 2019].

10 Airbuzz (2019). *The Magazine for Team Airbus.*

Studies have looked at the leadership style that would be most conducive to the implementation of a customer orientation in the company. They highlight a specific leadership style called transformational leadership[11]. The transformational leader succeeds in getting colleagues and collaborators to go beyond their personal interests, to converge in the same direction and to win their support by explaining and bringing meaning (Barabel and Meier 2015, p. 614).

ZEBOX is an international incubator-accelerator of innovative start-ups, located in Marseille, specialized in the transport, logistics, mobility and Industry 4.0 sectors.

Entrepreneurs are strongly committed to the development of their innovation in order to confirm the existence of a market, to demonstrate the adequacy between the latter and their offer and to attract customers. Their ability to do so will be a determining factor in their entrepreneurial success.

Nevertheless, there are several types of entrepreneurs, including those who are more business-oriented and those who are more "techno"-oriented. The business-oriented profile launches itself into the creation of a company following different professional experiences, which led him to the observation of a non-optimal or even non-existent response to an observed problem. The projects carried by this type of profile are generally relatively well aligned with the satisfaction of a need. A second profile, which could be called "technologist", develops a technological solution before specifying its potential on the market. The risk associated with such an approach is to see efforts pushed in a non-optimal direction because they do not address a real market problem.

A structure like ZEBOX, positioned on innovative projects, essentially dedicated to B2B, combines both types of profiles. In both cases, one of ZEBOX's missions, supported by its corporate partners[12], is to help entrepreneurs better understand the markets in which they are evolving (or will evolve) with regard to their specificities and their assets. The support on the strategic aspect of the project will make it possible for them to take the necessary distance to confront the market and exchange with multiple profiles of potential customers. This exercise will be an opportunity

---

11 The transformational leader theory was initiated by Burns in 1978 (Burns 1978). For a summary of work on this form of leadership, see Gotteland (2019).

12 ZEBOX relies on corporate partners who are leaders in their field: CMA CGM, Accenture, BNP Paribas, Centrimex, CEVA, CIMC, EY, GTT.

for them to refine their value proposition, thus maximize their chances of meeting their market and eventually make the decision to pivot as soon as possible.

The transition from the incubation stage to the acceleration one validates a certain maturity in the customer orientation of the entrepreneur and the start-up. Incubation enables the identification of a first strategic client or a key partner in order to better structure an initial business model. Acceleration builds on this first step to move towards a more ambitious implementation that will make it possible to develop a first portfolio of customers. The evolution of the project during the incubation phase, and then its transition to acceleration, will be all the better if the entrepreneur is able to capitalize on the network to which the incubator/accelerator gives him/her access.

Box 1.1. *Testimony of Matthieu Somekh (CEO and Co-Founder of ZEBOX, Former President of France is AI and Former Director of Entrepreneurship and Innovation at the École Polytechnique)*

Finally, it can be assumed that there are employees in an organization who have a sort of natural customer orientation at an individual level. These employees can then serve as role models and influence the level of customer orientation of their colleagues or their team (Lam *et al.* 2010). Empirical studies have confirmed that a leader's level of customer orientation influences the level of customer orientation of his or her colleagues (Liao and Subramony 2008), and this is particularly true in the context of sales management (Lam *et al.* 2010).

1.2. Marketing as the source of customer orientation

By putting customers and their satisfaction at the heart of its ambitions, customer orientation is intimately associated with marketing. Customer orientation can also be considered as the implementation of the marketing concept[13]. To better understand the marketing concept and its implementation is then a natural step to better enter in the customer orientation.

---

13 In the very first lines of their introduction, Kohli and Jaworski make it clear that "the term 'market orientation' means the implementation of the marketing concept" (Kohli and Jaworski 1990, p. 1).

1.2.1. *Marketing as a corporate culture*

The marketing concept and customer orientation are very similar in their cultural dimension, since they are both customer-centric business philosophies.

1.2.1.1. *The customer at the heart of the marketing concept*

Peter Drucker, the historical and essential author of management, was one of the first to approach the concept of marketing in the early 1950s. He emphasized that marketing is not a separate and specific function of the company, but a global approach of the company from the customer's point of view. In this sense, the marketing concept is close to a specific corporate culture based on a set of shared values and beliefs that put the customer at the heart of the company (Deshpandé and Webster 1989). Today, it is easier to speak of a marketing perspective as opposed, for example, to a product or production perspective that focuses more on the company's offer and its capabilities.

By holding marketing accountable for the return on investment of its actions, the company and its shareholders have pushed it to focus on and value two major assets: the customer and the brand. Customer equity, defined as the sum of a customer's lifetime values, and brand equity, are now recognized as key elements in the evaluation of a company. In B2B environments in general and service environments in particular, it is possible to hypothesize that customer equity plays a more important role than brand equity[14].

1.2.1.2. *The search for a balance between satisfaction and benefit*

Marketing and customer orientation are not seen as an expense but as an investment that needs to be skillfully managed by finding the right long-term balance between customer satisfaction and profitability for the company. If it is quite simple to satisfy the customer as it is also quite simple to reach a given level of profitability, the difficulty lies in maintaining the balance between satisfaction and profit. Some people will want to allow the occasional and exceptional "sales opportunity" that offers the company a much higher profitability than customer satisfaction. But this imbalance cannot be maintained over time without running the risk of exposing oneself

---

14 This hypothesis is proposed by Romero and Yague (2015), among others.

sooner or later to a competition that, either for the same level of profit, manages to offer the customer greater satisfaction, or for the same level of satisfaction, manages to lower the price with lower profitability. The opposite situation, where satisfaction is higher than profitability, is just as dangerous, since it is difficult to imagine the company maintaining its competitiveness over time with such an imbalance in its profitability.

When managers in B2B environments are asked about the percentage of business achieved at such a fine balance, they are often surprised by the proportion of those who acknowledge that they satisfy the customer more than the company. B2B seems to be much more characterized than B2C by an imbalance between satisfaction and profit in favor of the former. The duration of the relationship, the proximity with the customer, the passion for the job and the technical challenge can explain a lesser vigilance of managers on this balance. By wanting to please the customer, the employee often pleases himself/herself first. In this proximity to the customer, which is the basis of customer orientation, saying no to the customer is often difficult.

However, there are several reasons why a manager might say no to a client:

– financial and economic reasons: in order to achieve what the client requests, it would be necessary to commit resources (financial, technical, human, time, etc.) that would be too great in relation to the expected return;

– technical reasons: the provider is not sure to be able to bring the expected result to the customer;

– safety reasons: what the client asks for carries a risk both for his/her own employees and for the service provider;

– image reasons: what the customer asks for can damage the reputation of the provider.

However, we must distinguish between over-quality and customer delight, because while we must guard against the former, the latter is inherent to customer orientation. The notion of delight appears in the field of marketing through the notions of customer satisfaction and experience.

Customer delight, considered as a positive emotional reaction (Oliver et al. 1997), consists of surprising the customer, in going beyond his/her expectations (see Table 1.1 for illustrations of these differences between over-quality and enchantment).

Over-quality	Enchantment
– A superior performance that the provider brings compared to what is expected by the client or what was agreed upon.	– An additional value that the provider brings to its client that is not expected or asked for.
– The customer does not always perceive this superior performance.	– The customer clearly perceives this additional value.
– This performance has no real value for the customer.	– This additional value brings the customer an additional benefit.
– The customer is not willing to pay for this performance.	– The customer might be willing to pay to benefit from this value.
– The extra performance does not lead to increased customer satisfaction.	– Customer satisfaction is positively (and strongly) impacted.
– But it can mean an additional cost to the provider (direct or indirect, visible or hidden costs).	– It may involve additional cost for the provider, but it is a profitable investment.
– Example: cleaning an additional space that was not foreseen in the contract.	– Example: cleaning a site at the end of an intervention.

Table 1.1. *Over-quality and customer delight*

This issue of the balance between satisfaction and profit questions the relationship between the service provider and its client more broadly. In complex cases and relationships where the financial and technical stakes are high, the question of the commitment of the service provider and also of the client arises. The service provider is not the only one involved in maintaining the balance between satisfaction and profitability. This balance will also depend on the client's commitment to participate, to get involved in the long-term, to aim towards a partnership relationship. This will in turn justify for the service provider the investment in a relationship which, if it can be unbalanced at the beginning, because it requires taking a real risk, turning out to be more balanced in the long-term.

1.2.2. *Strategic marketing*

Strategic marketing will determine the company's long-term orientation by deciding on its positioning and its major strategic axes. Strategic marketing relies on a thorough analysis and knowledge of the market and the environment in order to align its structuring decisions.

1.2.2.1. *Knowledge of the market and the environment*

In accordance with a strategic methodology, the analysis of the environment is divided into micro- and macro-environments. The micro-environment is close to the notion of market and groups together actors with whom the company has regular interactions and who constitute its daily life: clients, customers, distributors and intermediaries, and influencers. On the other hand, the macro-environment has a less direct and more distant influence on the company, but it is just as real and can sometimes be very strong[15].

Analyzing one's environment means first of all locating and identifying each of the actors and then understanding their positions, their evolutions and their strategies in order to anticipate their impact on the company and also to think about collaborative perspectives or the ways in which the company can influence them. This will be the subject of the second part.

1.2.2.2. *Positioning the offer*

Positioning is the heart of strategic marketing by ensuring that the offer has a clear, distinct and privileged place in the customer's mind so that it is preferred over competing offers. Positioning is the ultimate step in strategic marketing that begins with market segmentation and continues with segment targeting. These key marketing concepts are essential to the implementation of a customer focus[16].

1.2.3. *Operational marketing*

Operational marketing refers to the implementation of the marketing strategy. The notion of marketing mix is very closely associated with operational marketing.

1.2.3.1. *The marketing mix*

The marketing mix is the set of tools available to marketing to act on the buyer's behavior in order to achieve the defined marketing strategy and reach the company's objectives. McCarthy's 1960 classification is widely

---

15 The PESTEL model summarizes the six main influencing factors in a mnemonic way: political, economic, socio-cultural, technological, ecological and legislative.
16 These principles are discussed more fully in Chapter 8.

adopted. It groups these tools into four categories called the "4Ps": product, price, place, promotion.

A good marketing mix must above all be coherent, coherent between actions and coherent with the positioning.

1.2.3.2. *Expanding the marketing mix*

While the "4Ps" model remains the reference model of operational marketing, the means of action of marketing have been progressively widened. In order to be in phase with the evolution of the markets, it is obviously necessary today to integrate the notions of experience, customer relationship, digitalization, social responsibility and sustainable development. Among the various extensions of the marketing mix concept and more specifically of the "4P" model, it is interesting to look at two of them: the "4Cs" model and the concept of the services marketing mix.

The "4Cs" model, proposed in the 1990s by Robert Lauternborn, is a sort of transposition of the "4Ps" model from the supplier's point of view to the customer's one (Lauternborn 1990). Each of the four elements of the 4Ps is translated into a customer benefit in the 4Cs model: customer needs, convenience of buying, cost to satisfy and communication. The "4Cs" model thus emphasizes the customer orientation of marketing even more explicitly.

The concept of the service marketing mix was developed in the early 1980s by service marketing specialists to better integrate the specificity of service[17]. Three other levers of action were added to the traditional "4Ps" model: people, physical evidence and processes. The people element takes into account the actors who play an essential role in the service relationship. These are the staff in contact, the customer and the other customers. The physical evidence reflects the importance of the physical environment in which the service takes place as well as the different tangible elements that are present during the relationship with the customer. The process refers to all the procedures, mechanisms, activities and flows necessary to provide the service. Each of these three service-specific levers is dealt with in the last part of this book.

---

17 This model of a marketing mix extended to the service, which is widely used, was first proposed by Booms and Bitner in 1981 (Booms and Bitner 1981).

1.3. The manager's customer orientation in response to marketing issues

We must distinguish between function and culture. If marketing as a function is now facing certain challenges, its original culture, that is, the customer at the heart of the company, is more relevant than ever. The customer-oriented company can neither be the exclusive project of a department, even if it is a marketing department, nor the strategic vision of the management committee alone. Making customer orientation a managerial skill is, therefore, a response to the challenges of marketing and a powerful lever for achieving the promises of a customer culture in the company.

1.3.1. Restricted marketing

1.3.1.1. Credibility crisis

Marketing suffers from many prejudices and is often referred to in a pejorative way in order to discredit or denigrate people, approaches and actions. It is considered vulgar, manipulative and even dishonest. In some sectors, it is now clearly in conflict with aspirations for sustainable development and greater social justice. In industrial, technical and scientific environments, where it is well established within large companies and organizations, it is still little appreciated by the players because it is probably not well known. Is it then to counter these negative energies that the title of Chief Customer Officer is now more easily given to the old-fashioned Chief Marketing Officer? Or should we see it as a final questioning of marketing's actual capacity to take an actual interest in the customer, so that it is necessary to integrate its *raison d'être* into its title?

1.3.1.2. Difficulty of implementation

It is not uncommon to hear marketers themselves complain about their difficulty in "getting their strategy down", implementing their plans and actions, and to encourage managers to use the tools they develop. These complaints are particularly common in service and B2B environments, because in these environments, marketing has difficulty achieving its objectives without the collaboration of field managers. Marketing undeniably suffers from being confined to its own function and department, which gives it a bureaucratic image, far from the reality of the field and the operational people. It is, therefore not surprising that its plans, strategies, actions and tools do not arouse much enthusiasm among employees. On the other hand, marketing and customer orientation have always recognized that they cannot be confined to one department or one function, but that they must be implemented with the support and involvement of the entire organization. It has, therefore, become a challenge for the marketing department to succeed in involving all the company's employees, and especially the managers, in the achievement of its own objectives. The interrelations and interdependencies between marketing, operations and human resources have always been at the heart of the specificity of service management. The questioning of the interrelationships between marketing and sales is going in the same direction, and we are witnessing a merger between the marketing function and the sales function, with the emergence of new marketing and sales departments.

1.3.1.3. *Customer orientation as an extension of marketing skills at the managerial level*

The solution to involve managers in the implementation of a marketing culture, strategies and tools would be to increase their competence in customer orientation. For companies without a marketing department, the customer-focused manager would become the key player in the deployment of a customer culture. The customer-oriented manager does not have to "do the job" of a marketing department, but must have the ambition to fully integrate the customer into his/her vision and actions. The marketing department and customer orientation will never be in competition but ideally in collaboration and synergy.

Increasing the manager's customer orientation skills also has the advantage of responding to aspirations for autonomy and freedom in relation to what is often perceived as diktats emanating from headquarters and of moving towards greater horizontality. Customer orientation, by valuing the customer and, therefore, the relationship with the other and the human being, gives meaning to the work that the manager often complains of having lost. If the manager's job no longer inspires dreams[18], wouldn't enriching it with

---

18 This managerial malaise is clear from a study conducted by IPSOS for BCG between June 14 and July 15, 2019, based on 5,000 respondents (1,500 managers and 3,500 managed). BCG and IPSOS (2019). The end of management as we know it? [Online]. Available at: http://media-publications.bcg.com/BCG_Theendofmanagement-vimpression.pdf   [Accessed 19 October 2019].

the confidence that the company has in them for maintaining its most precious asset, the customer, be likely to re-enchant it?

1.3.2. *Marketing exposure to technological challenges*

1.3.2.1. *The digital revolution*

The term digital revolution clearly indicates the impact that digital technologies will have on society in general and on business in particular. Marketing is one of the privileged targets of this digital revolution and cannot survive without integrating it. We talk about digital marketing or e-marketing to gather strategies, methods and tools that rely on the Internet. Digital marketing is an undeniable means for marketing:

– to have access to the market since it has become a common habit for each of us to go on the Internet to search for information on an offer or a company;

– to maintain or increase its market share since the share of online commerce is constantly increasing;

– to enrich the relationship and the customer experience since the customer asks for a digital experience in addition to, or sometimes instead of, a physical experience;

– to launch new offers that can even be based on new business models since the economic model of platforms is constantly conquering new sectors.

Indissociable from the Internet and the digital revolution, data and customer data in particular, poses a triple challenge for marketing: technical (how best to collect and analyze data), strategic (how best to transform this data to create value) and ethical (how to create value from customer data without compromising their freedom and respecting their rights). The data issue is particularly important for B2B services[19].

---

19 In an interview with *Les Echos*, Thierry Breton, European Commissioner, states, "the main future source of data is in industry, and more generally in B-to-B applications": Grésillon, G., Perrotte, D., Barré, N. (2020). Thierry Breton: "Pour accéder au marché européen il faudra accepter nos règles". *Les Echos*, January 8 [Online]. Available at: www.lesechos.fr/monde/europe/thierry-breton-pour-acceder-au-marche-europeen-il-faudra-accepter-nos-regles-1161004 [Accessed January 9, 2020].

Thus, initially adorned with many virtues, digital technologies pose new challenges to marketing: managing e-reputation, meeting the demand for transparency that the Internet has promised, working in the immediacy that the Internet allows for, rethinking the skills of marketers as well as salespeople, etc. But above all, the Internet questions the role that humans can retain in this immaterial channel of relationship to the market and the customer.

In a 2019 report[20], research firm Forrester notes:

> In reality, a flood of repetitive messages now inundates consumers. They're exhausted by the endless drone of bland ads that follows them around the Internet, clogs their inboxes, and interrupts their social media feeds. Over time, customers' receptivity to marketing has eroded, their interest has waned, and they're actively taking steps to block out the noise with tools like ad blockers and intelligent agents (e.g. Amazon's Alexa).

1.3.2.2. *Artificial intelligence*

Artificial intelligence (AI) is progressively penetrating companies to simplify, streamline and optimize many tasks and processes. Marketing is using AI to enhance the customer experience through, for example, chatbots, robots and other facial recognition technologies. In a recent study on customer evaluation of AI, Cap Gemini manages to show that customers are quite satisfied with the experiences they have with AI technologies but that human intelligence remains essential to build a truly exceptional experience[21]. In the same vein, Yann Le Cun, head of AI research at Facebook and a major researcher in this field, explains in his latest book that AI does not have a common sense or a global representation of its environment that would make it possible for it to react to new and unexpected circumstances (Le Cun 2019). Hence, human intelligence remains unique and essential today to analyze and react to new situations.

---

20 Forrester (2019). Embrace A New Marketing Era: End Dissonance And Drive Growth. Report, Forrester Research, Inc, p. 4 [Online]. Available at: https://go.forrester.com/marketing-strategies/ [Accessed 30 August 2019].

21 Capgemini research institute (2018). The Secret to Winning Customers' Hearts With Artificial Intelligence. Cap Gemini [Online]. Available from: www.capgemini.com/wp-content/uploads/2018/07/AI-in-CX-Report_Digital.pdf [Accessed 27 August 2019].

1.3.2.3. *The manager's customer orientation as the human face of marketing*

The challenges of digital technologies, data and AI are real and strong. The company must fully address them, and marketing is in the best position to integrate them into the customer's perspective: its status as a function attached to the top management, its resources as a major department of the company and its global vision of all the company's businesses and markets, more than authorize it to do so, oblige it to do so. And yet, human element, through its intelligence, sensitivity and proximity, remains necessary in the construction of a full customer relationship and can even become a valuable counterweight to the potential drifts of the all-technological approach. By effectively sharing the customer orientation with the manager, the marketing perspective regains or maintains its humanity. Nevertheless, the manager must remain vigilant in developing and maintaining a mastery of these technologies, which will be more and more essential in the exercise of his/her responsibilities.

2

Reality and Challenges of Service

2.1. Economy and service: from data to discourse

Service dominates the economies of developed countries and plays a major role in development. While economic analysis strongly emphasizes the weight of service in our economies, interpretations of this reality are far from consensual.

2.1.1. *The economic weight of service*

2.1.1.1. *Service in general*

The work of the British economist Colin Clark in the 1940s, taken up by the Frenchman Jean Fourastié, proposed classifying the economy into three sectors: the primary sector, the secondary sector and the tertiary sector[1]. This classification is the basis for our national accounts and INSEE today. But it must be recognized that service activities cannot be confined to the tertiary sector alone. If we look more closely at the activities of companies

---

1 The primary sector includes activities that exploit natural resources, mainly agriculture and fisheries, but mining activities are also often included in this sector. The secondary sector includes companies that process raw materials, mainly industry and construction. The tertiary sector is often defined by default in relation to the first two sectors and includes activities that do not belong to the first two sectors; it mainly includes services, distinguished into market and non-market services.

belonging to the first two economic sectors, we find two other types of service activities:

– internally deployed services such as research and development or the corporate university;

– services that the company combines with its products in order to position itself more advantageously in its markets or to benefit from additional financial income. The car manufacturer has long offered financing and after-sales services. The winegrower is increasingly interested in new activities such as wine tasting, cellar tours and the creation of an art center.

Without even including this tertiarization of the primary and secondary sectors, the tertiary sector has a major weight in all economies, and particularly in developed economies like France. In terms of value added, the tertiary sector accounts for 79.2% of the French economy and 56.8% if only the market services sector is taken into account. The primary and secondary sectors represent only 1.8% and 19%, respectively. In terms of employment, the hierarchy of sectors is the same; the tertiary sector accounts for 80% of total domestic employment, the secondary sector for 17% and the primary sector for 3% (INSEE 2019a).

2.1.1.2. *The B2B service*

Looking at the diversity of the tertiary sector, we see the vitality of a specific set of services, that of business services. This vast group of heterogeneous activities, which share the common denominator of offering services to companies rather than to households or consumers, represents a particularly dynamic field in the French economy. In the INSEE nomenclature, business services are not explicit, but they correspond broadly to scientific and technical activities and administrative and support services (see Box 2.1).

In its July 2019 note (INSEE 2019b), INSEE does not hesitate to describe business services as the main driver of growth, emphasizing the particular vitality of specialized scientific and technical activities.

This dynamism can be seen from the main economic indicators listed in Box 2.2.

The new nomenclature introduced in 2008 by INSEE does not define an explicit category for services rendered to businesses. INSEE considers that these activities correspond broadly to sections M and N of its nomenclature.

Section M includes scientific and technical activities:

– legal, accounting, management, architecture, engineering, control and technical analysis activities;

– scientific research and development;

– other scientific and technical activities (advertising and market research, veterinary activities, other specialized activities – design, photography, translation and interpretation).

Section N includes administrative and support services:

– rental and leasing activities;

– job-related activities;

– travel agencies, tour operators, reservation services and related activities;

– investigations and security;

– building and landscaping services;

– administrative and other support activities (including call centers, trade show and convention organization, etc.).

Box 2.1. *Business services according to INSEE*[2]

– **Number of companies**: nearly one in four service companies is a company that caters to the B2B market; 18% of companies in France are B2B service companies (INSEE 2018a).

– **Business creation**: the INSEE considers the business services sector to be the most dynamic in terms of business creation, ahead of trade. A quarter of the businesses created in France are in the field of business services (INSEE 2018b).

– **Number of jobs**: 10% of jobs are in the business services industry and they account for 13% of service jobs (INSEE 2018c).

2 www.insee.fr [Accessed September 4, 2019].

– **Job creation**: in its target scenario for job growth in France over the period 2012–2022, France-Stratégie-DARES considers the business services sector to be the largest contributor to net job creation (France Stratégie-DARES 2015). The business services sector has the largest number of job creations (INSEE 2019a).

– **Value added**: business services concentrate half of the value added of market services (47%) (INSEE 2018d).

Box 2.2. *Dynamism of business services*

2.1.2. *Discourses on service*

While the economic data are unambiguous and show a reality dominated by services, the interpretations can diverge and confront us with a multiplicity of discourses, often contradictory, on the contribution of services to the economy. Should we be enthusiastic or worried about this quasi-monopoly of services?

Analysts of the macroeconomic evolution of societies have established two opposing theses[3]: the post-industrial thesis and the neo-industrial thesis.

2.1.2.1. *Post-industrial thesis*

The proponents of the post-industrial thesis identify the growth of services as the major feature of contemporary economic history and support the reality of the transition from an economy dominated by the industrial sector to one dominated by services. Daniel Bell in the United States, Alain Touraine in France and, before them, Jean Fourastié have been the founders of this post-industrial society (Fourastié 1949; Touraine 1969; Bell 1973). The research studies of Engel and Baumol provide the main foundations of this thesis. Engel's law postulates that the increase in purchasing power leads to a shift in household demand from basic necessities (especially food) to mainly industrial goods and then to "higher" goods (health, education, leisure), which are essentially services. Baumol's work has established that productivity growth is on average faster in the industrial sector than in the service sector, justifying the irreversible decline in industrial jobs[4]. Today, major market trends, such as the aging of the population and the preference

---

3 These two theses are set out by the economist Jean Gadrey (1992, p. 21).

4 Although new technologies, such as digital technologies and AI, are now challenging the lower productivity in services.

of younger generations for use rather than possession, only amplify household demand for services. The behavior of companies, by outsourcing a growing number of activities, from the simplest (maintenance of green spaces) to the most complex (human resources management), also contributes to the dynamism of the services market.

In a complementary way, the industrial company feeds into this reality by backing an ever greater share of its added value with service activities. The "servuction" or tertiarization of industry are the terms commonly used today to indicate the potential of services to enhance and differentiate the industrial company's offer. The growing technical complexity of products naturally leads to the launch of specific services to support their marketing, distribution, consumption and recycling. This is one of the challenges of Industry 4.0, which relies on the Internet of Things and data to offer innovative services that generate new sources of profit.

Finally, at the very heart of development economics thinking, while industry has long been considered indispensable for growth, the idea is now also defended that a country can develop from its service activities without necessarily relying on a solid industrial sector. India illustrates this new path of economic development, with growth based in particular on the export of advanced services, rooted in new technologies (Kucera and Roncolato 2016).

2.1.2.2. *Neo-industrial thesis*

However, in the 1970s, and more recently during the 2008 crisis, given the slowdown in growth, an opposing trend emerged that attempted to re-evaluate the importance of industry. The "neo-industrial" thesis attributes a driving role in the economy to the industrial sector. According to this thesis, the tertiary sector cannot develop without maintaining a dynamic in the industrial sector. In the face of deindustrialization, the neo-industrial thesis displays the will – some would say the utopia – of reindustrialization. Reindustrialization seems to be a powerful political argument, since it is regularly used by actors from all sides of the political spectrum, up to and including Bruno Le Maire's recent statement that "France has not chosen to be a service economy"[5].

5 Statement by Bruno, the mayor: Vie publique (2019). Déclaration de M. Bruno Le Maire, ministre de l'économie et des finances, sur une politique économique en faveur du plein emploi, à Paris le 15 octobre 2019 [Online]. Available at: http://www.vie-publique.fr/discours/271205-bruno-le-maire-15102019-politique-economique [Accessed on October 21, 2019].

The neo-industrial thesis probably contributes to a certain distrust of service. In a 2013 book, Augustin Landier and David Thesmar denounced three preconceived notions that they believe are sinking France, to use the title of their book (Landier and Thesmar 2013):

– misconception number 1: a France without industry would be Disneyland;

– misconception number 2: to save jobs, one has to save the industry;

– misconception number 3: a real engineer works in a factory.

The economic and health crisis at COVID indirectly revives this debate on reindustrialization and gives new weight to the neo-industrial thesis.

2.1.2.3. *Towards complementarity between industry and service*

While the extreme positions around which the "post-industrial" and "neo-industrial" theses are developing are attractive, the fact remains that they leave a damaging void, that of the complementarity between service and industry[6]. Indeed, we are forced to admit that as industrial companies develop and become more complex, they not only outsource more and more of their activities (security, catering, etc.) but also call on increasingly sophisticated services (engineering, consulting, waste treatment, etc.). In this sense, industry is fueling the demand for services. But can we also reject the hypothesis that the dynamism, innovation, growth and sophistication of service activities support and assist industrial development? In particular, industrial companies cannot meet the digital challenge without the support of digital service companies to rethink their strategy, processes and offerings. Industry 4.0 will undoubtedly be both industrial, to meet the technological and environmental challenges of society, and "service-oriented", to deliver the value expected by the market.

The time is no longer to question the supremacy of service in our economies but to create synergies, complementarities and even mergers between the two.

---

6 This is precisely the path defended by Jean Gadrey (1992).

2.2. Defining the service

Services have historically been defined by default as activities that cannot be classified in industry or agriculture according to the usual INSEE nomenclature. Economic science has been particularly concerned with approaching a definition of service, with the desire to move beyond the debate between material and immaterial and productive and unproductive, and by focusing more on the conditions and characteristics of service production[7]. While it remains ambitious to try to define service, it is still necessary to understand it. Two complementary angles, the organizational angle and the market angle, can contribute to understanding it.

2.2.1. *The organizational angle: the concept of servuction*

Servuction[8] is one of the founding models in service management and remains an essential reference for understanding the reality and challenges of service at both a marketing and managerial level. This neologism, formed from the terms service and production, indicates the production system of a service. The model identifies the key elements necessary to produce a service and highlights the major role of the customer and the resulting managerial implications. The servuction model is shown in Figure 2.1.

2.2.1.1. *Elements necessary for the production of the service*

Five main elements make up the servuction model:

– the front-line employees in contact with the customer; these employees may disappear in automated or digitalized services; however, they remain essential in most service situations, if only to relay a failure of the technical system;

---

7 Gadrey then proposed the following definition: "a service activity is an operation, aimed at a transformation of state of a reality C, owned or used by a consumer (or client, or user) B, carried out by a service provider A at B's request, and often in relation to it, but not resulting in the production of a good that can circulate economically independently of the medium C" (Gadrey 2003, p. 18). This definition implies the impossibility of attributing a property right to a service, which fundamentally differentiates it from a good.

8 The concept of servuction was developed by Pierre Eiglier and Eric Langeard and presented in their first book in 1987 (Eiglier and Langeard 1987).

– the physical evidence is made up of all the material elements necessary for the production of the service and which can be used by the customer, by the front-line employees or by both at the same time;

– the internal organization system is the part that is not visible to the customer; often called the back office; it supports the front office, which is the part visible to the customer;

– the customer who, unlike the production model, is present in the service production model, participates in the production of the service;

– the service is the goal of the system, the result of the interaction between all the elements.

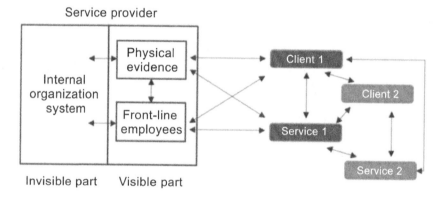

Figure 2.1. *Servuction (Eiglier 2004, p. 15). For a color version of this figure, see www.iste.co.uk/mathieu/services.zip*

2.2.1.2. Co-production of the service

The notion of co-production is an essential specificity of service management. It indicates that the service cannot be produced by the service provider alone but that it is co-produced with the client. Co-production not only signals the clients' participation in the production of the service but also seals the necessity of their presence in the production of the service. The notion of co-production is linked to that of customer participation, which underlines the role that the customer must play in the process in order to obtain the service he or she wants. Servuction being a system, if we remove one element, the client in particular, the system will no longer function. This property of systems demonstrates the necessary presence of the client in the production of the service; without the client, there can be no service.

The customer is, thus, the central issue in service management. Not only must customers be satisfied as clients, but they must also be integrated as co-producers. The service provider must not only meet their expectations to satisfy them but also manage their participation to ensure that his or her service production system works as well as possible. The fourth part of this book returns to this point in depth.

2.2.1.3. *The B2B manager facing servuction*

To be fully relevant in the B2B context, servuction must integrate two specificities. The first one is a stretching of its temporality; B2B servuction starts well before the production of the service and extends downstream with the maintenance of a relationship within which a next business opportunity can germinate. The second specificity of B2B servuction is an inversion of its spatiality; much more than a client going to the service provider, it is often the service provider who goes to the client.

The temporal specificity of B2B servuction refers to the reality of a service relationship that takes place over a long period of time. In B2B, servuction will often be the result of a first stage of interaction between the service provider and the client, that starts with a contact, then moves towards a purchasing and negotiation process[9]. In this stage upstream of the usually described servuction, the provider and the client take the time to get to know each other and define, specify or clarify, both the service and the servuction. It is not uncommon, for example, for the client to ask the service provider for the intervention of particular collaborators, thereby influencing the operating mode of the service. On the other hand, the duration of B2B relationships contributes to stretching out the servuction over time, which then tends to evolve and change. Contracts are signed over several years, even over 10 years, 20 years and sometimes even more. This long time span requires adaptations of the servuction.

In the original model, the servuction takes place in the physical location of the service, which is the place where the company welcomes the customer in order to perform the service (the post office, the supermarket, the hotel, etc.). In most B2B services, it is the service provider who moves to the customer's premises, and the service is no longer performed entirely at the service provider's premises. This is the spatial specificity of B2B services.

---

9 The purchasing phase is presented in Chapter 5, and the negotiation phase is presented in Chapters 5 and 6.

The manager is responsible for his or her servuction. His or her performance will be directly linked to the performance of the servuction for which he or she is responsible. The performance of the servuction is inexorably linked to the long-term maintenance of customer satisfaction, the involvement of the front-line employees and the excellence of the service. Three key competencies will enable him or her to achieve this goal: marketing skills to satisfy the customer, leadership skills to involve his or her team and technical and organizational skills to maintain service excellence. It is undoubtedly a real managerial challenge to develop and maintain these three skills concurrently. Usually, marketing skills are in the hands of marketers and technical and organizational skills are in the hands of engineers, technicians and operational managers. Customer orientation is, therefore, an essential skill for managers to meet this challenge.

Two main profiles are found in B2B services:

– managers who owe their position to a track record of technical and operational excellence. These managers may lack marketing and leadership skills. These profiles are found particularly in technical, scientific and engineering departments;

– managers who have less technical and more generalist backgrounds or training and who, therefore, have more natural marketing and leadership skills, but who may lack technical and operational confidence in tricky situations or when dealing with customers and teams who are more experienced in these areas.

These weaknesses can obviously be worked on. It is essential for the manager to be aware of them by identifying them after an introspection or with the help of HR diagnostic tools such as 360 degrees. These weaknesses can then be addressed through training and also through mentoring and internal coaching.

2.2.2. *The market angle: a process and an outcome*

If servuction defines service from an internal organizational perspective, the customer will have a different approach to service.

2.2.2.1. *Letting the client speak*

To find out how the client perceives and defines the service, the easiest way is to ask the client simple questions about their perception and evaluation of the service. When letting customers express themselves in this way, one will see that they have a vision that at first glance seems disjointed, mixing what is incidental and what is essential in the eyes of the provider.

Clients state items that can be grouped into two categories[10]:

– elements related to the result of the service, that is, the main benefit obtained, which is often related to the core of the provider's offer;

– elements related to the service delivery process.

In most cases, we will find that clients cite many more process-related elements than outcome-related elements. In fact, it is not unusual for clients to not even mention an element related to the result.

The examination of these elements is then particularly instructive. We will discover in particular that:

– some elements are not identified by the provider;

– what matters to the customer is not always what the company invests in first;

– what counts for the customer is not always what makes the eyes of the engineer, the technician or the manager shine;

– the provider spends energy to be efficient on points that are not taken into account by customers.

What customers tell us is really the experience they have had throughout the service.

2.2.2.2. *Customer experience issue*

Service is often defined from the customer's point of view as a lived experience. This experience is built from the observations that customers make voluntarily or involuntarily during the service, from the actions that they are led to perform, from the human or material interactions in which

---

10 This distinction was conceptualized by Grönross by distinguishing "process consumption" from "result consumption" (Grönross 1999).

they participate or from the emotions or feelings that are generated within them. This notion of customer experience has been widely addressed in the B2C field but seems to be breaking through more timidly in the B2B field. This can be explained on the one hand by a culture naturally focused on service, results and technical and business aspects. On the other hand, the belief in the rationality of B2B markets makes the notions of emotions, feelings and, more broadly, customer experience suspect. However, the simple question asked to the customer about the service clearly shows the importance of the experience. We should not neglect the fact that B2B customers are also B2C customers who appreciate positive experiences in the context of their personal consumption and who will tend to translate this performance into expectations in their professional sphere. B2B customers are also Amazon or Apple customers who offer a fluid, simple and responsive experience.

A study of a large sample of B2B and B2C customers conducted by Salesforce Research in 2019 sheds light on the importance placed on experience by B2B customers[11]:

– 89% of B2B respondents confirm that the experience a company delivers is as important as its products and services; the rate is 84% for B2C respondents;

– 82% of B2B respondents say they are willing to pay more for a better experience; only 59% of B2C customers are willing to do so;

– 82% of B2B respondents say that a great experience with one company increases expectations of other companies; 69% of B2C respondents make the same claim.

However, it must be admitted that the understanding of the experience is much more complex in a B2B environment than in a B2C one. If the B2C customer experience is that of an individual, the B2B customer experience is that of a company. First of all, the customer experience takes place over a long cycle. It begins with the first contact between the service provider and the customer in a pre-purchase phase, the duration of which increases with the complexity of the service. Then, many services are provided on the basis of multi-year contracts with a high level of interaction between the service

11 Study conducted in April 2019 by Salesforce Research on a sample of over 8,000 customers and over 15 countries in Europe, Asia and North America; 28% being B2B customers and 72% being B2C customers (Salesforce Research 2019).

provider and its client. To this temporal dimension, we must add that the experience is the result of a face-to-face meeting between a large number of actors on the client and provider sides.

While the manager cannot be responsible for the entire customer experience, he or she must nevertheless be careful to deliver the elements that he or she and his or her team control, in order to contribute to a positive experience for the customer. This includes the interaction between the customer and the front-line employees, who by their customer orientation will contribute to the creation of a positive service experience.

2.3. Characteristics of the service

Service has characteristics that distinguish it from a product[12]. Beyond the knowledge of these characteristics, the manager must manage the implications that have specificities in a B2B context.

2.3.1. Intangibility

2.3.1.1. Two dimensions of intangibility

Services are intangible. We cannot use our five senses to approach them. One cannot see, touch, smell, hear or taste a consulting service or a technical maintenance service as one can for raw material or a machine tool. This is the physical dimension of intangibility. The second dimension of intangibility is of a mental nature; the client has difficulty in forming an idea of the service he or she is really going to obtain, in appreciating its quality before the realization of the service and sometimes even after. From the client's point of view, the perception of risk stems from this uncertainty attached to the purchase of a service.

---

12 The first researchers in marketing and service management were exposed to criticism of their work, which focused on the validity of a distinction between product and service. In this context, four generic differences between product and service were proposed: intangibility, simultaneity, heterogeneity and perishability (Sasser *et al.* 1978). These characteristics are still widely cited, although they are regularly criticized as being too general. To be closer to reality, each of these characteristics should be understood as a *continuum*, on which a particular service can be positioned; some services are very intangible (consulting), while others are less (works and maintenance).

2.3.1.2. *Managing the client's perceived risk*

Managers must then manage this risk as perceived by the client. They can choose to rely on it openly if they believe that they can use it as a competitive advantage, by demonstrating that they are the players best able to manage this risk[13]. Alternatively, it can engage in a more discreet and indirect approach by seeking to reduce the client's perceived risk.

In the case of a client with whom they have already been involved, they will have to skillfully bring out past elements of the relationship that contribute to reassure the client. In the case of new clients, it will be necessary to make the service tangible in order to give the client signs of the value and quality of the service[14]. The premises, the material, the documents given, the telephone reception, the website, the collaborators themselves and the brand or the network are for the customer so many signs on which they will rely to infer professionalism, seriousness and quality.

In a B2B context, the diversity of people involved in the customer's purchase decision must also be taken into account. Not all of them will have the same perception of risk; the intensity and nature of the perceived risk often vary between the people in the buying center. Managers must, therefore, understand these variations and provide personalized responses in order to reinforce the negotiation strategy.

2.3.2. *Simultaneity*

2.3.2.1. *Direct consequence of servuction*

Simultaneity is a direct consequence of servuction. It indicates that the service is performed and consumed at the same time. The front-line employees are at the heart of this simultaneity, interacting more or less strongly depending on the nature of the service. Hence, the customer attaches so much importance to the service process. The challenge of this simultaneity is to manage this interaction between the service employees and the customer in the best possible way so that it brings value to both the company and its customer.

---

13 This approach is presented in Chapter 7 as a way to counteract the commoditization of supply.

14 Theodore Levitt, professor of marketing at Harvard Business School, was one of the first to speak of the tangibilization of service (Levitt 1981).

2.3.2.2. *Managing the interaction between the client and the provider*

The reality of provider–client interaction is particularly complex in a B2B context. It is not a single person on the provider's side who acts with a client, but a large number of collaborators on the provider's side who act with many people on the client's side[15]. These people will be different depending on the phase of the relationship (during the decision process, during the service, after the service). The stakes of the interaction will also differ according to the phase of the relationship, leading to different relational modes. During the decision-making process, the actors interact in a negotiation mode. During the service, the interaction is naturally more collaborative. At the end of the service, we find ourselves in a more administrative and relaxed mode if the service went well or, on the contrary, clearly conflictual if there were dysfunctions on the client's or service provider's side. Managers must, therefore, not only ensure that they are present, even to varying degrees, throughout the relationship, but also adapt their interaction style to each phase of the relationship.

2.3.3. *Heterogeneity*

2.3.3.1. *Heterogeneity factors*

Because of its simultaneity, meaning that it is produced each time it is consumed, the service varies from one performance to another. The factors that explain this heterogeneity are numerous: depending on the employee who performs the service, depending on the client who participates in the service, depending on the time during which the service is performed and even depending on the place where the service is performed. The consequence is a variation in the quality of the service. Depending on these factors, the service provider may deliver an excellent service or a catastrophic one. The manager's objective is to control these factors as well as possible, based on the knowledge of the customer's expectations, in order to ensure the most consistent level of service possible.

2.3.3.2. *Managing service quality*

B2B service contracts often include performance objectives in order to limit the risk of heterogeneity. In the context of a B2B service, the manager can act in two directions. The first is to work on the service process to ensure that all the elements of this process that can be formalized, and, therefore,

---

15 This reality is elaborated in Chapter 6.

likely to be standardized. This is similar to the principle of operation sheets, like a worksite preparation sheet, for example. The other line of work concerns the service employees, a strong factor of heterogeneity in a large number of service situations. It is then up to managers to make their teams aware of this reality and to support them in order to neutralize this drift.

2.3.4. *Perishability*

2.3.4.1. *Lack of stock*

Because of its intangibility and also because it is consumed at the same time as it is realized, the service cannot be stored. This is the interpretation of the perishability of the service.

The consequence is that, over a given period of time, a given service unit has only a given capacity to perform services. At its maximum capacity, a new business opportunity cannot be seized by the service provider. On the other hand, the unit may find itself under capacity at a given moment due to a lack of contracts, leaving a certain number of employees unoccupied. It is obviously these two extreme situations that managers must anticipate in order to avoid them as much as possible.

2.3.4.2. *Managing the service capacity*

In a B2B context, there is also the notion of seasonality to which is added the reality of economic fluctuations specific to the activity of particular sectors of activity. Service providers working directly with the oil sector, particularly on research and development, engineering and even works and maintenance assignments, were quickly and strongly affected by the drop in the price of a barrel of oil in the second half of 2014 and the spring of 2020. Political, economic, regulatory and health factors can quickly affect the manager's unit activity in a positive or negative way. A diversified client portfolio in terms of industry sectors is an excellent hedge against these types of contingencies.

But there is a situation in B2B that is just as delicate for managers, when a loyal customer asks for new services when their unit is at maximum capacity. The risk of disappointment, misunderstanding or even loss of customer loyalty is high. Outsourcing may appear to be an option, but it also has its risks. If managers have no real room for maneuver to respond to the client, they can only count on the strength of their relationship and their proximity to the client to limit the latter's disappointment.

The Ortec Group is a French company providing services to the industrial, public and tertiary sectors. It is present in 24 countries and employs 11,000 people. It provides its clients with innovative and responsible solutions to support them in their various design, implementation and development projects

A service environment is essentially different from a production environment by the immaterial nature of the offer. In this respect, service is a perception, an appreciation specific to a particular sensitivity. Many variables will interfere in the perception of the quality of a service. This immateriality makes the client particularly sensitive to the various tangible proofs associated with the service. A poorly maintained and untidy construction site induces negative perceptions in the client, whereas new, modern work clothes, worn with pride by the field staff, will reinforce the provider's brand image. Moreover, in services, because of their intangible nature, there are many opportunities for development and innovation.

The human element is also an essential characteristic of service activities. People are at the heart of service. The service is provided by men and women who arrive at work each morning in varying degrees of fitness, perhaps worried about a child who has been ill during the night, or tense on certain days due to difficult transport conditions. The service rendered to the client will necessarily be impacted by these personal conditions. The service will be different every day, since every morning it is a new construction site that has to be started, with a different customer, in a particular environment, with organizational, technical and human constraints that are always specific. While the world of production is one of series, duplication and repetition, the world of service is one of variability, where adaptability and responsiveness are essential. The human factor cannot be reproduced identically. For a product as for a service, high standards, rigor and organization are essential skills, and the human qualities of the collaborators are precious resources for any company. Nevertheless, this human dimension is prevalent in services because it contributes to the realization of the service.

It is then up to managers to take the full measure of the human dimension of the service by making it resonate both within their team and in their relationship with customers. On the one hand, the human dimension of service makes managers dependent on their team. If they are not supported by their team in responding to market requirements and competitive issues, then they will not be able to do anything on their own. They have no other choice but to unite all the components of their team around them, in order to release the value of the service. By becoming the leader of their team and developing one's communication skills, they will be able to exercise a natural authority and inspire the necessary confidence so that their colleagues follow them on the path of customer and service requirements. On the other hand, managers will have to build and maintain a quality human relationship with their client, which will be the cement of trust. Beyond the service rendered, the client becomes attached to his or her service provider because he or she feels listened to and understood, that an interpersonal chemistry has been created and that a feeling of sympathy has been experienced. It is this relationship of trust that will make the client want to collaborate with a manager and his or her team in particular. The client trusts not only the professionalism of the manager and his or her team but also the quality of the relationship, solidified by transparent communication and the willingness to maintain a dialogue.

Customer orientation, in the service industry, is fully realized in this attention to the human being. Operational efficiency and economic performance are obviously the *sine qua non* conditions for a manager's success, but nothing is possible in service, and especially in B2B, without this customer orientation. And yet, the manager is not really prepared for this requirement and this service culture. The company's mission is to accompany the employee in his or her assumption of responsibility, in order to bring him or her to be a true customer-oriented manager in the service industry, beyond the mere mastery of a trade. Human investment must complement material investment. Investing in people means recognizing the contribution of each individual to the creation of value and competitive differentiation, sending clear signals of recognition and sharing the fruits and results of the group. The Ortec Group supports all its employees through career paths built in the spirit of the group, which reinforce the feeling of belonging and attachment to the company. Field personnel are motivated and valued by internal training courses that reinforce technical skills and structure a level of professionalism. In addition, management training courses accompany employees throughout their career development. However, the manager must develop his or her own curiosity, in order to trigger the customer relationship, and be willing to question himself or herself, in order to maintain this relationship at the highest level. By being able to intervene at different stages in the life cycle of a project, the Ortec Group encourages its employees to broaden their vision, in order to be able to make proposals to the customer.

Above all, a sense of service must be a state of mind shared by all employees. This state of mind will be all the more widespread in the group if a service culture, supported by clear values, is strong.

Box 2.3. *Testimony of Bernard Greder (Managing Director of the Ortec Group)*

Markers of B2B

3.1. Reality of the market

Buying on the market is much more of an option in B2B than in B2C. If in practice, the household can only produce a small number of products or services necessary for its consumption, the company in theory has this possibility, and it is then by choice that it calls upon the market. At the same time, by buying on the market, the company involves its service provider in an industrial sector that he or she must know and master.

3.1.1. *Market option*

3.1.1.1. *Outsourcing, the driving force behind service companies*

Daniel Cohen explained that it was by interfering in the management of the firm that, starting in the 1980s, the shareholder challenged the rules of historical industrial capitalism, in particular by limiting the firm's activity to what is the core of its business and by calling on the market for everything else (Cohen 2018, p. 97). The firm then has a choice between making or having made. We are entering the era of subcontracting and outsourcing, which concern service activities as much as the manufacture of all or part of a product. Whether in the 1950s and 1960s, there were still cooks, guards, gardeners and switchboard operators among the staff of companies, these tasks have been long entrusted to specialized service providers. More and more jobs are being outsourced; today's administrative staff, accountants, tomorrow's human resources managers or financial managers. This concerns both industrial and service companies. However, while the opposition *"make or buy"* works quite well for the production of a tangible product, it is less convincing for a service. Indeed, given the reality of the co-production of a service and the necessary participation of the client, as described in Chapter 2, it is legitimate to propose a third way: *making* with. Neither *making* nor totally *buying*, the use of a service provider should indicate the client's willingness to work with the service provider, who thus becomes a partner. The terms used to describe the relationship between the company and its service provider refer to various realities (see Box 3.1).

Subcontracting is a term that has a legal framework and a precise definition. The "principal" entrusts an operation or a "subcontracted" work to a "contractor" who must "conform exactly" to the "directives" contained in a "technical specification" in order to "execute" the tasks that are "entrusted" to him[1]. The subcontractor is clearly in a situation of dependence, constraint and submission. Subcontracting has an unflattering and often pejorative connotation. While the term comes from the world of industry, it is also used for services.

The provider and the service delivery are terms dedicated to the service environment. We speak of the beneficiary of a service or the client of a provider in a neutral or positive perspective.

The partner would then be the most accurate term to illustrate the need to work with the client to achieve the service.

Box 3.1. *Revealing semantics*

Outsourcing has several motivations:

– The company wishes to concentrate on what it considers to be strategic, its core business, and entrusts all other activities to the market. Historically, the outsourcing movement has its roots in this desire, as illustrated by the catering sector.

– The company engaged in a cost reduction strategy outsources some of its activities in an effort to reduce their cost of execution. The relocation of call centers to low-cost countries makes it possible for the company to reduce the cost of handling customer complaints.

---

1 www.insee.fr/fr/accueil [Accessed on October 16, 2019] and *Larousse Dictionary* (translated entry for *sous-traitance*, "subcontracting").

– The company is looking for a specialized player that will make it possible for it to benefit from a specific expertise that it cannot afford to deploy internally. The specialized investment bank will come to advise a client from time to time in the context of a company takeover, for example.

– The company, subject to fluctuating business cycles, relies on contractors to acquire the flexibility needed to adapt to its markets. Temporary staffing companies thus enable their clients to absorb their activity flows.

Depending on the reasons why the company calls on the market, the provider's position will be more or less comfortable, particularly because of the importance attached to the price of the service. However, it should be understood that these motives are rarely exclusive. In reality, several factors contribute to the company's decision to call on the market. In addition to cost, there are often criteria of expertise, responsiveness and flexibility. It is then an in-depth work of knowledge and understanding of the customer and its environment that will make it possible for the manager to decipher the real expectations of his customer. This is the subject of the second part of this book.

3.1.1.2. *Transaction costs theory*

The transaction costs theory makes it possible for us to approach the exchange between the service provider and his or her client from a particular angle.

The transaction costs theory was developed by Oliver E. Williamson[2] from the pioneering work of Ronald Coase[3] on the justification of the existence of the firm. Transaction costs, which are different from and complementary to production costs, reflect the reality of costs linked to the necessary coordination between the firm that buys and the firm that sells, in order to make the transaction. These costs are divided into *ex ante* costs (search for information, negotiation of the contract, etc.) and *ex post* costs

---

2 Oliver E. Williamson was awarded the Nobel Prize in Economics in 2009 for his work on the transaction costs theory (Williamson 1975, 1985).

3 In 1937, Ronald Coase published the famous article "The Nature of the Firm" in the journal *Economica*, in which he introduced the concept of transaction cost. He received the Nobel Prize in 1991.

(policy and enforcement costs, necessary adjustments between the actors, etc.). These costs are borne both by the firm that buys (e.g. the search for information on the quality of offers) and by the firm that sells (e.g. the search for information on the solvency of the customer). Ronald Coase, thus, managed to justify the existence of the firm by its capacity to reduce these transaction costs and, thus, to be more efficient than the market. Nevertheless, the firm generates organizational costs, such as recruitment costs, management costs and support costs. It is, therefore, the comparison between transaction costs and organizational costs that determines the choice between outsourcing and insourcing, or between using the market or the firm. The firm should be preferred as long as organizational costs are lower than transaction costs. Oliver E. Williamson proposed, in addition to the two extreme forms of governance, the market and the firm, hybrid forms such as the alliance or the contract, which have the main virtue of reducing transaction costs.

This work is, therefore, particularly interesting in the B2B field, since these transaction costs are additional costs, both to the production cost borne by the firm selling and to the purchase cost borne by the firm buying. These transaction costs tend to be particularly high in the case of a service because of the inherent specificities of the service. The difficulty of comparing services between providers, which makes the market less transparent, the asymmetry of information that may exist between the provider and his or her client, and the uncertainty of the outcome that is linked to the intangible nature of the service, increase the investment of both parties in the preparation, execution and monitoring of the exchange, and, therefore, have an impact on transaction costs[4]. These transaction costs can even, in extreme situations, be higher than the cost of production; this is the case, for example, of a fairly trivial service, such as a one-off maintenance or repair operation for a client, but for which the costs associated with ordering, monitoring and invoicing are high. It is acceptable to assume that the actors will try to reduce these costs in order to move towards a more efficient relationship. The relationship between the client and the provider, its quality, intensity and duration, is a particularly effective way of reducing these transaction costs.

---

4 For a discussion of the application of transaction costs to services, see de Bandt (1995, pp. 123–126).

3.1.2. *Derived demand*

The phenomenon of derived demand is specific to B2B markets. It indicates that a company's demand is always derived from a demand in the final consumption market. The activity of furniture design agencies, for example, is conditioned by the consumption of furniture goods by households. The industrial sector is, therefore, a translation of this notion of derived demand, which always starts from the final market and goes up through the various intermediate actors.

3.1.2.1. *Concept of the industrial sector*

The industrial sector is a rich and complex concept. It can be used to describe and analyze an economic activity in order to reflect more precisely on the industrial policy of a country; for example, we will speak of the French nuclear sector. In a more technical approach, the industrial sector is defined as the succession of transformation operations that a raw material undergoes to become a consumer product. The textile channel is described in this way, starting with the basic material, a natural fiber or a chemical fiber and ending with the finished product, like a garment. The industrial sector is approached here in a more pragmatic way; all the actors upstream and downstream of the service provider as well as those on the periphery. We start from the service provider itself to define the industrial sector, and it is the actors who structure the sector and not the activities or operations.

Figure 3.1 illustrates the industrial sector of a new aircraft painting company. A first simplified description of this sector reveals three downstream actors, the manufacturer, the company and the passenger, upstream actors who are its suppliers of tools and materials, as well as two of the main peripheral actors, namely the expertise and control organizations on the one hand, and the state and state organizations on the other. The sector, thus, broadens the notion of customer, since it reveals in the example three types of customers:

– the direct customer who buys the service, that is, the aircraft manufacturer;

– the indirect customer who is the customer's customer, that is, the airline which is the manufacturer's customer;

– the final customer who is always the consumer, that is, the passenger who travels on the airline.

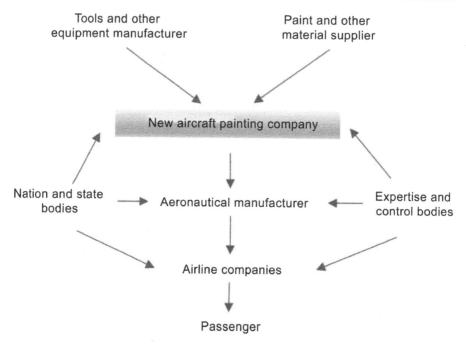

Figure 3.1. *The new aircraft painting service industry. For a color version of this figure, see www.iste.co.uk/mathieu/services.zip*

3.1.2.2. *Risks and opportunities associated with the industrial sector*

The existence of a sector in which the service provider is involved entails both risks and opportunities for him.

The main risk is linked to this notion of dependence inherent in derived demand. The industry relies on the end market as well as on actors from whom the supplier is often literally and figuratively distant. It is difficult for actors located upstream in the sector to really decipher the behavior and intentions of actors located downstream in their industry. There is also the risk of inertia specific to the sector; a small variation in final consumption has strong repercussions upstream in the sector. In the previous example of the aircraft paint company, while it has long benefited from sustained growth in global air traffic, the health crisis of spring 2020 has put it in a much less favorable situation. As for the expertise and control bodies, they are putting in place procedures and constraints that weigh on its activity.

While service providers overcome this complexity in understanding the industry, real opportunities open up. By having several types of customers, direct, indirect and final, they can bring to each of them a specific value or use their knowledge of the different actors with their direct customers in order to reinforce their competitive position. This requires the manager to develop a real ability to listen to his or her different customers and to have a very good knowledge of his or her sector[5].

Veolia is a French group with 178,780 employees located on five continents. The group assists cities and industries in the management, optimization and recovery of their water, energy and waste resources.

Over the past five years, listening to customers has become a major focus for the development of the skills of the group's managers. On the one hand, this can be explained by a significant change in the customer portfolio; from a situation in which 80% of contracts were with mayoral customers, by the end of 2019, there was an almost even split between industrial and mayoral customers. When approaching a new customer, it is imperative to ask questions about their expectations and negotiation methods. In addition, an employee survey conducted in 2013 among 5,000 people, representing about a quarter of the group's top management, revealed the excellence of the group's competitive positioning on the technical dimension of its offer and also a tendency for employees not to listen sufficiently to the customer and to retreat into an essentially technical stance. The survey thus revealed the need for a cultural evolution, from a technical orientation to a customer orientation, anchored more in listening to the customer.

This evolution was successfully achieved thanks to a support around three main axes:

– A department for innovation and markets was created in 2013, which was a strong signal. This new strategic department, focused on marketing, sales, markets and customers, has supported the group's reorientation towards this new industrial customer, and has enabled managers to integrate this new customer-oriented culture. Teams from this new department took part in integration days to make new employees aware of the challenges of customer orientation.

– A sales academy has been set up to provide managers with tools for portfolio analysis, segmentation analysis and customer analysis. Specific modules have been developed on listening to customers and their key expectations, preparing for calls for

---

5 The analysis of the pipeline is discussed in Chapter 4.

tender and negotiation. At the same time, these training courses have been enriched by encouraging the sharing of best practices between countries and between markets.

– The net promoter score (NPS)[6] has been introduced as one of the 18 key indicators for steering the *raison d'être* of the Veolia Group. As the customer is one of the stakeholders in this *raison d'être*, customer and consumer satisfaction has become a major objective. The NPS is integrated into the bonus policy of the managers in order to clearly include listening to customers and customer satisfaction as managerial performance indicators, in a multi-faceted approach to this performance.

This customer focus was not limited to the direct customer but considered a broader ecosystem in order to take into account all stakeholders. In a household waste collection service, for example, listening to the customer cannot be limited to the technical director of the mayoral service. In the perspective of a caring relationship, listening will also be directed towards the final consumer and the citizen. Real citizen panels can be proposed to municipalities in order to gather the expression of the final customer. A particular territory may have specific issues and lead to an expansion of the technical solution to a more environmental solution. This wider listening of the actors can then sometimes make it possible to come back to the direct customer in order to enrich and adapt the offer (B2B2C2B). The contract gains in depth by going beyond its technical core. The added value of an offer is not limited to the simple service and can also reflect the consideration of social, societal and environmental issues. The customer, whether mayoral or industrial, has a broader vision of their needs. Customer orientation must lead managers to integrate an analysis of the risks in their entire ecosystem (e.g. knowing the working conditions of their subcontractors) in order to measure their responsibility.

In parallel with the expansion of this external ecosystem in which the manager must take an interest, customer orientation, in order to be fully realized, must also rely on a broader internal ecosystem. In order to increase the social, societal or environmental dimensions of his or her technical offer, the manager must collaborate with colleagues with complementary skills in social integration, sustainable development or human rights, for example.

Listening to the customer leads the manager to be a responsible entrepreneur, capable of managing the risk of a necessary development.

Box 3.2. *Testimony of Olivier Carlat (Director of Training and Social Development, Veolia Group)*

---

6 The NPS is an indicator of customer satisfaction. It is presented in Chapter 6.

3.2. The relational issue

The customer–supplier relationship is the central concept of B2B marketing. The B2B exchange is considered as a relational exchange. The concept has historically been updated from the important empirical work carried out by the European research group IMP (Industrial Marketing and Purchasing Group), based on the hypothesis that exchanges between organizations are different from exchanges between a company and a consumer[7].

3.2.1. *Framework of the client–provider relationship*

3.2.1.1. *Characteristics of the relationship*

Duration is often highlighted as a strong specificity of the B2B relationship. An average duration of about 10 years is often put forward[8], and it is widely accepted that close and long-lasting links go beyond the simple relationship between a client and its provider.

Daniel Michel, Robert Salle and Jean-Paul Valla, active members of the IMP group, draw on the empirical work of this scientific community to summarize the essential characteristics of the inter-firm relationship, understood as a dyadic relationship and no longer limited to a single actor (Michel *et al.* 1996):

– the supplier and his or her customer are active in the relationship in order to make it live and evolve. Both can make efforts to adapt;

– the supplier and its customer make investments in order to create, maintain and develop the relationship. These investments are essentially human, technical and financial;

– each company engages a large number of people in the relationship. There is a sales center on the supplier side, and a buying center on the

---

7 See in particular Häkan Håkansson and his early work with the IMP group (Håkansson 1982).

8 One of the first observations on the duration of the B2B relationship was made by Jean-Paul Valla. It concerned 139 supplier–customer relationships in Europe, and the average duration was established between 9 and 13 years depending on the type of product (Turnbull and Valla 1986).

customer side, who will interact[9]. These numerous relationships that are established between different people will increase the exchange of a social dimension. It is not only technical or financial exchanges that are carried out but also social exchanges;

– the supplier and his or her customer tend to maintain the relationship over time, if only to make the investment that has been made profitable.

3.2.1.2. Relationship as an investment

Because of the characteristics of the B2B relationship, the notion of investment is often associated with it. This investment is borne by both the supplier and the client, and is not always clearly identified by the actors. In the context of a service provision, this investment is made first upstream when the relationship is opened and the purchase decision is made, and then throughout the process of providing the service. This investment can be approached through the concept of transaction cost developed above. By going back to the nature of these different transaction costs, we can assume that they decrease in proportion to the duration of the relationship:

– *Ex ante* costs can be reduced or even eliminated if the client remains loyal to the provider. For example, the client will no longer have to bear the cost of searching for potential providers and the provider will be able to reduce the cost of setting up preliminary projects.

– *Ex post* costs will also be lower; on the client's side, the costs of monitoring compliance with the contract should be reduced and the cost of adapting the provider to comply with the contract should also be reduced by relying on its experience with the client.

Opportunism, which is one of the main factors explaining transaction costs, must be included here (Williamson 1985). Opportunism is defined as the explicit violation, by one of the actors in the exchange, of either an explicit contract or a relational contract. Opportunism is the search for self-interest; it is a calculated effort to deceive, misinform or mislead one's partner. Opportunism can be an active and voluntary approach by one of the parties (time billed less than the actual time, reduction of investment to maintain a formalized level of quality, etc.) or be of a more passive nature

---

9 In the context of service delivery, it will be necessary to add actors who will appear during the realization of the service. These actors refer to the notion of the service target, which is presented in Chapter 6.

(one of the parties hides information from its partner or does not inform its partner of a change in conditions, etc.). The higher this risk of opportunism is considered by the partners, the more resources are invested in controlling and monitoring this risk. Opportunism and transaction costs move in the same direction; the higher the perceived risk of opportunism, the greater the resources to control it. While the contract is traditionally used by the firm to limit its partner's opportunism, it also hinders the ability of the parties to evolve a strategic exchange naturally marked by uncertainty and complexity. Given this limitation of the traditional contract, the actors may be led to turn to a contract of a more relational nature[10]. The social dimension of B2B exchange can be put forward as a moderator of the tendency to opportunism[11] – what if the relationship and proximity between the client and his or her service provider made individuals less opportunistic?

3.2.2. *Relational excellence*

Since relationships are at the heart of B2B exchanges, it is necessary to build a real relational strategy in order to increase performance. There can be no lasting relationship without trust, and this relationship will only be truly human if emotion finds its place.

3.2.2.1. *Building trust*

Trust is defined as an expectation, a belief, a feeling, a behavioral intention and a behavior (Guibert 1999). Trust leads us to expect that our partner will fulfill his or her obligations (Dwyer *et al.* 1987) and to believe that he or she will keep his or her promises and words (Anderson and Weitz 1989). Two types of trust are usually distinguished, interorganizational trust and interpersonal trust. While the manager is not at the heart of interorganizational trust, he or she is the actor in the interpersonal trust that he or she builds with the client during the relationship. Interorganizational trust often comes before interpersonal trust. Before knowing one's partner, one knows the company to which he or she belongs. Depending on the reputation and image of the company, and the experience one has had with

---

10 The need for a renewal of the traditional contracting approach seems to be emerging (Frydlinger *et al.* 2019).

11 Granovetter in particular, by recognizing that the economic transaction is embedded in a social relationship, nuances the risk of opportunism, which is at the heart of the transaction costs theory (Granovetter 1985).

it, one has built up trust in the company before moving on to interpersonal trust. On the one hand, trust makes it possible to improve the relational climate (better communication, greater cooperation, fewer conflicts, etc.), and on the other hand, to improve the quality of work. In B2B exchanges, trust is a key factor in the success of the business relationship. In B2B exchange, it will stabilize the relationship, ensure its continuity and make it difficult to replace a supplier with a competitor (Turnbull and Wilson 1989).

The manager will succeed in building this trust by maintaining a regular relationship with his or her client, stretching beyond the simple commercial relationship (being present before the call for tenders) and service relationship (maintaining the relationship once the service is completed). Listening, relevant communication and proactivity are the major ingredients in building trust.

Trust is never fully established and must be continuously maintained through a sustained and positive relationship.

3.2.2.2. Rehabilitating emotion

It was in the early 1980s that the rationality of the consumer was seriously questioned and that emotions made their appearance in the B2C field[12]. In B2B, there is still a tendency to consider that the actors, and in particular the buyers, are dominated by reason because of their professional identity. The myth of rationality and cold logic still dominates. It is not a matter of questioning the rational and reflective dimension of the B2B exchange, but of admitting that emotions also have their place in this exchange, since they are human beings interacting in a relationship that is often, as we have seen, deep and lasting.

Recent research in psychology and neurology, as well as in economics, has led us to reconsider the role of emotions in the functioning of the brain. Going beyond the traditional framework of cognitive psychology, which made little room for emotion, new currents have gradually become interested

---

12 It was Hirschman and Holbrook who paved the way for experiential marketing in the early 1980s by placing emotion at the heart of consumption (Hirschman and Holbrook 1982).

in the role of emotion[13]. Neurosciences are now able to demonstrate that emotions are crucial for the functioning of the brain and the life of the mind and that reason and emotion are complementary[14]. In the field of economics, the new trend of behavioral economics opposes the classical *doxa* by maintaining that *homo œconomicus* is not a totally rational agent. We have an emotional brain that plays a very important role in our behavior[15]. Emotional and cognitive processes are, thus, linked and act together to guide our attention, our evaluation, our behavior and our decisions.

There is no reason not to accept the idea that the buyer and, more broadly the client, even if they are professionals, analyze, decide and act under the action of their emotions, because they are above all human beings. In order to respond to the emotional dimension of the customer, the manager must develop his or her skills and emotional intelligence.

Dedalus, as a publisher and integrator of health solutions, supports public and private health institutions in the transformation of their information systems.

The human and social dimension of customer relations is essential. It is a long-term process, with public contracts lasting five to seven years and tacitly renewed for a minimum of three years, which can extend to about 20 years. In addition to the quality of the offer and its implementation at the customer's site, the

---

13 We can refer to the work of Richard Davidson, professor of psychology at the University of Wisconsin. In one of his founding experiments, by observing the brain activity caused by emotions, he highlighted the role of the prefrontal cortex in emotions. "And here we were pointing to the prefrontal cortex. This region was considered the seat of human reason, the place of foresight, wisdom, rationality, and other cognitive functions that distinguish us from 'lower' animals. We, on the other hand, argued that it also directed our emotions, and that psychology's barricade between reason and emotion had no real basis" (Davidson 2018, p. 72).

14 The famous professor of neurology, Antonio Damasio, has shown how emotion can guide reasoning and decision-making (Damasio 2003).

15 The idea of this emotional brain was proposed by the psychologist Daniel Kahneman, winner of the Nobel Prize in Economics in 2002 and at the origin of the new behavioral theory. Following his work on analysis and decision-making, he proposed a theory based on the opposition between two systems of thought that coexist in us; a "system 1", fast, automatic, emotional, instinctive and intuitive, which goes directly to the conclusion without taking the time to think and without integrating logical elements, and a "system 2", which takes the time to analyze, calculate, reason and think. If these two systems communicate and act together on the behavior, it is often the "system 1" that takes the upper hand because it is faster and consumes less energy. In this respect, emotions play an essential role in decision-making (Kahneman 2011).

capacity for innovation and the mobilization of research and development, customer relations must be a priority at all levels. Excellence in customer relations must be sought at all stages of the business cycle, from design to support, including sales and deployment. There are many opportunities for interaction with the customer; an employee from the research and development department, who has an innovative idea, may take part in a sales meeting; during the deployment of the software solution at the customer's site, consultants, project managers and project directors are on the customer's site or providing remote support; the support teams have the opportunity to meet with the customer's representatives. The support teams naturally have a very strong interaction with the customer. These day-to-day relationships will contribute to building a global relationship with the customer. A difficult and chaotic customer relationship will be a hindrance to the enrichment of the commercial relationship, and in extreme cases may even put an end to it. The relational proximity, and the trust that goes with it, will encourage the customer to exchange very early with a collaborator of the provider on a project or a subject of reflection.

Not all employees have the same relational ease. Those with business, management and marketing backgrounds seem to be more at ease, while those with a more technical profile may be less agile in managing this relationship. If customer relations are integrated as an essential issue by the sales teams, this is not always the case for the other departments of the company. Customer relations are, thus, becoming a real point of vigilance, especially since it is mainly technical profiles, often with an engineering background, who are in contact with the customer once the sale has been concluded. For certain personalities, there may be an intrinsic difficulty in managing human relations, but there is also a simple lack of training and awareness of this relational issue.

The relationship will be built in harmony with the customer based on real efforts in three main directions:

– Cultivate a listening and empathetic posture. Such a posture will give clients the feeling that we care about their needs, that we are interested in the specifics of their work and that we are truly willing to help them by simplifying their daily life.

– Make sure you adapt to the person you are talking to. First, it is essential to adapt your level of language to the profile of the person you are speaking to. A person from the client's IT department will be comfortable with technical language, while medical staff will be impervious to such jargon. It is also important to be flexible in order to maintain a constructive dialogue with the person you are talking to, and to avoid being too rigid in your approach to the client's requests.

– Be proactive with your interlocutor. It is preferable to initiate short regular contacts rather than limiting yourself to an episodic formal contact. Do not hesitate to come back to clients regularly to inform them of the project's progress. The lack of continuous feedback and information can create uncertainty and frustration for the client.

There is a real need to make all teams and colleagues aware of the challenges of customer relations.

Box 3.3. *Testimony of Guillaume Reynaud*
(Sales Director France, Dedalus)

PART 2

Knowing the Customer

Introduction to Part 2

Customer knowledge is the foundation of customer orientation. It is a foundation that must be continuously maintained to remain solid. But which customers are we talking about? Who is this customer that we need to discover and know?

The industrial sector is the strong specificity of B2B that radically distinguishes it from B2C. Beyond their direct market, managers must broaden their analysis to include many indirect players that can have an impact on their activity and performance. Managers may feel that they are straying too far from their business and their environment and that they are discovering territories that are totally unknown to them, without always being convinced of the benefits of this approach. However, through this effort to structure their sector, managers are enriched by a vision in terms of the risks and opportunities borne by each of the players.

After having broadened their customer approach to the entire sector, refocusing on the direct customer makes it possible for managers to prepare their posture in purchasing and negotiation situations. Understanding purchasing means first of all identifying the people who will be involved in the purchasing decision and understanding their expectations, their positions and their constraints.

Finally, the last client to be known will be the one with whom managers and their teams will be in contact during the execution of the service. The client becomes a service target. These service targets will be the client's employees, or people in the client's environment.

The knowledge of the customer must, therefore, be oriented in these three directions in order to best support the manager and their team in building the three essential relationships in B2B service. Modeling the industrial sector will help strengthen the business relationship with the ecosystem. The commercial relationship will be structured from the understanding of the purchase from the customer's point of view. The service relationship will be better anticipated thanks to the identification of targets.

Modeling the Industrial Sector

4.1. Direct market

A manager may be in charge of a single major account or, on the contrary, have a portfolio marked by a strong geographical or sectoral dispersion. Whatever its size or complexity, this is the manager's market. It does not always overlap perfectly with the company's overall strategic analysis. Hence, it is important for managers to conduct their own analysis of their market.

4.1.1. *Knowing one's market in its entirety*

The first thing a manager should do is to build a big picture of his or her market, by representing it around the few most salient points.

4.1.1.1. *Defining it*

First, it is important to define one's market in a qualitative way. Naming one's market is not always easy and the terms used often indicate the way in which the manager approaches it. Do managers define it in terms of the service they offer, the markets they serve or the solution they provide (see Table 4.1)?

The approach that managers adopt to name their market impacts not only the size and value that will be attributed to it but also the competitive perception that one has of it and the value that one believes one must bring to it.

The managers' territory must clearly appear in the definition of their market. Is it a simple geographical territory or a more precisely defined territory in terms of business, client and activity sectors?

	From the service offered	From clients served	From the the solution provided
Consulting company	Consulting market	Market of the CAC 40 companies	Support in the digital transition
Cleaning company	Cleaning market	Market for offices and head offices	Well-being of employees
Transport company	Goods transportation market	Food companies market	Integrated logistics

Table 4.1. *Defining one's market*

The simple and summary definition of their market will make it possible for managers to not only have a clear discourse with their prospects, their customers and their team but also clarify with their hierarchy the objectives that are given to them.

4.1.1.2. *Evaluating it*

After this first phase of approaching the direct market in a qualitative way, it is necessary to move towards quantification. In particular, one will try to get an idea of the number of potential clients for our service and, more broadly, to assess the value of our market. The limited number of clients is often cited as a key characteristic of B2B markets. The reality is actually much more complex. From a single customer (as can be found in the nuclear engineering sector) to a large portfolio of customers (as in the case of express parcel delivery), market valuation can be more or less rapid.

It is essential not to limit one's market to one's current customers but to build an ambitious and, at the same time, realistic vision of one's market potential. When questioning managers, one realize that many of them are unable to give a quantitative indicator, even if it is not very precise, of the size of their market within their perimeter and to approach the share that they capture. Managers must make an effort to provide figures for their own areas of operations, as Sophie Bellon, Chairman of the Board of Directors of Sodexo, clearly stated in the Group's 2017–2018 Reference Document: "Sodexo's future is very promising. The market potential for our activities is estimated at

900 billion euros, or nearly 45 times our current revenue"[1]. These estimates that managers manage to make also have the advantage of positioning their territory in relation to their company as a whole and in relation to other territories. Are managers in a particularly dynamic territory or is it stagnating? Are they not well established in a territory that needs to be conquered or, on the contrary, well established in a territory that needs to be protected?

Finally, managers must add a more strategic dimension to their thinking by identifying the factors that structure the evolution of the market. In fact, it is often factors belonging to the macro-environment that provide an overview of the market (see Box 4.1).

Veolia: presentation of the group and its strategy[2]

The environmental services market is a growing market driven by:

– increasing demographics and urbanization of cities (70% of the world's population will be urban by 2050)[3];

– the need for access to drinking water and sanitation remains high in the world (nearly 700 million people still do not have access to drinking water and more than 2 billion do not have access to sanitation services)[4];

– an awareness of the need to act in favor of environmental protection, with a general tightening of the regulatory framework;

– the cost constraint for services, associated with performance requirements, favoring the outsourcing of services to specialists;

– a change in consumer behavior: increasingly initiated and demanding on health, environmental protection and lifestyle changes for a better quality of life, increasingly sensitive to recycling and collaborative economy functions and wishing for a more transparent governance of services.

Box 4.1. *Growth factors in the environmental services market*

---

1 Sodexo (2018). Document de référence 2017–2018. Report, p. 12 [Online]. Available at: www.sodexo.com/files/live/sites/sdxcom-global/files/PDF/Finance/Sodexo-Document-Reference-2017-2018.pdf [Accessed on November 10, 2019].

2 Veolia (2018). Document de référence 2018 : rapport financier annuel. Report, p. 14. [Online]. Available at: www.veolia.com/sites/g/files/dvc2491/files/document/2019/04/Veolia-Document-de-reference-2018-Rapport-Financier.pdf [Accessed on November 15, 2019].

3 According to a March 31, 2015, United Nations report.

4 *Ibid.*

4.1.2. Segmentation

Marketing segmentation is an essential step to better understand the diversity of one's market. It consists of reducing the inherent heterogeneity of markets, particularly high in B2B, by forming customer segments. A segment groups together customers who share common characteristics (profile, expectations, behavior, etc.) and who should, therefore, be approached and satisfied in a similar way. This approach makes it possible for the service provider to be more efficient both in its commercial approach and in the execution of its service by optimizing the resources deployed on each segment served.

4.1.2.1. Specificities of B2B segmentation

In a B2B context, the principles of segmentation are identical to those initially developed in B2C. It is mainly the criteria used to form the segments that will be specific. For consumer markets, it is consumers that one seek to group into customer segments, whereas in B2B markets, it is both organizations and individuals who are members of these organizations and who participate in the purchasing process that one need to bring together in the most homogeneous segments possible. Organizational variables, such as the size of the firm or its sector of activity as well as more individual variables, like the decision-making process, must be taken into account in order to understand the heterogeneity of the market.

To integrate these different segmentation variables, a two-level, two-step approach specific to B2B has been proposed: an initial macro-segmentation followed by a micro-segmentation (Wind and Cardozo 1974). Macro-segmentation focuses on the characteristics of the client organization (size, location, sector of activity, etc.) and on the purchase situation (new purchase, repeat purchase, etc.). Micro-segmentation requires a more detailed knowledge of the market, focusing on the buying center for each macro-segment and the individuals that make it up (buying criteria, buyer's attitudes, etc.).

4.1.2.2. Challenge of segmentation in service activities

The specificity of service production reinforces the urgency of segmentation. Because of the customer's participation in the service, a given service can only be suitable for a homogeneous set of customers in terms of their participation. One cannot imagine a given service process that could satisfy customers with different expectations, behaviors and profiles in terms of their participation in the service. From a more pragmatic point of view, this indicates that one cannot limit segmentation to the customer who buys, but that one must increase it by segmenting the customer who participates in the service. While in B2C, the customer who buys and the customer who consumes the service are generally the same, in B2B, the people involved in the purchase relationship are most of the time different from those who will interface with the service provider to perform the service[5]. The segmentation of a market for a B2B service must then integrate this duality; segment the market that buys and segment the market for which and with which the service will be performed, segmenting the market by taking into account both the characteristics of the customer who participates in the purchase decision and the characteristics of the customer who participates in the performance of the service. It is proposed that a distinction be made between a commercial segmentation and an operational segmentation, which makes it possible to articulate a double duality of segmentation for B2B services (see Table 4.2).

	Macro-segmentation	Micro-segmentation
Business segmentation	**Segmentation of companies in order to better understand their buying behavior.** *Examples of segmentation criteria*: company size, company sector of activity, novelty and stakes of the purchase. *Example of market segments*: in the school catering market, public institutions will have a different purchasing process than private institutions.	**Segmentation of companies' buying centers to better understand their buying behavior.** *Examples of segmentation criteria*: purchase criteria, composition of the buying center. *Examples of market segments*: in the intellectual services market, it will be relevant to distinguish between companies that have buyers dedicated to the purchase of intellectual services from those who do not.
Operational segmentation	**Segmentation of companies in order to better understand their behavior during the delivery of the service.** *Example of segmentation criteria*: corporate culture. *Example of market segments*: in the neo-banking market, entrepreneurs will have a specific and different behavior from even an SME.	**Segmentation of the employees involved in the delivery of the service with the provider.** *Examples of segmentation criteria*: socio-demographic characteristics, status and function in the company. *Examples of market segments*: in the reception market, the service relationship will differ between the headquarters of a CAC 40 company and its provincial production site.

Table 4.2. *Dual segmentation for B2B services*

---

5 This particularity of the B2B service is more fully elaborated on in Chapter 6.

4.1.2.3. *Managers facing segmentation*

Beyond the legitimacy of marketing segmentation in the context of implementing a customer orientation, managers must be convinced of its usefulness and use it to act on their performance. Segmentation first makes it possible for managers to understand their market, this time not in its entirety but through the particularities of the customers who make it up. Segmentation is a tool for managers to decipher, analyze and anticipate, in order to deploy a better relational excellence throughout the relationship with their clients: to better structure their approach to the purchasing and negotiation process, to better accompany the client in their participation in the service and to better manage potential conflicts during and after the service. Segmentation offers managers a real perspective on their market and their customers.

However, to take full advantage of this segmentation approach, managers must remain vigilant on the following points:

– Always start by turning to the marketing department or functional departments to learn what the company already knows about the marketing segmentation of its markets.

– Not segmenting one's market based on internal criteria such as the turnover achieved with a customer. In this case, it would be a simple customer typology and not a segmentation in the marketing sense of the term.

– The market should not be restricted to current customers but extended as much as possible to all potential customers. The challenge is to have a broad vision of the market. This is a real challenge for the manager who must strive to see further than his current market.

– Do not assume that segmentation cannot be applied to a single-client context. An intra-client segmentation can often be relevant. Indeed, having a single company as a client does not necessarily mean that one works for a single team, a single entity or a single department of this client. There may be opportunities for business development within the client company. It is, therefore, useful to consider the heterogeneity of the various potential internal clients.

If managers are responsible for both sales and service production, they will be directly concerned by the duality of segmentation – commercial segmentation and operational segmentation – and will be able to articulate both in their customer relationship. On the other hand, if managers are only in charge of the commercial or operational part, there is an actual issue of reconciliation and integration of these two segmentations, which should be an additional argument for close collaboration between the two managers.

4.1.3. *Targeting*

4.1.3.1. *Principle of targeting*

Targeting consists of deciding which of the various market segments that will be served. Identifying the customers one does not want to serve is just as important as identifying those one does want to serve. This targeting is based on a joint analysis of the characteristics of the segments and the company's capabilities and the company's willingness to serve them. The objective is to identify the segments that best fit the company and that can, therefore, be addressed most effectively by the company. Most of the time, the company identifies several target segments including a priority target. Each target is approached and served in a specific way. The notion of priority target is particularly important:

– it is supposed to have the most impact in terms of sales, results or development;

– it must, therefore, be the subject of particular attention, especially in the context of a service activity for which the performance of the service is linked to the client. Operational decisions, like investment choices in particular, should, therefore, be made with this target in mind.

Finally, the definition of the targets makes it possible to identify the direct competitors and the key success factors that must be mastered in order to be effective on the chosen targets.

4.1.3.2. *Challenges of targeting for managers*

This targeting process first gives managers the opportunity to critically analyze his or her client portfolio (see Box 4.2).

When responding to calls for tenders, targeting allows one to go faster and with more objectivity on two essential questions:

– Bid/no bid? That is, deciding whether or not to respond to the call for tenders depending on whether or not it falls within a predefined target. The decision thus becomes constructed and reflected;

– How to respond? The segmentation will have first identified the key variables of customers (their expectations, their decision style, etc.), which will make it possible for managers to build a more relevant response.

A few simple questions allow for a quick initial analysis of a client portfolio with regard to the defined targeting:

– What is the share of customers[6] who belong to the priority target?

– What is the share of customers who do not belong to identified targets?

– Are there any identified targets that do not fit into the client portfolio?

– How much time is spent with the priority target customers?

– How much time is spent with customers who do not belong to identified targets?

Box 4.2. *Client portfolio analysis*

Targeting is certainly a necessary reflection, but it should not prevent managers from keeping an open vision of their market; segments that are not in the target today could become so tomorrow, just as competitors positioned on segments not targeted by the company could attack its targets tomorrow. Managers find themselves in a well-known situation of double bind (Ancelin-Bourguignon 2018): exploring new potential targets and exploiting the defined targets.

4.2. Indirect actors

A service provider is never "only" in a B2B relationship. Managers must be careful not to lock themselves into an exclusive relationship with their only direct client. In reality, the company is embedded in a vast network of players, which could lead any service provider to define itself, with a touch of audacity, as a business-to-society service company, following the example of Bureau Veritas[7].

---

6 The customer share is calculated in terms of number of customers, turnover and result.

7 www.bureauveritas.fr/qui-sommes-nous/notre-mission [Accessed on September 8, 2019].

4.2.1. *Identifying the actors*

4.2.1.1. *Vertical players*

In the classic approach to a sector, one first look at the vertical players, distinguishing between those located downstream from its position and those positioned upstream.

Three categories of downstream actors can be distinguished: the direct customer, the indirect customer and the final customer. The direct customer belongs to the company's direct market, introduced in the first part of this chapter, and will be discussed more extensively in Chapter 5. The indirect customer is the customer of the direct customer or of an indirect customer depending on the length of the channel. Finally, the end client is the consumer. In the simple case of painting new aircraft, illustrated in Figure 3.1 in Chapter 3, the manufacturer is the direct customer, the airline the indirect customer and the passenger the final customer. The greater the distance between the company and the downstream actor, the more difficult it will be to detect signals in order to anticipate scenarios of change in the industry as a whole or in the behavior of the direct customer in particular. These downstream actors, beyond the direct customer, are to be evaluated in relation to their power of influence on the sector and their capacity to influence the company's activity. The end client in particular can become a target of attention. For Sodexo, for example, understanding the end consumer is essential:

> One want to better understand our consumers' needs so one can meet them. At the same time as they become an important source of additional revenue, they have the power to influence the decisions of our B-to-B customers.[8]

The upstream actors are the company's suppliers and service providers. In the context of customer orientation, these players are becoming particularly important, since by directly influencing the company's CSR performance[9],

---

8 Message from Sophie Bellon, Chairman of the Board of Directors of Sodexo: Sodexo (2018). Document de référence 2017–2018, pp. 12–13 [Online]. Available at: www.sodexo.com/files/live/sites/sdxcom-global/files/PDF/Finance/Sodexo-Document-Reference-2017-2018.pdf [Accessed on November 18, 2019].

9 CSR, corporate social responsibility, defined by the European Commission as "the responsibility of companies for their impact on society"; www.diplomatie.gouv.fr/IMG/pdf/Communication_of_25_October_2011_by_the_European_Commission_on_CSR_cle434613.pdf [Accessed on September 8, 2019].

they can become relevant support points for the service provider in its relations with its customer and, more broadly, its industry. Customers are increasingly sensitive to these issues with the rise of the concept of responsible purchasing. These upstream suppliers and service providers can also have an impact on the quality of the service delivered to the customer, and managers must, therefore, integrate them as players in their customer orientation.

4.2.1.2. *Horizontal actors*

Beyond this first approach of the sector around its different vertical actors, it must be admitted that at each level of the sector, peripheral actors, that one call here horizontal actors, form in their turn a kind of transversal sector to the main sector. The control bodies specific to the aeronautical sector are one of these horizontal actors, major, for a provider of painting of new aircraft. These horizontal actors are numerous, and it is not easy for managers to identify them.

The concept of a business ecosystem can be useful to better understand this broader approach to the industry. The concept appeared in the 1990s. Referring to its ecological meaning, it emphasizes the idea of interactions between actors in a common environment (Daidj 2011). The more recent emergence of "platform"-type environments, and their growing importance in many markets, is reactivating interest in this concept (Adner 2016). The business ecosystem is mainly characterized by the heterogeneity of the actors that comprise it, mixing market actors (companies) and non-market actors (institutional organizations, administrations, research centers, interest groups, associations, professional groups, lobbies, etc.). The notions of industry and sector are no longer relevant, since the business ecosystem brings together actors from different sectors and industries. Within these business ecosystems, formal and informal relationships enable the dissemination of knowledge and information, and the emergence of coordination and collaboration processes that promote innovation and strengthen the competitiveness of the various actors.

The notion of proximity has always been at the heart of the concepts of networks and ecosystems . However, if historically one started from a proximity of a geographical nature (the industrial district, the cluster, the competitiveness cluster), one are now sliding towards the notion of an organizational proximity (Assens and Ensminger 2015). The business ecosystem, thus, tends to be defined as a social community in which actors come together around shared economic and industrial issues and ambitions. Ecosystems are often illustrated in broad and global environments: the cell phone ecosystem, the IT industry and technology platforms. Managers' task is to apply this notion of ecosystem to their perimeter, without attempting to describe the more global ecosystem of their company or industry in an exhaustive manner.

4.2.2. *Managers' responsibility towards indirect actors*

The indirect actors are, therefore, numerous, and this can petrify the manager. However, this multiplicity of actors represents as many opportunities for action for the manager. Customer orientation can be deployed on other actors than the direct customer, thus contributing to a better performance of managers.

4.2.2.1. *Assessing actors*

After having identified the various players in the sector and his ecosystem, a manager must evaluate them and identify the main issues. First of all, it is the capacity of each player to influence the sector in general, and its direct client in particular, that must be evaluated, distinguishing between key players and more secondary players. The key player in a sector is not systematically the direct client that generates the most financial revenue but the one that is indispensable in the creation of value. For LinkedIn, for example, even if it is clear that individual members contribute very little to its financial revenues, they are, on the other hand, essential in the creation of value, since they are the ones who make the site attractive to paying customers, that is, recruiters. The key player may be located further downstream in the value chain, but it may also be located in the ecosystem and quite far from the heart of the sector, without necessarily being a market player. This analysis must be carried out on different time scales. In the short-term, for example, in the context of negotiating a call for tenders, key players are very often in the immediate environment. On the other hand, in a longer-term analysis, key players may be further away, such as the end client, who often gains weight in a more global strategic vision.

In addition to identifying the key players in the sector in terms of influence and actions, it is also necessary to enrich one's knowledge of the various players by asking questions about their roles and issues. By enriching its vision of the sector, this approach also strengthens the service provider's position *vis-à-vis* its direct client. By being able to provide their client with precise knowledge and information about their own client and, more broadly, about the sector and the ecosystem, managers open up the scope of the relationship with their client beyond the service that is exchanged.

With a better knowledge of the sector and of the specificities of the different actors, the service provider also has the means to propose a more innovative offer to its client (see Box 4.3).

A manufacturer of wooden garden sheds contacts a documentary engineering service provider in order to dematerialize its technical assembly documentation. Before responding to this simple request from its direct client, the service provider identified the main players in this sector. It then realized that its client's technical documentation is actually used by different actors: the indirect client, which is represented by the network of resellers, the end client, which is the consumer, and horizontal actors such as architects or installers. Each of these actors does not use the technical documentation in the same way and on the same media. For example, while end clients may appreciate being able to consult the technical documentation on their smartphone or tablet, the architect will be attracted to being able to integrate it directly into his or her own design software. The service provider then offers its customer, in addition to a general digitalized technical documentation (DOC), four versions of this documentation specific to the constraints of each indirect actor.

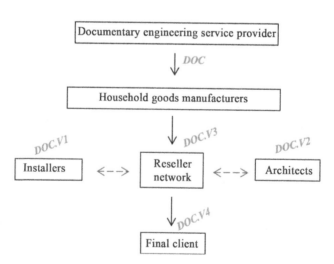

Figure 4.1. *Supply chain of a home goods manufacturer. For a color version of this figure, see www.iste.co.uk/mathieu/services.zip*

Box 4.3. *Sector vision to enrich the offer*

4.2.2.2. Deploying a relationship strategy

Establishing relationships with the players of his industry and his ecosystem is undeniably a priority in managers' business strategy and an essential support for maintaining operational and relational excellence with the client. For example, it is in the interest of a thermal engineering service provider to maintain excellent relations with the inspection bodies responsible for validating the conformity of an installation, in order to be able to lift any reservations directly with the body without the client necessarily being informed. The client will be reassured by the serenity of the end of the construction site and will retain a good image of the provider.

In this relational strategy, managers must first choose the actors with whom it seems relevant to establish relationships, as it is illusory to enter into a relational strategy with all the actors in the ecosystem. This choice is in fact the direct result of the analysis and knowledge of the actors described above. Once these actors have been selected, one must find the best way to contact them. In addition to direct contact, more indirect actions can be imagined: being put in contact by other actors, participating in professional meetings, joining professional networks, organizing events, etc.

This stage undeniably requires a lot of time and energy. Managers must try to rely as much as possible on their team, on internal resources of their company and more widely on their personal network.

4.2.2.3. Diversifying its anchor points

With a deeper understanding of the industry and their ecosystem, and having established relationships with certain key players, managers can realize that it is possible to approach and influence their client more indirectly. In this way, they anchor themselves to other players in order to strengthen their position *vis-à-vis* their direct client and to better manage the risk of dependency.

It is often by relying on an indirect customer, or the end client, that many B2B companies build innovative approaches in their markets. One of the best-known examples is Intel, which, by making it possible for computer brands to put the *Intel Inside®* sticker on their hardware, has relied on pressure from the end client to encourage its direct customers to buy its microprocessors rather than those of its competitors. This strategy was largely successful given Intel's dominant position in its market. In the textile sector, many industrial brands such as Lycra® or Gore tex® have the same strategy of focusing on the end client.

The indirect client may be sensitive to the providers chosen by its supplier, especially when these providers are likely to have a direct impact on its performance. In this case, it is perfectly legitimate to rely on the indirect client in order to strengthen its position with its direct client. This support of actors other than the direct client can take the form of lobbying actions or go as far as more voluntarist approaches such as the construction of alliances or the establishment of contracts.

However, these strategies must be used with caution, taking into account the possible reactions of its direct client.

4.2.2.4. Building an offer

Finally, the most daring approach consists of building a service offer for players other than the direct client.

This may be a service offering that the service provider usually provides to its direct client and that it extends to an indirect player. For example, a technical study service initially addressed to powerful clients can be deployed to the subcontractors of this client. Some service providers go so far as to design particularly innovative offers for indirect players (see Box 4.4).

SUEZ, On'Connect™ generation

Suez is a world leader in water treatment and waste management. Its activities include the construction and operation of water networks and infrastructure; the collection, sorting and recovery of waste; and the production of local and renewable energy. Circular economy model is widely promoted by the group. Convinced that one are only just entering the era of digital utilities and that the digital revolution is still in its infancy in the environmental businesses, Suez is very committed to digital technologies in order to develop intelligent solutions.

On'Connect™ is a technology that connects objects, in particular water meters, and collects and processes data. This is known as a smart or communicating water meter. This data makes it possible for Suez to develop digital platforms and design new services (an alert, for example, in the event of a suspected water leak) for various actors in a given territory. According to Suez, these services have a dual purpose: to increase the well-being of users and to encourage more responsible consumption.

On'Connect™ generation is one of these platforms. Its objective is to promote home support for the elderly by offering a preventive support service for isolated elderly people. It is aimed at caregivers and social structures of communities (CCAS). Based on the principle that water consumption is a good indicator of the person's activity, On'Connect™ generation collects data on the elderly person's water consumption. This data enables real-time identification of a change in consumption and weak signals such as taking a shower in the middle of the night or stopping household chores that may indicate a loss of autonomy. Notifications are then sent to caregivers or social structures. Partnerships with tele-assistance or tele-health companies can further enrich the offer.

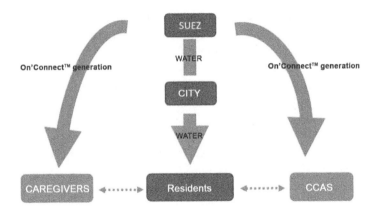

Figure 4.2. *Supply opportunities for the water supply chain. For a color version of this figure, see www.iste.co.uk/mathieu/services.zip*

Box 4.4. *Building an offer for indirect actors*[10]

10 Box 4.4 was written from the following sources: Suez (2016). On'Connect : une nouvelle ère pour la ville connectée. Press release [Online]. Available at: www.suez.fr/fr-fr/actualites/communiques-de-presse/on-connect-une-nouvelle-ere-pour-la-ville-connectee [Accessed on November 28, 2019]; Suez (2018). Pollutec Trade Show: SUEZ supports cities by launching two digital solutions for tourism and to help seniors living at home. Press release [Online]. Available at: https://www.suez.com/en/news/press-releases/pollutec-trade-show-suez-launches-two-digital-solutions-on-connect [Accessed on November 28, 2019]; Suez (2019). Publications [Online]. Available at: www.suez.com/fr/actualites/publications [Accessed on November 28, 2019].

Green Gas International designs, develops and operates solutions for gas extraction and upgrading in Central and Continental Europe (Germany, Poland, the Czech Republic and Slovakia). Mine gas is the mainstay of Green Gas International's business due to the large number of coal mines in its markets. The gas is first removed from the mine to ensure the safety of the miners while respecting environmental constraints. The extracted gas is then either sold directly to industrial customers or transformed into thermal and electrical energy by the cogeneration system.

The direct customers are mainly industrial companies, local authorities and the electricity network for the electrical energy produced by the cogeneration.

The mine is a complex actor to understand in this particular context, being simultaneously a customer and a supplier. As a supplier, the mine sells the material essential to its activity to Green Gas International. As a customer, it buys a high value-added service that makes it possible for it to maximize its income from the sale of its gas and which also offers Green Gas International better volumes of gas to be recovered. The relationship, thus, has a strong partnership dimension with strongly joint interests. Managers may find it difficult to embrace this relationship in all its depth. This player also poses an identified threat, since coal mines are due to disappear in the more or less short-term.

The citizen, as a consumer of electricity or heating, or as a customer of the industry, is an end client who may be sensitive to the nature of the energy used.

Beyond the vertical sector, the ecosystem is wide, mixing European, national and local actors. The European Commission sets a global framework for energy policy in which each of its member states must participate. The regulation may appear as a threat for Green Gas International, but it is the responsibility of its managers not to interpret it as a fatality. Customer orientation, based on an analysis of market evolution, must accompany managers to help them imagine their market of tomorrow. The threats identified in the ecosystem must lead managers to break out of an overly restrictive vision of their market: the vision of their market should never be limited to what the company knows how to do, to the tools it possesses and to the skills it masters. It is from the market targeted by managers that skills, tools and techniques can be adapted or acquired. At the national level, professional federations and chambers of commerce are intervening with legislators to make them aware of the extent of the environmental challenge represented by mine gas and the need to continue extracting it. In addition to these major European and national players, local anchoring must be maintained, by being present with the major local decision-makers, cities and regions. These local players contribute to building managers' network, can be allies at key moments' and are also potential clients. Finally, one must take into account competitors who do not always have rational strategies but who can deploy maneuvers to satisfy their egos.

In an international environment, the implementation of customer orientation must take into account the cultural dimension that shapes employees. In Central and Continental European countries, pragmatism is strong and the operational capabilities of the teams are solid. However, the vision is more short-termist with a tendency to fatalism. It is, therefore, necessary to help teams to better project themselves and to imagine possible futures. Exchange, proximity, pedagogy and a certain humility are the best allies for managers to bring their local teams to a true long-term customer orientation.

Box 4.5. *Testimony of Laurent Barrieux (Managing Director and Chairman of the Board of Green Gas International)*

Understanding the Purchase

5.1. Buying center concept

The buying center is the term that designates all the people who are involved in the process and decision to purchase a product or service in a B2B context. Not all companies have a purchasing or procurement department, but every B2B purchasing process involves a buying center. This buying center can be limited to one person in the simplest situations or for the purchase of specific services, or it can include many people for more complex purchasing situations.

5.1.1. *Composition of the buying center*

5.1.1.1. *Roles*

The buying center is made up of people with specific roles in the buying process and often different expectations towards the provider and its offering. The following main roles are usually distinguished:

– The initiator: triggers the need and is thus at the origin of the purchase. The more important the strategic and financial dimension of the service is for the client, the more the initiator tends to have a high hierarchical position. A president or CEO is usually the initiator of ambitious projects and investments. The human resources department takes the initiative to call on a recruiting firm. A maintenance manager of an industrial site initiates the consultation of construction companies. A product manager expresses the need for a graphic designer to help him/her in the implementation of his/her communication plan. The initiator can be confused with the user or the buyer in certain purchasing situations but this is not systematic.

– The user: this is the employee of the client company who benefits from the service. In the case of training, the user will be the participant who is not systematically the initiator. The notion of user is discussed in more detail in Chapter 6.

– The advisor or influencer: he or she guides the buying process and the choice of service provider without necessarily being an employee of the client company. For technical maintenance or repair services, the client's technical services undoubtedly have an advisory role. However, a design office, a control agency, an assistant to principal, often have a great influence on the choice of the service provider.

– The prescriber: has a more formal role than the advisor in imposing or proscribing a service provider. The prescriber is generally an internal actor but can be independent in more constrained environments. The nuclear safety agency in France (ASN), for example, plays the role of prescriber for all services provided in the nuclear sector. The client's legal department may exclude a contractor because of a risk related to its sustainability.

– The gatekeeper: a person who stands between the service provider and the members of the buying center. The purchasing or procurement department is often cited as a filter for access to users, or management assistants who can limit access to the decision-maker.

– The decision-maker: makes the final purchasing decision, alone or collectively. Whatever their hierarchical level, from a general manager to a department head, the decision-maker has a definite managerial position.

– The buyer: often mistakenly confused with the decision-maker. In some cases, the buyer may simply apply the decision of their general management without having any impact on the decision. Their main mission is to ensure that buying procedures are adhered to and, in particular, that the buying process runs smoothly. However, it would be simplistic to describe him/her as a simple purchasing administrator. It is important to distinguish between purchasing situations, which are increasingly common, in which the buyer belongs to the purchasing department, and those in which the purchasing process is handled by another department. For purchases of intellectual services in particular and services in general, the purchasing department is not always the main contact.

5.1.1.2. *Diversity of profiles and expectations*

It is imperative to have a broad knowledge of the buying center without limiting yourself to the person who may seem the most important, the decision-maker or buyer. Each can provide valuable information and enable managers to refine their approach strategy and increase their chances of success. It is important to identify as clearly and as precisely as possible the people who make up the buying center: their identity, role, contact details and profile. The objective of defining the profile is to provide a whole set of information that will allow for a better understanding of the person, and to better prepare to build a relationship with him or her. In this sense, elements related to the person's education, professional background, family situation, hobbies and also more detailed elements likely to better characterize their psychological profile, become precious information to better understand their problems and expectations.

When it comes to buying center expectations, it is tempting to simplify them around the traditional price, quality and delivery trilogy. Although this trilogy remains essential in B2B, we must strive to broaden it to better approach the complexity of our customers' expectations, beyond what is written in a specification or verbally formulated. This understanding of customer expectations is particularly complex, firstly because of the diversity of the members of the buying center, who do not all have the same expectations, as well as because of the difficulty for the customer to make their expectations for a service explicit, that is, to project themselves onto the result. Hidden, unspoken expectations, more personal and emotional factors, further increase the difficulty in grasping the customer's real expectations. Anxiety, for example, when faced with a complex decision, can lead the client to favor providers capable of simplifying their decision-making[1]. Especially since expectations are always at two levels: expectations to satisfy the general interest of the company, and individual expectations to satisfy our own interest, the two types of expectations not always converging. The time spent with the different members of the buying center, well before the offer, the quality of the listening, the professionalism of the relationship, are the best allies in this quest for the real expectations of

---

1 A large study of thousands of executives involved in complex B2B solution buying processes found that for 40% of these purchases, the client would experience post-purchase anxiety; terms such as "difficult", "awful", "frustrating", "painful", "minefield" are used to describe complex buying processes; there would then be a 62% greater chance of closing a high-value sale for the supplier that makes the buying process simpler (Toman *et al.* 2017).

the customer, which alone guarantees the commercial success in the first instance, and the quality of the service in the second instance.

In a global approach to the buying center, it remains essential to identify members who are enthusiastic about the offer and the provider, those who are hostile to it, and those who seem neutral. These positions can evolve over time, at different phases of the purchasing process until the final stage of the negotiation.

Faced with this diversity of profiles, expectations and positions, the success of the sales approach depends on the development of a discourse, approach and response adapted to each member of the buying center. Each member of the buying center must be approached at the right time, with the right discourse and with response elements that are specific to them.

5.1.2. *The buyer*

As described above, the buyer is not the only actor in the purchasing process and may even be absent in some commercial negotiations. Nevertheless, in many purchasing situations, buyers are key players, and they depend on a role that carries a lot of weight with the customer. It is all the more important to better approach buyers as they are, for many managers, a poorly known and often feared actor.

5.1.2.1. *Reality and challenges of the purchasing department*

It is commonly accepted that purchases represent on average 50% of turnover in European companies, and in some sectors[2], this figure can rise to 70% and even more. In the automotive industry, for example, buying represents 75% of the value of the final product[3]. Services and intellectual services have long been outside the scope of the purchasing function, but are now gradually being included in the same way as the purchase of goods and products. Business, operational or functional departments, which have

---

2 Gouttebroze, B. (2017). Panorama de la fonction achats [Online]. Available at: www.decision-achats.fr/Thematique/strategie-achats-1236/Dossiers/est-que-fonction-achats-metier-acheteur-processus-achats-formation-remuneration-313312/decouvrez-differentes-familles-achats-317465.htm; and CDAF Formation (2019). Qu'est-ce qu'un acheteur ? [Online]. Available at: https://www.cdaf-formation.fr/quest-ce-quun-acheteur/ [Accessed on September 26, 2019].

3 This percentage is announced by Thierry Sauvage, professor at ESLI and director of the public interest grouping campus ESPRIT: www.meilleurs-masters.com/master-achats.html [Accessed September 26, 2019].

historically had control over the purchase of intellectual services and services, may still be reluctant to work with purchasing department, preferring to maintain direct contact with familiar and known suppliers. For example, the purchase of legal services is still largely the preserve of the legal department, just as strategy consulting services are the preserve of general management. Although the buying role is now considered essential for traditional product purchases and is becoming increasingly important for service purchases, service providers must nevertheless remain vigilant with regard to the weight of other departments in the purchase of certain services (see Box 5.1).

People in charge of purchasing services:

– the purchasing or procurement department for 68% of the buying professionals surveyed;

– business departments and prescribers for 17% of the professionals surveyed;

– human resources for 15% of the purchasing professionals surveyed.

Box 5.1. *Actors in service procurement[4]*

The traditional prerogatives of the purchasing department are:

– gathering information on the different products, services and solutions that exist on the market to meet the company's needs;

– referencing of suppliers and service providers;

– drafting of specifications and calls for tenders;

– follow-up of the suppliers and service provider responses and their pre-selection through the establishment of a short list;

– participation in the negotiation and final selection.

---

4 Survey conducted in 2016 by e-purchasing solutions provider Ivalua on trends in purchasing among more than 390 European and North American purchasing professionals from large international companies: Ivalua (2016). Intellectuelles & Services : les Achats prennent le lead [Online] https://fr.ivalua.com/newsroom/prestations-intellectuelles-services-les-achats-prennent-le-lead/ retrieved from Décision-Achats.fr: www.decision-achats.fr/Thematique/category-management-1229/Breves/Prestations-intellectual-services-purchasing-prennent-lead-304599.htm [Accessed on October 1, 2019].

The purchasing function has undergone a profound change over the last 20 years, moving from a simple support function to a strategic function, and going beyond a simple formalization of purchasing with a search for value. Aware of its importance, it has become more independent and is now increasingly attached to general management. At the same time, it has become more professional, with a level of recruitment that is becoming more widespread at the master's degree level, made possible by the proliferation of specialized masters. Since the end of the 1990s, purchasing has integrated new tools from digital technologies such as e-procurement[5] and e-sourcing[6].

The purchasing role has also become more professional through the acquisition of real expertise in specific purchasing families, and in particular in the purchase of services. It is no longer rare to find buyers in purchasing departments who are experts in service purchasing, sometimes even specialized in specific services. In its barometer of consulting purchases, Consult'in France established that 65% of consulting buyers are expert buyers dedicated to the purchase of intellectual services[7], and consultants believe they go through purchasing department in 61% of cases[8]. Bertrand

---

5 E-procurement, that is, the administrative management of a company's purchases, using information technology and in particular the Internet. The objective is to streamline purchasing procedures as much as possible while reducing costs. In the best case, the company will manage to set up an automated procedure. E-procurement can also be the subject of a collaborative approach between several companies, always with a view to shared cost management. This can lead to the creation of electronic marketplaces. The term is sometimes used by professionals in its contracted form "e-proc". www.e-marketing.fr/Definitions-Glossaire/procurement-241694.htm [Accessed on October 4, 2019].

6 A company's purchasing strategy, which consists of identifying and selecting suppliers (producers, central purchasing agencies, importers, etc.) by making the best possible use of information technology, particularly the offers and dedicated platforms available on the Web. According to Marc Filser: "Marketplaces are already a tool for improving the efficiency of distributors' purchasing activities. They simplify relations with suppliers through the use of tools like electronic catalogs, and they speed up the negotiation process through auction sessions. Their impact on the relationship between suppliers and distributors has yet to be analyzed: the marketplace may indeed be perceived by the industrialist as an additional weapon in the distributor's toolbox". www.e-marketing.fr/Definitions-Glossaire/sourcing – 241724.htm#80bF1bp9Xo2EbJZA.97 [Accessed on October 4, 2019].

7 Consult'in France, Baromètre des achats de conseil (2017–2018). Consult'in France, Syntec Stratégie et Management, Paris, p. 9.

8 EMI Conseil (2019). Baromètre des achats de Consult'in France 2017, p. 12 [Online]. Available at: https://emiconseil.fr/barometre-des-achats-de-consultin-france-2017/ [Accessed on June 4, 2020].

Malguet, partner of MLA Conseil and director of Consult'in France, underlines the interest for service providers to increase the skills of buyers[9]:

> Today, we are increasingly faced with professionals specifically trained in buying intellectual services, and more specifically in management consulting purchases, who have made a career in purchasing [...]. The fact that we have buyers who understand what consulting is, what it is used for and how it contributes to performance, makes it possible for us to save time and to move upmarket.

Clients are, therefore, acquiring expertise in the purchase of services. Understanding what a service is, how it operates from the provider's point of view, how it fits into its organization and contributes to its performance can only foster better relations between the client and its provider. The service provider must accompany its client in this rise in skills by encouraging the construction of common interpretations of services[10]. This is a posture that can enhance its value and enable it to establish greater proximity with its client.

5.1.2.2. *From the cost killer to the value incubator*

The buyer does not generally have a good reputation. He has a negative image as a cost killer, haggler, harasser or manipulator. The recent report of the parliamentary commission of inquiry on the relations between the large-scale distribution and its suppliers underlines that "the persistence of exchanges marked by a certain harshness, even based on intimidation and psychological pressure" are not to be excluded between the buyers and their suppliers[11].

---

9 https://emiconseil.fr/barometre-des-achats-de-consultin-france-2017/ [Accessed on October 5, 2019].

10 For example, the Consult'in France purchasing group has built a matrix for analyzing a consulting service that makes it possible for buyers to better understand the skills required according to the consulting phase (Consult'in France, Baromètre des achats de conseil (2017–2018). Consult'in France, Syntec Stratégie et Management, Paris, p. 38).

11 Report of the parliamentary commission of inquiry into the situation and practices of large-scale distribution and its groupings in their commercial relations with their suppliers (2019), p. 59 [Online]. Available at: www2.assemblee-nationale.fr/15/autres-commissions/ commissions-d-enquete/commission-d-enquête-sur-la-situation-et-les-pratiques-de-la-grande-distribution-et-de-ses-groupements-dans-leurs-relations-commerciales-avec-les-fournisseurs/ (block)/RapEnquete/(instance_leg)/15/(init)/0-15 [Accessed on January 10, 2020].

However, the buyer's position is changing, and the importance given to price is not as overwhelming as we sometimes imagine[12]. The buyer must remain one of the guarantors of the margin, while also gradually becoming the artisan of an extended firm by building strategic partnerships with his/her suppliers, subcontractors and service providers, in order to consolidate the sources of innovation of his/her company. Subcontractors and service providers directly or indirectly contribute to the competitive differentiation, innovation and continuous improvement of their customers' processes and offers. It is, therefore, up to the buyer to act as a value incubator, in order to create a context and environment with its subcontractors and service providers that is conducive to the release of these potential sources of value. Purchasing services is a strategic category of purchasing for the company, with complex financial, technical, legal, organizational and human issues at stake. Purchasing departments must convince the various internal customers of their added value in order to overcome their reluctance to collaborate on certain categories of services. Often, internal customers themselves see purchasing as a mere cost killer, which is a real source of conflict.

The purchasing department must then find its rightful place alongside the other departments involved in the purchase of the service. It must stick to its core business and agree to work in tandem with the internal customer, without trying to impose a process or a choice on departments that have a wealth of know-how and experience. In the specific case of training purchases, for example, the buyer must collaborate with the HR department to draw up the specifications, identify potential suppliers and develop the negotiation strategy. The buyer must recognize that training is a purchase in which the trainee, the business line and the human resources department are essential stakeholders. The purchasing department is obliged to internally sell itself by highlighting other skills and other objectives beyond cost reduction.

Finally, in the growing context of responsible purchasing, the buyer is asked to control the supplier risk, even going so far as to impose a duty of

---

12 Only 68% of purchasing departments put cost reduction as their top priority for 2020, a percentage down 7 points from 2019. Study conducted among 682 buyers by AgileBuyer in partnership with the 10,000-member National Purchasing Council and reported in an article in *Les Échos* (Dupont-Calbo 2020).

vigilance in accordance with the Sapin II law[13]. The buyer becomes a stakeholder in the construction and protection of the company's image by guaranteeing ethical, sustainable and responsible purchasing. Box 5.2 shows the importance given by companies to responsible purchasing.

Faced with these changes in the purchasing function and the challenges they pose for the buyer, managers can skillfully position themselves as a true partner of their buyers to support them in their new role as a value incubator.

A quantitative study conducted online with a sample of 185 decision-makers in the field of sustainable procurement shows that **sustainable procurement is a strong and real concern of companies**:

– 9 out of 10 organizations surveyed have a responsible purchasing policy;

– for 48% of the organizations surveyed, sustainable procurement is a priority;

– strong evolution of responsible purchasing skills: in 2009, 46% of companies declared having a good knowledge of responsible purchasing; in 2019, 87% of companies declare having a good knowledge of responsible purchasing.

Box 5.2. *Sustainable procurement[14]*

5.2. Buying process

After identifying the various people involved in the purchase, it is necessary to identify the different stages of the customer's purchase in order to adapt to them as best as possible.

From the customer's point of view, the buying process is broken down into different stages. The manager must identify them in order to adapt to them as best as possible. Depending on the nature of the purchase (strategic, technical, routine) and its scope, the purchasing process will be more or less formalized. B2B purchasing is a long process that generally takes weeks or months and can extend over several years. For example, it was after three years of competition, with eight competitors at the start, that ADP Ingénierie finally won the competition for the architectural design of the

---

13 A French law relative to transparency, the fight against corruption and the modernization of economic life.

14 ObsAR (2019). Baromètre des achats responsables. OpinionWay pour l'ObsAR. 10th edition [Online]. Available at: www.obsar.asso.fr [Accessed on September 30, 2019].

Beijing–Daxing airport[15]. The purchasing process is structured around stages in which the client's stakes and stance change, which must lead the manager to adapt.

5.2.1. *The launch*

Three key stages structure the launch of the purchase for the customer: recognition of a need, specification of the service, sourcing. For their part, managers must establish a relationship with the client as soon as possible in order to anticipate the release of the call for tenders.

5.2.1.1. *Recognition of a need*

This is really the very first step in any buying process. The need is revealed by the initiator. Initiators most often belong to an operational or business department, but they can also depend on a functional department. Because of their proximity to the customer, service providers can participate in this recognition and can even reveal a need to their customer. This is one of the consequences of customer loyalty: by remaining present at the customer's site, the established service provider is particularly well placed to participate in the recognition of a need or to be quickly informed of this first phase of the purchase. The entire team, present at the customer's site, must feel concerned and alert to these precursor events, likely to trigger a purchase. Some companies have set up challenges for their employees on customer assignments, with bonuses that can amount to several hundred euros, if a need is detected and results in an assignment.

Providers who develop particularly innovative services, as is the case for an entrepreneur or a start-up, are confronted with the absence of this very first stage among their potential clients, because the need is still too latent. The position of such providers is even more complicated as they are generally not known by these potential clients. In this case, the channel approach presented above can be relevant.

---

15 Schaeffer (2019). Ces entreprises françaises qui ont tiré leur épingle du jeu pour le nouvel aéroport de Pékin. *Les Échos*, September 25 [Online]. Available at: www.lesechos. fr/industrie-services/air-defense/these-french-companies-who-have-pulled-their-own-game-for-the-new-airport-in-Beijing-1134539 [Accessed on September 26, 2019].

5.2.1.2. *Service specification*

It is at this stage that an initial, more or less formal, set of specifications will be drawn up in order to specify the nature of the need and the expected benefits of the service. In a more formalized process, the client can also specify the commercial conditions and the selection criteria of the service providers. In structured companies and for significant purchases, the purchasing department is very often the major player in this stage, in association with internal prescribers or users. In certain situations, for specific services, this stage can be carried out in direct relation with the user or the initiator.

The formalization of the service is a step that remains difficult for customers because it is often difficult to really specify their expectations and to detail them around precise and objective criteria, due to the nature of the service. It is also both the process and the result of the service that must be specified. This requires a real competence in the service from the client. If the service addresses issues that are new to the customer, the difficulty of specifying the service is even greater. A service that is poorly specified by the customer will be a source of tension and dissatisfaction, not only during the buying process, but also during the implementation phase. Faced with the difficulty experienced by clients in truly clarifying their request, it may be in the clients' interest to remain with a more flexible definition of their needs. Service providers, by making their service more legible, can become a kind of Maieutician of their clients' needs.

5.2.1.3. *The search for providers*

Sourcing, referencing and approval are used not only to seek out potential service providers but also to make an initial selection by eliminating those who do not meet the minimum requirements. These eliminatory criteria generally revolve around the capacity and technical competence of the service provider, insufficiently fulfilled legal conditions or limitations in terms of financial solvency, for example, or presenting a risk of economic dependence. The purchasing function will actively participate in the sourcing process by making its contribution to departments that are reluctant to collaborate with it. The list of potential suppliers is generally drawn up on the basis of recommendations from the various internal departments, professional networks and information gathered on the Web. For many services, sourcing is often poor due to a lack of knowledge of the service concerned. There is a debate about the benefits and limitations of referencing for both the service provider and the client. Clients recognize the need to keep non-referenced providers in order to maintain flexibility, while providers, especially the smaller ones, complain that this step is cumbersome.

In particularly formalized purchasing procedures, notably within a specific legal framework, the client may have to launch a call for application before a call for tenders. The call for application is essentially an administrative phase, but it nevertheless allows for an initial selection of service providers. The selection is not yet based on the content of the service but on legal conformity, qualifications and references.

5.2.1.4. *Manager's mission: upstream lobbying*

While the start-up i-Sea has been chosen by the European Space Agency to lead Space for Shore, a consortium of 10 European companies and universities, with a budget of 1.5 million euros over three years, it is thanks to its strategy of responding to calls for tender. Its director considers that "it is crucial to be informed well in advance of the official publication of the call for tenders"[16]. The more the service provider is present before the call for tenders is issued, the better its chances of success. This presence as early as possible in the tender process is intended to get to know customers and their needs better and also to build or strengthen a relationship outside of a strict commercial relationship, and, thus, establish a more solid trust. Before the tender is issued, it is easier to meet the various players in the purchasing center, to take the time to discuss with them and to strengthen our knowledge of the customer. These exchanges and this relationship before the tender issued have a real impact on the purchasing decision.

Through these contacts, managers and their team will seek to better understand customers' needs, their buying criteria and the way they view the buying process. The various members of the buying center can be identified and then approached. In this long-term approach, which is based on in-depth work and mobilizes resources, managers must know how to surround themselves with their team and also how to approach other managers and

16 Matas, J. (2019). Appel d'offres : la start-up I-Sea a convaincu l'Agence spatiale européenne. *Les Échos Entrepreneurs*, September 23 [Online]. Available at: https://business.lesechos. fr/entrepreneurs/marketing-sales/0601896022334-appel-d-offres-la-start-up-i-sea-a-convaincu-l-agence-spatiale-europeenne-331836.php [Accessed on September 23, 2019].

other departments in their company that have already built a relationship with the customer.

In this approach, it is appropriate to go further than simply collecting information. The service provider must be proactive by providing clients with information and advice, and by accompanying them in the difficulties they may encounter, particularly in specifying the service. If the service provider has succeeded in establishing a real proximity with the client, they can accompany clients formally or informally in the drafting of the specifications, or in their review, and advise them on legal or contractual clauses. Service providers also acquire the legitimacy that will make it possible for them to propose services, define types of services, help clients to become aware of new needs and to formalize them. If the analysis of the sector has highlighted key players in the ecosystem, it is now time to get closer to them.

This positive and constructive presence of the service provider before the call for tenders is issued, although it represents a heavy investment, also has the advantage of preparing and simplifying the delicate phase of responding to the call for tenders.

5.2.2. Call for tenders

A call for tenders or a consultation is a process for selecting a supplier set up by the client. There is a wide variety of calls for tender: some are very heavy and very formalized, comprising several hundred pages, while others are more flexible, or simply triggered by a simple phone call or e-mail, or even limited to an oral request. The call for tenders is launched by a company called the principal.

5.2.2.1. General characteristics of the call for tenders

In its general principle, the main objective of the call for tenders is to organize the competition in order to select the best supplier. It allows for consulting a group of suppliers who submit a commercial and technical proposal based on a common set of specifications. It has become a common practice in B2B, whether for the purchase of products or services. It is a compulsory procedure from a certain financial amount. However, not all business is settled by a tender process. The urgency, the impossibility of changing supplier and the low financial stake of the purchase can lead the customer not to resort to a call for tender procedure.

The invitation to tender is drafted by the client or principal, sometimes with the help of a service provider such as an assistant to principal. It is structured around the following main headings:

– presentation of the company and the general context of the invitation to tender;

– definition of the need;

– description of the specifications of the expected services in terms of functionalities, expected benefits, specific requirements, volume, deadlines;

– notification of planned information meetings with bidders;

– explanation of the supplier selection process: procedure, rules, selection criteria and key dates;

– sharing a rating grid.

A distinction is usually made between public and private invitation to tenders. The public invitation to tender is said to be more cumbersome from an administrative and legal point of view, often discouraging smaller companies from bidding. This is why the legislator decided to raise the threshold at which public purchasers must use the public procurement procedure when buying from the private sector from 25,000 to 40,000 euros.

From a commercial point of view, the private invitation to tender is little different from the public ITT. In both cases, the service provider can establish a relationship with the client before the contract is awarded. As regards, for example, oral presentation, it is amusing to note that it is not prohibited by the public procurement code, whereas in the context of private tendering, some buyers are reluctant to do so.

5.2.2.2. *Manager's mission: writing the proposal*

When the tender is published, the manager must first decide whether or not to bid (bid/no bid). The earlier the tender is anticipated, the easier this decision will be. It depends on the evaluation of the capacity to respond from a commercial and technical point of view, the chances of success and also the capacity to carry out the service with an expected financial result.

If the decision to bid is made, the response must then be prepared. First of all, a team must be mobilized and organized according to the different technical, commercial, legal and financial dimensions of the tender. Depending on the complexity of the ITT, other departments may be involved in preparing the response, in particular the legal and financial departments. External partners, subcontractors and co-contractors may also be involved.

Reading and clarifying the ITT is an essential step before working on the response. The document does not always spell out what one needs to know to bid well. Knowledge of the client in general, and of the ITT in particular, is a considerable asset in interpreting the document.

Once these steps have been completed, the team can prepare its response by mobilizing all its knowledge of the client.

5.2.3. *From short list to contract*

On a date set by the client, all providers send their responses. The client then enters the active stage of provider selection.

5.2.3.1. *Creating a short list of providers*

Based on the responses received, a multi-criteria analysis of the offers will enable reduceing the number of service providers to a short list. After having made an initial selection on the basis of eliminatory elements, taking into account performance, cost, deadlines and a broader set of additional criteria, will not only make it possible to retain only a few service providers, but also to explain the final choice internally and externally.

5.2.3.2. *Negotiation*

The buyer, as a well-trained professional, and more generally the client, will take particular care in preparing the negotiation. Clients will first ensure their position in the negotiation by collecting a maximum of information on the service provider and by acquiring a detailed and appropriate knowledge of their offer. Then, they will develop their negotiation strategy by selecting the main points of the negotiation and by adopting a negotiation method. Clients, and especially buyers, manage to break down the price of the service by distinguishing between direct costs (often salaries directly linked to the performance of the service) and indirect costs (linked, for example, to the service provider's structural costs). This way, they ensure that the indirect costs invoiced are not too high. Securing the contract becomes a key point of negotiation for services that are difficult to control, such as, for example, a clause prohibiting a headhunting firm from poaching employees after having placed them[17].

5.2.3.3. Contractualization

This stage is the result of the negotiation where the client and the provider have agreed on the terms of the final agreement. It takes the form of a purchase order or a purchase contract between the client and the service provider, which establishes a legal bond between the two parties. In this stage, the lawyer teams up with the buyer to draw up the contract. These contracts are becoming increasingly dense and go beyond the purchased service and risk management, including contractual obligations based on documents and clauses not directly related to the purchased service: charter of ethics, adherence to a sustainable development policy or code of ethics[18].

5.2.3.4. Manager's mission: to be reactive

After the offer has been submitted, the manager and their team must remain attentive to maintaining a quality relationship with the client. The client may return to the service provider for additional requests, to obtain clarifications, to propose an oral presentation of the proposal or even to start a negotiation. It is then necessary to be reactive, to remain attentive, to keep in mind the diversity of the buying center and the expectations. The service provider's discourse and actions must remain anchored on the knowledge of the customer acquired before the call for tender.

It may also be advisable to attempt to take action. The knowledge of the customer and the different actors of the buying center should make it possible for the manager to judge the opportunity of such a more proactive approach. Is it possible to make contact with the various players in the buying center? Is it possible to propose to come and present the offer? Is it possible to propose meetings with other customers and visits to customer

---

17 Commercial negotiation is discussed in more detail in Chapter 9.

18 See the interview with Stéphane Larrière, legal director for purchasing at Atos Group, published on the Décision-achats.fr website: www.decision-achats.fr/Thematique/strategie-achats-1236/breves/les-acheteurs-vont-prendre-main-contrats-260879.htm [Accessed on September 29, 2019].

sites? Just as the buyer prepares for the negotiation, the manager must also prepare for it[19].

Finally, regardless of the outcome of the tender, post-tender analysis is absolutely necessary. In case of success, it is necessary to know the criteria that really made the client decide. It is important to know whether objective reasons won the day (price difference, quality, deadlines, etc.) or more subjective reasons that the client will tend to summarize around the notion of trust. Of course, we must take the time to celebrate the victory with our team. In case of failure, the analysis, if more difficult to do, is also more important. It is absolutely necessary to make the effort to call back the customer, who remains a customer after all, and to try to better understand the reasons for their eviction. There is also a lot of work to be done to re-mobilize the team. The employees involved in the bidding process may feel responsible for the failure and feel a certain anxiety, frustration and demobilization. This is a key moment where the manager's leadership must assert itself: being able to objectively analyze the reasons for the failure, to draw the possible consequences and also to reassure and remobilize the team.

Flyin'Chef is a provider of customized culinary events. The company designs, markets and carries out these events for different types of clients:

– shopping centers to animate their galleries and attract visitors;

– companies for their internal operations (team building activity to animate, thank and develop loyalty of their employees) or commercial (to attract prospects or thank and develop loyalty of customers);

– organizers of fairs and exhibitions and their exhibitors;

– event agencies that are more generalist and that turn to specialists for more specific events.

Regardless of the type of customer, there is never any real contact with the purchasing department. Some customers, such as shopping centers, do not even have a purchasing department. We may have to work with the purchasing department after the event for administrative follow-up or referencing, but the purchasing department is never the decision-maker. Moreover, when the company refers a potential service provider to its purchasing department, it is generally a bad sign. Service providers will enter a catalog from which they will generally never leave!

---

19 This point is developed in Chapter 9.

For the corporate customer, the service provider is in contact with a manager throughout the purchasing process. Managers, team managers, department managers or company directors are also the initiator of the event. Together with their assistant, they are the sole interlocutors of the service provider during the different stages of the process. For the agency client, the service provider is in contact with project managers who set up the event for their own client. In the case of professional organizations, a marketing and event manager may be the sole contact.

Referrers can play a role in some cases. They are often freelance event planners who can recommend particular providers to their clients.

The service specification stage is particularly crucial. In general, the client is interested in the service but has a lot of trouble formulating the objectives and purpose of the event. It is then up to the service provider to help the client formulate its objectives. The shopping center would be the client who would most clearly formulate its objective in terms of attendance of the target population (e.g. to attract 150 children during the day).

Depending on the customer's profile, expectations vary. The shopping center has an expectation that is expressed in economic terms with quantified indicators like the price of the service in relation to the person reached. For the company, a culinary event is a costly operation. The buying process starts when the customer is aware of the reality of the price. The company wants to be reassured and is looking for an all-inclusive operation. As for the trade show client or the agency, it is the quality of a customized and turnkey service that is expected.

The organization of an event is a service for which the client generally has high expectations associated with the perception of a risk. The service provider must be particularly careful to convince the client that the promise will be kept during the execution of the event. References are an undeniable asset in the commercial phase. The process must be formalized so that the service provider can explain and communicate it to the client, for example, by sending a summary document to the technical manager of the shopping center containing the main technical data related to the organization of the event. Finally, service providers must make an effort to adopt the customer's language, which makes it possible for them to demonstrate their understanding of the customer's problem.

Box 5.3. *Testimony of Antoine Imbault (ANCuisine Manager, Flyin'Chef Franchisee)*

Identifying Service Targets

6.1. Different types of targets

The targets of the service appear during the delivery of the service. This notion of service targets refers to the people who come into contact with the service provider and its teams during the service delivery stage. While most of the service targets are generally found with the direct client, others, some of whom may be at the heart of the service relationship, belong to other players in the sector. The manager must first identify them and then anticipate the issues related to their satisfaction.

6.1.1. *Targets within the direct client organization*

Even considering a simple service, performed by a single person over a short period of time, in contact exclusively with employees of its direct client, the number and nature of the targets are surprising (Box 6.1).

This situation, described in Box 6.1, reveals three different targets: the beneficiary, the facilitator and the observer.

Samir arrives well in advance this morning at his client's place. He likes to have time to get acquainted with the place, set up, check that everything is working well, and especially to welcome the first participants.

Samir works in a large national training group and specializes in safety at work. His company won a tender with a manufacturer to deliver two days of safety training to its managers and supervisors. The training is to be repeated at the client's five largest production sites. Today, Samir is starting the training on the first site, which is acting as a pilot site.

A month ago, one of his colleagues in the sales department put him in touch by e-mail with the head of training in the client's human resources department in order to prepare the training day. During the negotiation, it was agreed that the trainer would have a conference call with the company's group safety manager to fully understand the issues and the specificity of safety for the client, and to be able to convey the key messages. It was the training manager who put Samir in touch with Etienne Michel, the safety manager. The teleconference, which was initially scheduled to last one hour, ended up lasting more than two hours. Samir and Etienne Michel discovered that they had worked in the same industrial group in the past, but at different times, and they both shared a strong and real commitment to workplace safety. Finally, Etienne Michel suggested to Samir that he contact the managers of each of the sites so that they could drop by during his training to reinforce his message. Samir thought this was an excellent idea. Samir called the training manager to tell her about this exchange with Etienne Michel and to ask her to put him in touch with a contact person at each of the sites in order to prepare his day of intervention. So about two weeks ago, Samir called Nicole, the assistant to the director of the first site that had been chosen, to be his contact person. Samir had specific questions to ask Nicole: how to get to the site, where the training would take place, how the room would be set up and equipped, where and when the breaks would be, who would be in the group, etc. Several exchanges by email and telephone followed in order to settle the training as well as possible. On a specific point of computer connectivity, Nicole preferred to put Samir in direct contact with Aline, a person from the technical department who offered to come and join him in his room at the start of his training to make sure that everything would work well. This reassured Samir.

It's 8:00 am this morning and Samir is about to enter the client's site. The first guard, whom Nicole had warned about Samir's arrival, checks his identity and lets him access the visitor's parking lot easily enough. At the reception, Nicole is waiting for him and accompanies him directly to the room, giving him some practical information about the site. Samir is reassured and immediately feels at ease. Nicole suggests calling Aline to make sure everything is working. The first participants arrive. There will be 20 of them. Samir is used to organizing a practical activity during his training, lasting about an hour, to observe the safety conditions on site. The activity was prepared in great secrecy with Nicole to choose a place and a situation that would not put any of the participants at odds. It is a workshop of about 10 people surrounded by a team leader who will be visited. An informal exchange with the team leader and the workers will be very instructive. Lunch will be taken in the canteen of the site where this group of 20 "chefs" around a stranger will not go unnoticed! As planned, the director of the site will come by at the end of the first day for an exchange with the participants. He will arrive a little before the scheduled time of his intervention and will attend about 15 minutes of Samir's intervention. He will come back the next day to listen to Samir's debriefing of the training with the participants. The person in charge of the training will also come for the debriefing of this first training.

Box 6.1. *Direct client service targets*

6.1.1.1. *The beneficiary*

The beneficiary in context of a direct client is the target that should be the easiest to identify because it is to them that the service is addressed and for them that it is performed. Trainees are the beneficiary of a training course; employees are the beneficiary of their company restaurant; just as traveling executives are the beneficiary of an airline, a car rental company and a hotel. It should be noted that all of these service providers are very rarely chosen by beneficiaries themselves, but are usually negotiated upstream by the purchasing department or by management. The service described in Box 6.1 reveals 20 beneficiaries, that is, the 20 participants in the training. In this particular case of a personal service (training), the beneficiary is easily identifiable. The beneficiary of a service to an object (repair) may be more difficult to identify since the main beneficiary of the service is the good before being a person[1]. In the case of an asset that is strongly linked to a collaborator, used directly by the collaborator in his or her professional activity, it is possible to go back to the beneficiary of the asset to identify the indirect beneficiary of the service. The asset can be that of a particular employee (his or her company car), of a unit (the green spaces of a head office, the machine tool of a production line) or of the company as a whole (its IT system). Finally, in the case of a service offered more widely to the

---

1 This distinction between people processing and possession processing was proposed early on by Lovelock in order to better understand the managerial and marketing implications of each type of service (Lovelock 1996, pp. 28–32).

company as a legal entity (a consulting or auditing service, for example)[2], the beneficiaries are made up of a set of diverse stakeholders.

6.1.1.2. *The facilitator*

Facilitators collaborate with providers in a more or less formal way at different stages of the service in order to help and accompany them in the delivery of the service. Providers have difficulty identifying facilitators because they are often too focused on the beneficiary alone. These facilitators are numerous and scattered throughout the client organization. In Box 6.1, six different facilitators appear throughout the service relationship:

– the training manager who puts the trainer in contact with the right people;

– the safety director who exchanges with the trainer and obtains the collaboration of the site managers;

– the assistant of the site manager who will settle the practical details of his/her intervention and welcome him/her on the site on the day of his/her training;

– the person from the technical department who helps the trainer with his/her computer connections;

– the guard who gives access to the site;

– the site manager who comes by during the training to support the trainer's message.

In addition to these visible facilitators, there are invisible facilitators who are even more difficult to identify. The provider will only think of them in case of an incident or difficulty. For example, if the trainer arrives in the morning in a room that has not been reorganized to accommodate 20 people, leaving an insufficient number of chairs, they will be somewhat irritated with the maintenance department.

It is clear that the facilitator has a strong impact on the service and on the recipient.

---

2 Lovelock introduced a specific service into his typology of services, which is largely found in professional services and in business services, and which he called information processing because of the actions carried out from and on information. The author took as examples of this type of service financial services, legal services, management consulting and marketing studies (Lovelock 1996, p. 31). Taking up Lovelock's typology, Eiglier identified three beneficiaries: the person, the object and the company (Eiglier 2004, p. 4).

6.1.1.3. *The observer*

Observers do not really participate in the delivery of the service. They are voluntarily or involuntarily exposed to the service or the provider. They may even be active observer in the sense that they put themselves in a position of evaluation, interested in the progress, and the realization of the service. In this case, they have often participated in the purchasing process as members of the buying center, buyers, decision-makers, influencers, or prescribers, and participate in the evaluation and control of the provider's performance.

In the situation described in Box 6.1, two rather passive observers appear: the workers and the team leader of the workshop visited by the group during the training, and the people present in the canteen during lunch. Two other observers are more active: the site manager when attending the trainer's presentation and the debriefing, and the training manager, who also attends the debriefing.

Thus, the observer forms a conscious or unconscious impression of the provider that will contribute more or less strongly to the overall evaluation of the provider. In this example, the site manager and the training manager will likely have a significant impact on the overall evaluation of the trainer, whereas the impression of the passive observers might be expected to be ignored. However, the passive observer may in some cases have a real impact on the evaluation of the provider, especially in the context of close proximity to the decision-maker.

6.1.2. *Targets in the sector*

The reality of the sector reappears in the service delivery stage in the sense that the targets of the service can also be found among actors other than the direct client, whether it be the indirect client or other actors even further down the sector.

6.1.2.1. *Targets in the indirect client organization*

Two types of services lead the provider to carry out the service with targets belonging to the indirect client:

– the service is performed for the indirect client;

– the service is performed in the presence of the indirect client.

In the case where the service is performed for the indirect client, the indirect client is the beneficiary. The direct client has selected a provider to perform a service that will benefit its own client. Box 6.2 illustrates the challenges for the provider of direct contact with an indirect client.

Multi Tec[3] is a company that carries out multi-technical work and maintenance (plumbing, heating, air conditioning, electricity, etc.) for mainly tertiary clients (shopping centers, offices, clinics, hospitals, etc.). A year ago, Multi Tec won a tender with Blue & White, a luxury hotel chain comprising three mountain hotels and five seaside hotels. Part of the tender included on-site maintenance for each of the eight hotels with a 24/7 presence during the operation of the establishment. Serge Duchoy, Multi Tec's operations manager, has just come out of a meeting with the technical director, the purchasing director and the general manager of Blue & White. The meeting was more than tense, and the contract is seriously in question. The meeting only dealt with a dozen or so customer comments sent to headquarters at the end of the season. Serge Duchoy rereads the one he would have found amusing, if it were not likely to trigger a breach of contract and cast a pall over Multi Tec's image in the industry:

> We had a very pleasant stay in your hotel but we were surprised by the attitude of your service man in an establishment like yours. At the beginning of the week, the bulb of the beautiful lamp that lights the coffee table in the living room of our suite burned out. We reported it in the morning to the reception. In the afternoon my wife and I decided to have tea in our room after our day of skiing. We were relaxing in our living room in our ski tights when there was a knock on our door. It was your service man who offered to change the bulb in our lamp. He wasn't sure whether he could come back later, maybe tomorrow... We preferred to do it right away even though it wasn't really convenient. He then made some room on our table, pushing our cups and plates, took off his shoes and then climbed on the table to replace the bulb. He was having trouble unscrewing the bulb. He cursed a bit and at one point a small screw of some sort fell into one of our tea cups! Without really apologizing but swearing a bit more, he retrieved it with a small spoon! He finally managed to change the bulb. He got back down from the table, put his shoes back on, and then left!

Box 6.2. *A client tells his story*

---

3 Multi Tec is a fictitious company; the facts re-transcribed are inspired by real events.

In this example, the true beneficiary of the service is the hotel's client. The provider then has two service relationships to manage: a relationship with its direct client and a relationship with the indirect client who is the true beneficiary of the service. The direct client is often the first to be exposed to a bad relationship between the service provider and the indirect client. In the case of social landlords, for example, tenants who are dissatisfied with the service providers in charge of the maintenance of buildings and common areas will tend not to pay their rent.

Services where the indirect client is simply present during the performance of the service are all situations where the service is performed on the premises of clients who host their own clients. The construction sector is regularly confronted with issues related to disturbances caused by their activities on sites that are communal or open to the public.

6.1.2.2. *Broadening our vision of targets*

It is necessary to keep an eye on the sector as a whole, in order to identify service targets. Keeping in mind that a target can be a beneficiary, a facilitator or an observer, we should identify a number of targets within the channel and beyond the direct client. The identification of these targets is essential because, as we have just seen, they contribute to the quality of the service, participating in the overall assessment of the service provider and they can even directly contribute to impacting the client's activity. The direct client will always be sensitive and attentive to the fact that the service provider takes into account actors who are close to the direct client or important to him/her.

6.2. Target satisfaction challenge

Identifying and knowing the targets of the service is essential to prepare to satisfy the customer, that is, to satisfy the variety of these targets.

6.2.1. *The notion of satisfaction*

Satisfaction is a theme that has quickly become central to service management and marketing. Largely studied in a B2C context, it is now necessary to examine the specificities of service satisfaction in B2B.

6.2.1.1. *Reference framework*

Customer satisfaction is an essential element of company performance (Ngobo and Ramaroson 2005). First of all, a positive relationship is recognized between customer satisfaction and customer loyalty[4]. This relationship is not systematic, but it is all the more robust the higher the satisfaction and the longer it is established (Seiders *et al.* 2005). Customer satisfaction also has an impact on the financial performance of the company[5], since customers will accept to pay more for a service if it brings them greater satisfaction[6]. This certainly explains why an investment company like Trusteam Finance chooses its targets according to their satisfaction index, and announces on its homepage that "customer satisfaction drives financial performance"[7]. It is widely accepted today that satisfied and loyal customers not only reduce their sensitivity to price, but also tend to buy more, to practice positive word-of-mouth more often, and the company is more efficient in its actions and in its relationship with them, as it knows them better[8]. This link between satisfaction and performance is reinforced by the fact that loyalty strategies are generally recognized as less costly than conquest strategies.

Satisfaction is a positive or negative impression that a customer feels during a purchase or consumption experience. The literature distinguishes between an affective dimension (Westbrook 1987) and a cognitive dimension (Oliver 1980) in the concept of satisfaction, while recognizing that the two dimensions combine to different degrees to form customer satisfaction (Homburg *et al.* 2006). The affective or emotional dimension refers to pleasure, surprise, contentment or, on the contrary, disappointment, regret and anger. The cognitive dimension indicates that clients evaluate, judge and compare in order to form their satisfaction. Satisfaction is the result of a comparison between expectations and performance: customers

---

4 This relationship between satisfaction and loyalty has been widely studied in the literature (Anderson and Sullivan 1993; Reichheld 1996; Goderis 1998; Oliver 1999).

5 A summary of studies describing a strong link between customer satisfaction and company profitability is proposed in 2006 by Gupta and Zeithaml (Gupta and Zeithaml 2006).

6 This price premium strategy, enabled by high customer satisfaction, is regularly proposed in the managerial literature and validated in research articles (Gruca and Rego 2005; Fornell *et al.* 2006).

7 www.trusteam.fr [Accessed on October 10, 2019].

8 These relationships, which have been widely discussed in a B2C context, have also been studied in a B2B context (Rauyruen and Miller 2007).

have expectations that are confirmed or not by the performance of the service[9]. If the perceived performance is equal or superior to expectations, customers will be satisfied. On the contrary, they will be dissatisfied if the performance of the service is below their expectations. Customer satisfaction thus poses two major challenges to the company: to know customers' expectations, on the one hand, and to approach their perception of the service performance, on the other. Expectation, performance and perception are recognized as complex constructs in the literature. Although the process of expectation formation is not completely known, it is, nevertheless, admitted that the customer relies on factors that are for some under the control of the provider, such as price, communication or commercial relationship, and for others that the provider is not alone in controlling, such as the customer experience, their basic needs and purchasing situation, word of mouth or the offers of competitors (Parasuraman *et al.* 1985). As for performance, since it is a perceived performance, it is clearly to be distinguished from the objective or technical quality of a service. Moreover, this perceived performance relates not only to the result but also to the service process.

The challenge of satisfaction for the service provider comes down to a good alignment of the performance of its service with the client's expectations. It is the expectations considered as the most important by the customer that should be satisfied first and foremost, even if it means performing less well on expectations that are less important for the customer.

6.2.1.2. *The specific context of B2B services*

In a B2B context, the approach to customer satisfaction must integrate two specificities that increase its complexity: the decoupling of the service purchase process from its delivery and the multiplicity of targets.

Two strong and distinct moments organize a customer relationship: the commercial relationship, which takes place during the buying process, and the service relationship, which focuses on the delivery of the service. The stakes for the client and the service provider are different at these two moments, but are nevertheless linked. Getting the deal remains the challenge for service providers in terms of the commercial relationship, that is, for a service to present the most attractive promise and for the client to find the

---

9 Oliver proposed the disconfirmation model to illustrate the process operated by customers to formalize their satisfaction (Oliver 1997).

right service provider. The challenge of the service relationship then becomes for the service provider to deliver the promised service, and for the client to ensure that the promised service is actually delivered. The actors involved in these two moments are not the same. The client's buying center becomes more discreet during the service relationship to make room for the service targets. On the provider's side, the operational people appear during the service relationship, whereas they were often absent from the commercial relationship. Manager, on the other hand, can remain present throughout the relationship if their scope covers sales and operations. It is then legitimate to think that the context being different, satisfaction will be built differently during the commercial relationship and the service relationship. Managers must remain vigilant in building satisfaction with both the commercial and the service relationship, without unbalancing one to the detriment of the other, but on the contrary, building on one to reinforce the other. The customer relationship will be in its entirety a combination of commercial and service relationships.

The multiplicity of targets described in the previous paragraph leads to multiple impressions and feelings of the service. Each target will have its own evaluation of its satisfaction. How will all these evaluations be combined? Is there a global satisfaction for the customer that takes into account all these evaluations? Our knowledge of B2B markets, and more specifically of services, does not enable us to answer this question today. We can admit that the satisfaction of certain targets will be more important than others. For example, we can think that the observer will be less important than the beneficiary. But as noted earlier, if observers have a particular proximity to the decision-maker, then their impression of observing and feeling will be particularly important. It is likely that the beneficiary will have a major impact on the evaluation of the provider, but the beneficiary's evaluation must be known and taken into account. This hypothetical global customer satisfaction, which would be a learned combination of the different evaluations of all the targets of the service, is still opaque, fragile and unstable. Managers remain in the best position to manage this uncertainty: knowledge of their perimeter and customers enables them to identify the targets whose satisfaction must be a priority and to detect targets that are more discreet but nonetheless essential in the evaluation of the service relationship.

6.2.2. *Measuring satisfaction*

6.2.2.1. *Methods*

Several methods are used by companies to measure satisfaction. The following are among the most common:

– Traditional satisfaction surveys aim to measure customer satisfaction on a certain number of items related to the service received and their experience. Some of these surveys are required as part of specific certifications. The more representative the sample, the more reliable the measurement. Some companies systematically send out a satisfaction questionnaire once the service is completed. Thanks to the significant size of the sample, specific statistical processing is possible, allowing for in-depth analysis of the results. The Internet is increasingly chosen by companies as a means of administration. Quantitative indicators are obtained by this method and make it possible, for example, to announce that 95% of customers are satisfied.

– The face-to-face interview makes it possible for clients to express themselves more widely on their feelings and on the experience they had with the service provider. The interview can take place at the end of a service or during a long service delivery, thus allowing for a regular review of the relationship. Clients will be sensitive to the hierarchical level of the collaborator who takes the time to listen to them. This method is ideal for obtaining client *verbatim* and understanding in depth the client's feelings.

– The net promoter score (NPS). It has now become a widely used indicator of company satisfaction in all sectors. It consists of a single question on recommendation intention: "Would you recommend this company to your friends and family?" The answer is given on a scale of 0–10. Between 0 and 6, respondents are considered detractors, from 7 to 8 as passive and only respondents at 9 and 10 are really promoters. To obtain the net score, the NPS subtracts the percentage of detractors from the percentage of pro drivers.

These methods are now well formalized in companies, often deployed by central departments or entrusted to external service providers. However, managers can supplement these data with more targeted measures for their area. The customer satisfaction interview can be a way to strengthen the relationship while getting feedback from the customer on their expectations and the service. The NPS is a very easy tool to implement. Managers can also involve their team to bring back information from the field.

6.2.2.2. *The gap model*

The gap model developed by Zeithaml, Parasuraman and Berry in the 1980s has become a reference tool in service management. Its longevity and popularity are due as much to its theoretical soundness as to its managerial relevance (see Figure 6.1).

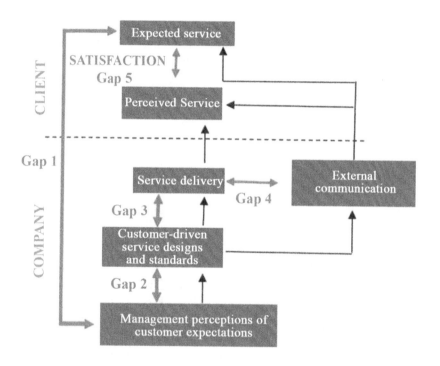

Figure 6.1. *The gap model (Parasuraman* et al. *1985). For a color version of this figure, see www.iste.co.uk/mathieu/services.zip*

As its name suggests, the model proposes approaching satisfaction from five gaps[10]. Achieving customer satisfaction consists of reducing and "closing" each of these gaps. The basis of the model, the customer gap, is the

---

10 These discrepancies are extensively developed by Zeithaml and Bitner in their seminal and regularly republished book in services marketing (Zeithaml *et al.* 2017).

gap between the expected service and the perceived service (gap 5). A good knowledge of the customer is essential to work on this gap. Gap 5, beyond sufficient customer knowledge, is also the consequence of four other gaps, the provider gaps: the listening gap (gap 1), the design and service standard gap (gap 2), the service performance gap (gap 3) and the communication gap (gap 4). It is then essential to recognize the specific responsibility of the manager in each of these gaps.

The manager participates in reducing gap 1 by maintaining a strong relationship with their clients and by mobilizing their team on the sensitivity and the feedback of the client's expectations. Customers cannot be approached only in a global way by the company; they must clearly appear to each manager from their specificities which can distinguish them from a global customer profile. This specificity of their customer perimeter must lead managers to participate in the elaboration of the service and in the definition of its standards in order to reduce gap 2. In a long-term service relationship, which is difficult to standardize perfectly, managers must keep a daily eye on service standards, which complement the overall design of the service, usually thought out beforehand. Managers are then the guarantor of the alignment between the standards and the delivery of the service. As gap 3 is strongly linked to the involvement of the team and the client, managers are again in the front line to ensure that their team and their clients play their respective parts correctly. Finally, by engaging in horizontal communication and monitoring the promises that they and their team make to clients, particularly during the commercial relationship but more broadly throughout the service relationship, managers will contribute to reducing gap 4. Managers must be able to articulate a global promise of their company to the market, with a promise that they know they can keep within their own perimeter.

It is, therefore, by working on these gaps within their perimeter, in addition to a global approach of their company, by integrating the specificity of their local market, that managers will achieve this customer excellence concentrated in satisfaction.

> B2B service relationships are long-term and have a certain depth. The relational surface is particularly important. Many people from different teams, departments and services, both on the provider's and the client's side, interact. The service provider is in contact with a complex system made up of many people with multiple and sometimes contradictory expectations. In order to deal with this client system,

service providers have to modulate their relationships according to those who interact with them, and find the best possible compromises in the client's interest.

The service relationship in many B2B businesses is very procedural, built around SLAs (Service Level Agreements). Nevertheless, true customer satisfaction often goes beyond the mere respect of a contract. It is the initiatives or daily attentions of the staff, often insignificant, that can delight the customer. Of course, it is not a question of deviating from the rules of the contract or cutting into the company's margin. The staff, who are often active on the customer's site, are in an ideal position to observe and take initiatives that may satisfy the customer beyond the contract. In this context, in-depth feedbacks are rich in lessons learned. They show that a successful business deal is the result of a sum of micro-decisions based on a strong human dimension, in order to resolve issues related to people, much more than just technical issues. The success of the business and the satisfaction of the client are based on trust, mutual esteem and even, let's say it, the pleasure of working together.

In order to support the excellence of the service relationship and promote customer satisfaction, the manager must meet two challenges. The first challenge is the feedback of customer information in order to maintain maximum reactivity in the face of the hazards of a business relationship. Managers must have a strong will and a solid commitment to get feedback from the field, from their teams, from the customer and even from the customer's customer. It is by listening to their collaborators with confidence, by regularly seeking their feedback, that managers will manage to have a clear vision of the real situations experienced in the customer relationship. They will then be able to better anticipate the actions that can be taken to satisfy or delight the customer or, on the contrary, to support their team in order to put them in a position to say no to the customer, always with a respectful attitude. The second challenge for managers is to encourage positive emotions such as esteem, trust and respect for the customer within their teams, in order to create an environment that is conducive to the development of a feeling of pleasure in working with the customer. Without these positive energies, there is a great risk of generating fear and inhibiting individual initiatives that are meaningful and valuable to the customer.

Box 6.3. *Testimony of Christian Mayeur (Director of Development and Innovation, AFNOR Group)*

Making the Most of the Offer

Introduction to Part 3

For managers and their team, the knowledge of the customer constitutes the best preparation for making the most of the offer.

First of all, it must be admitted that, in a more and more competitive environment, managers are confronted increasingly with the commoditization of the offer, which reduces the commercial negotiation to the price variable alone. The knowledge acquired about their clients and their environment makes it possible for managers to evaluate this risk of commoditization and then to identify the strategies that will enable them to better protect themselves.

In a more constructive and less defensive posture, enhancing the value of the offer involves paying attention to its formalization, which prepares it for marketing and presentation to the client. Because of its structure and plasticity, the service offer gives managers some leeway to align it as well as possible with the client's expectations.

While it is true that not every manager is responsible for the commercial development of his or her area, it is widely accepted that every employee is a potential salesperson. In any case, customer orientation must be linked to the sales approach: knowing their customer is preparing a sales approach, and satisfying their customer is securing it. Integrating the tools and principles of the sales approach is undeniably enriching their customer orientation skills.

Acting Against the Risk of Commoditization

7.1. Understanding the phenomenon of the offer commoditization

The commoditization of offer seems to be an inevitable phenomenon in the evolution of any market (Greenstein 2004; Olson and Sharma 2008; Reimann *et al.* 2010). While commoditization initially concerned raw materials, it gradually spread to product markets (consumer goods, capital goods), then to services (air transport, mobile telephony) and finally to skills (Holmes 2008). It is manifested in two concomitant realities: the offer becomes a simple commodity reduced to a few standard elements without any real distinctive character for the client, and the price becomes the almost unique element of the negotiation. No sector, no company is really immune to the comoditization of its offer.

7.1.1. *Characteristics of a commoditized market*

A commoditized market has four characteristics (Reimann *et al.* 2010):

– Homogeneity of offers: the products and services are standard, the technologies are identical, there is no variation in the quality and performance of competing offers.

– Price sensitivity: customers pay a lot of attention to price, choose based on price and look for the lowest prices.

– Customer disloyalty: the costs associated with switching suppliers are low, make it possible for the customer to change suppliers quickly, easily and without risk.

– Stability of the industry: customer preferences change very little, suppliers are stable, technology and product obsolescence evolve slowly.

The level of commoditization of a market can then be assessed on the basis of the intensity of these four dimensions.

7.1.2. *Explanatory factors*

A better understanding of the factors that drive a market towards commoditization enables managers to better anticipate the trap that this situation sets for them. Three main factors explain the trend towards commoditization of the offer: the evolution of customer behavior, the transformation of the market and the digital revolution.

7.1.2.1. *Evolution of client behavior*

Customer profiles and characteristics are changing over time. New segments are emerging and some historical customers may already be moving to other, more innovative markets. Expectations are being restructured as the customer gains experience and, therefore, expertise. The client has accumulated knowledge about the market as a whole, about the players and about the service itself. If there is a natural gap in expertise between the service provider and the client in a new market, this gap narrows over time. The client no longer hesitates to go into the details of the service provider's offer and to negotiate more precisely on different dimensions. While they used to accept a global price for a global offer, they are gradually becoming capable of entering into each line that makes up the price of the offer, thereby putting service providers in competition on the components of the offer. The lowest bidder on a particular line forces its competitors to match its price level. This expertise also makes it much easier for clients to identify the elements of the offer that are not essential or not very dependent on the core offer. They can then ask their provider to remove those elements from the latter's offer or to reduce them. This expertise that customers gain with the maturity of the market is used by them in the negotiation with their provider.

The maturity of the customer is also accompanied by the globalization of sourcing, that is, sourcing and purchasing that are no longer limited to a local market but extend to the world market. The globalization of purchasing is a specific consequence of the globalization of trade. While it was initially product purchasing that was affected by this globalization, today, we are witnessing the globalization of service purchases: the relocation of call centers to North Africa, India and the Philippines, and the purchase of information technology services in India or Eastern Europe. Companies that globalize their service purchases are generally looking for service providers that have lower costs than local providers with equivalent levels of expertise. It must be admitted that today, companies and buyers are less and less afraid to turn to global providers. Some clients even specify in their tender the percentage of the service to be performed in a low-cost country. This is particularly true for human capital-intensive services. Knowledge, skills and intelligence are now as much in Asia as in Europe or the United States, as is particularly the case in technology-intensive services. The market for skills is, thus, becoming more global and competitive, as the cost of human resources can be lowered. The globalization of procurement inevitably contributes to increased price pressure for domestic providers. Nevertheless, the health crisis in the spring of 2020 following the COVID-19 pandemic, by re-launching the debate on globalization, could modify offshoring and purchasing strategies.

7.1.2.2. Market transformation

The market itself, by transforming itself, can create a new environment conducive to the movement of commoditization of the offer.

First, there is the natural transformation of a market, which is the maturity phenomenon. The maturity phase of a market is characterized by a slowdown in growth. Thus, the environment becomes tenser for the players involved. Maturity is also associated with a certain harmonization in the companies' offer. While there were good and less good service providers, and while it was possible to appreciate different levels of quality and performance between competitors, maturity has brought order to the market and only the most competent players have resisted. We are witnessing a convergence of offers in terms of both quality and content. As all players tend to offer the same service, the customer can then focus on the only variable of difference still available, the price. Added to this is the phenomenon of mergers and acquisitions, a consequence of slowing internal growth, which is being compensated for by external growth. As the size of the players increases, cost advantages are being structured, which also maintains competition on price. This phenomenon of commoditization associated with the maturity of the market is all the more worrying as maturity is arriving increasingly quickly.

It is also necessary to consider a transformation of markets under the action of exogenous variables. Regulation and technology are two of these variables that strongly and very rapidly modify a market. The deregulation of a market as a whole (air or rail transport market, certain professional service markets) accelerates the phenomenon of commoditization. New technologies help open up markets to new players with both a strong capacity for innovation and a customer focus, exposing traditional players to the commoditization of their offerings[1].

Finally, a market can be transformed by new entrants who change the rules of the competitive game that seemed established. Low-cost players enter a market with a business model that is radically different from the models deployed by traditional players, thereby trivializing traditional models and offers (Kumar 2006). Uberization, defined by the *Petit Larousse* as "the questioning of the economic model of a company or a sector of activity by the arrival of a new player offering the same services at lower prices", is very close to the *low-cost* model. Services are particularly affected by uberization and few are really protected (Viot 2018). Both uberization and low cost are even stronger threats as these business models are no longer exclusively associated with lower quality offers but are also recognized as carriers of innovation (Santi and Nguyen 2012).

7.1.2.3. *Technological change*

New technologies favor the emergence of new players and new business models. They represent a threat to traditional players.

Digital technologies are at the forefront of this technological change. The digital revolution is a generic term that encompasses a diversity of technologies and practices, from artificial intelligence to the Cloud and Big Data, via the Internet of Things. It concerns the service sector as well as the industrial sector. Digital technologies have been shaking up the industry for

---

1 The European payment services market is particularly affected by this phenomenon (Hausladen and Zipf 2018).

some time and have a direct impact on its service providers and subcontractors. For example, Industry 4.0, based on the Internet of Things, Big Data and Cloud technologies, is turning the maintenance sector upside down by opening the way to predictive maintenance[2]. New approaches to service professions are emerging such as consulting 4.0 (Courtecuisse 2018). The consulting sector, as well as all intellectual professions (engineers, lawyers, doctors), is being impacted by new technologies, in particular machine learning. This technology enables the machine to learn by itself by developing a cognitive capacity, thus increasing the capabilities of the consultant and more broadly the intellectual worker.

All these technologies have two facets: optimization or enrichment. They undoubtedly enable us to enrich our offer and innovate as well as to optimize, rationalize and reduce production costs. In this way, they activate the commoditization of traditional offerings, either by making their functionality basic and standard, not to say outdated, or by significantly lowering the price of the service. In the cleaning market, players who succeed in installing presence sensors in the offices, linked to the agents' schedules, should be able to optimize their work and significantly lower the cost of their offer. We are waiting for the next service provider who will succeed in robotizing all or part of the cleaning service!

7.1.3. *The commoditization trap*

Commoditization is a threat that should be taken seriously by any company, as it leads to price wars (Davenport 2005) and erodes the profitability of suppliers and providers (Matthyssens and Vandenbempt 2008). The best way to avoid it is to be prepared: detect the first signals of commoditization at a very early stage, evaluate the risk of commoditization and, of course, consider a response strategy.

7.1.3.1. *Verifying the reality of commoditization*

Some elements moderate the threat of commoditization. It is the most standardized offers that are the most sensitive to commoditization because the client does not identify real differences between providers. In the same vein, if the client perceives a cost associated with a change of provider,

---

2 The impact of these technologies on the industry of the future was notably described in a 2015 Boston Consulting Group study (The Boston Consulting Group 2015).

competition can be contained. The services market, and particularly the market for complex services such as intellectual or technical services, may be characterized by more imperfect competition overall[3]. This is essentially due to the difficulty that clients have in obtaining objective information that would enable them to compare the price and quality of service of different providers. It is, therefore, necessary to evaluate the reality of this imperfection in the market and to anticipate its evolution.

More pragmatically, the following questions must also be answered in order to truly measure the threat of commoditization:

– What is the reality of purchasing for the customer? The Kraljic matrix, widely used in the purchasing field, classifies purchases according to the supply risk and the impact on the company's profitability (Kraljic 1983). Purchasing is considered to be all the more strategic when the supply risk and the impact on profitability are high. On the other hand, a low supply risk associated with a low impact on profitability characterizes non-critical purchases for which the offers tend to be standard and where competition is strong. The latter situation is obviously conducive to commoditization.

– Is this reality shared within the buying center? The more members of the buying center come closer to a strategic perception of buying, the less strong the forces that push for commoditization of the offer. Knowledge of the buying center is a considerable asset in this assessment.

– Is this reality shared within the sector? In the same way, the challenge is to know how the service is perceived within the sector, if there are actors who slow down the commoditization of the offer because of their profiles or their expectations, and to evaluate their weight in the negotiation.

– Is this reality verified in the prices charged? By comparing the decision taken by the client with the characteristics of the offers submitted, we can refine the hypothesis of the commoditization of the offer.

Finally, the conditions of commoditization are evolving very rapidly, in one direction or the other. We can even witness phenomena of "de-commoditization". This is what we are seeing in the relocation of certain activities. The aeronautical maintenance sector, for example, is moving away

---

3 In his description of service markets, de Bandt made this clear: "if in the case of services, market or competition mechanisms function, they do so according to particular modalities, more imperfect than elsewhere" (de Bandt 1995, p. 97).

from low-cost countries in Asia in order to save on the price of fuel needed to bring the aircraft to its maintenance site (Frachet and Mercaillou 2019).

7.1.3.2. *Falling into the trap or avoiding it*

The worst situation is when one falls into the trap, that is, when one gives in to the price pressure exerted by the customer without any adjustment, either in one's cost structure or in the content and process of one's offer. The degradation of profits is then inevitable. Two strategies are possible to avoid falling into the trap of commoditization. One is to work on its cost structure in order to compete on price. The other is to enhance the value of its offer to avoid, or at least weaken, price competition. In this case, it is managers' customer orientation that will enable them to make the best use of the offer within the scope of the company and for customers.

Of course, not all players will be able or willing to move towards a low-cost or uberization model. However, in a competitive climate that is becoming tighter, no one can afford to ignore an analysis of their cost structure and operational efficiency. Differentiation does not exclude the need to remain in the market, that is, to be able to offer its customers a price that is acceptable compared to those charged by the competition. Beyond the rationalization and efficiency plans that are deployed by more and more service providers, managers must remain vigilant and agile within their scope. Remaining attentive to the organization of their team's work, fully integrating the customer into the service process and finding a partner capable of taking over part of the service provision more efficiently are some of the levers that managers can use to keep their cost structure at an acceptable level[4].

Customer intimacy is undoubtedly a strong alternative in markets that are becoming commoditized. A study of 146 business units in 10 different industries showed that the more commoditized a market is, the more relevant the customer intimacy strategy becomes compared to other options (Reimann *et al.* 2010). Customer intimacy makes it possible for one to better understand one's customers and to better respond to their expectations, which, according to the authors of the study, becomes the only winning strategy in highly commoditized markets.

---

4 These approaches are discussed more fully in Chapter 11.

Garig is a family-owned company that has been present in the foodservice market for 12 years. It has 240 employees and a turnover of 21 million euros. It operates in the southern region of France and addresses three segments: daycare and schools, companies and government agencies, and medical and social services. It promotes a more human, more committed and more gourmet approach to catering by working with organic and fresh products from local producers.

Garig operates in an ultra-competitive market with international companies such as Sodexo, Elior and Compass. In these markets, many customers are looking for the lowest possible price. The players have capacities that enable them to position themselves on offers with very low prices. However, if Garig is still present in this market, and can even congratulate itself on never having lost a customer, it is because it manages to extricate itself from the competition on price alone. So, it's not just about price!

First of all, you have to be careful about the selection of customers. Customers who only talk about price, who do not show interest in the quality of the products, are not in the company's target. You have to know how to stay in your place, the one where you are the strongest. Knowing customers, listening to them, identifying their deepest expectations are obviously essential before submitting the offer. As the buyer is generally under the orders of the decision-maker, it is necessary to distinguish in the specifications, which are often voluminous, that which is incidental from that which is essential, to identify the component of the offer that will be decisive for the decision-maker.

Customer relations are at the heart of Garig's ability to withstand competitive pressure. Upstream of the bid, this customer relationship makes it possible to win a consultation. During the contract, it secures the chances of winning the next consultation. Customer relations are built on proximity, responsiveness and proactivity. Proximity is the result of the time we spend regularly with the customer. Customers are sensitive to the fact that they always find the same contact person and, therefore, can truly build a long-term relationship with him. Customers trust the person in front of them. This person is essential in the purchase decision. Reactivity is demonstrated on a daily basis, by modifying a contract, adapting an offer or releasing an investment. Proactivity, on the other hand, makes it possible for us to animate the customer relationship, in particular by making the offer evolve and by loosening the constraints of the initial framework.

Finally, the speech of the director or manager is essential in competitive environments dominated by the price variable. During meetings at Garig, there is very little talk about money, but rather about quality, the customer, the smile, the cleanliness, etc. Meetings are marked by questions such as "Have you seen your customers?" and "What are they asking you?". If we only talk to employees about money and results, they will in turn only talk to customers about prices. But above all, we must not only talk about price, but also be a force of proposal in the service and envision what the company can bring more to its customer.

Box 7.1. *Testimony of Martin Dubar (Managing Director, Garig)*

7.2. Countering the commoditization of the offer

Countering commoditization by enhancing the value of the offer has the immense advantage of being the only possible path for all companies that are not destined to become low cost or Uber. It is a rich path in the sense that it opens several possible strategies and can be practiced at different levels. This path will be all the more effective if managers have acquired a good knowledge of their customers and their business ecosystem.

7.2.1. *Strategies for presenting the offer*

Without modifying the offer in depth, managers can enhance their existing offer by demonstrating to their client their capacity to reduce various potential risks or to act on their profitability.

7.2.1.1. *Enhancing the value of the offer through risk*

Buying behavior was historically defined by Bauer as risk-taking (Bauer 1960). The notion of risk is also at the heart of the first approaches dedicated to B2B (Valla 1978), and it is a direct consequence of the specificity of the service (Eiglier 2004, p. 201). Perceived risk refers to the possible negative consequences of a bad choice, as felt by clients, and to the degree of uncertainty in which they find themselves in making a choice. If the provider is able to identify the risks perceived by its client, if it has the capacity to reduce them better than its competitors and if it is able to demonstrate this capacity to its client, then it has a first protection against price competition. Being the risk-reducing provider counterbalances the price.

In the general context of consumer products, the main risks identified are functional, financial, physical, psychological or social risk (de Baynast *et al.*

2017, p. 89). While these risks remain relevant in the specific context of B2B service, the approach can be enriched.

Convinced that "uncertainty or risk perceived, shared, or sensed to varying degrees by members of the buying center, is the driving force behind customer buying behavior", Michel, Salle and Valla developed the risk approach as a method of analyzing and understanding this behavior (Michel *et al.* 1996, p. 138). The approach reveals the main factors that influence risk: the newness of the purchase, the stakes involved and the characteristics of the market. It also incorporates the notion of the buying center to emphasize that its members will have different perceptions of risk. Finally, two types of risk are distinguished: the risk incurred, which is an objective risk, and the risk perceived by the customer. The perceived risk is not always an objective risk, just as objective risks are not always clearly perceived by the customer, or are differently perceived by the members of the buying center. While it is obvious that managers have a duty to reveal to the customer an objective risk that the customer has difficulty in perceiving, it may seem more difficult to find the right course of action for a perceived risk that has no objective basis. Should he demonstrate to clients that their perceived risk is not real, or on the contrary take advantage of clients' misperception? True customer orientation is undoubtedly more aligned with the first position.

The risk approach is still of great interest due to its pragmatism and its ability to be implemented by the manager. Nevertheless, an additional line of risk linked to environmental, social and governance issues (ESG risk) should be included to keep in step with the evolution of purchasing practices of companies, since the majority of companies that implement a responsible purchasing policy carry out an ESG risk analysis[5]. There is a professionalization of buyers in risk management.

Finally, to be fully relevant in the specific context of a B2B service, the risk approach must go beyond the sole risk associated with the purchase decision to also include the risk associated with the delivery of the service and involve other actors than just the members of the buying center. There is indeed a risk associated with the delivery of the service that will be

---

5 In its 10th barometer of responsible purchasing, the *Observatoire des achats responsables* with OpinionWay indicates that 83% of companies that have implemented a responsible purchasing policy have an ESG risk map or analysis. ObsAR (2019). Baromètre des achats responsables. OpinionWay pour l'ObsAR, 10th edition [Online]. Available at: www.obsar.asso.fr [Accessed on January 27, 2020].

perceived more directly by the customer's service targets. Although some of the risks perceived by the buying center are an anticipation of the delivery of the service, service providers must have an explicit approach to these risks in order to be able to integrate them into their commercial approach.

Once the risks have been identified, managers must take action to convince the client that they are the providers best placed to reduce the latter's risk. The client will then weigh the price of the service against the risk and uncertainty that each provider is able to reduce. Box 7.2 illustrates the position that a provider may adopt in response to a particular risk.

Improper subcontracting is a risk to which many services are exposed. It is a real and significant risk to which the client is not always alerted. Service providers can then be real advisors to their clients on the prevention of this risk, which, in order to be effectively anticipated, requires specific actions and investments from the service provider. Skillfully managed, particularly in the drafting of the commercial proposal and in the methods used to carry out the service, the risk of improper subcontracting positions service providers as valuable partners, and enables them to circumvent overly stiff competition on price, by justifying an enhanced service.

Improper subcontracting is a form of illegal work punishable by the French *Labor Code*. It is considered as a loan of labor, clearly forbidden by law, except for specific authorized activities (temporary work, wage portage, work sharing companies, etc.).

Article L.8231-1 of the French Labor Code prohibits improper subcontracting, defined as any profit-making operation involving the supply of labor that has the effect of causing harm to the employee concerned or of evading the application of legal provisions or the stipulations of a collective labor agreement. More precisely, three criteria characterize improper subcontracting:

– Transfer of the subordination link: the employee of the service provider works under the authority of the client company and no longer of his or her employer.

– Profit-making purpose of the operation: the subcontracting company benefits from the operation.

– Violation of the employee's rights: there is unequal treatment between the employee on assignment and the employees of the client company, particularly in terms of salaries and non-application of the collective agreement.

Improper subcontracting directly concerns all sectors that provide their clients with additional employees. It is, therefore, understandable that subcontracting companies or service providers are concerned by the improper subcontracting, and particularly the intellectual services and IT services sector.

Improper subcontracting must be taken particularly seriously because the penalties can be severe for both the service provider and the client company: criminal penalties (imprisonment and fines), civil penalties (the employee can take the matter to the industrial tribunal to claim compensation for damages) and administrative penalties (reimbursement of public aid, for example).

In order to avoid the risk of improper subcontracting, it is important to understand that the judge will rely on a set of indicators in order to establish whether the sole purpose of the contract is the lending of labor and whether there is a relationship of subordination between the employee and the client company. The elements that the judge will take into account are generally the content and the purpose of the contract, the know-how of the service provider, the method of remuneration of the service provider, the provision of means to carry out the service and the actual hierarchical link of the employee:

– The purpose of the contract, explicit or implicit, must not be the loan of employees. The contract must clearly define a task to be performed for which the loan of labor is only a means. This task must fall within the subcontractor's particular competence, justifying that the know-how of the personnel made available does not exist in the client company. The object of the sale must in no case be the employee. Deliverables, deadlines and commitments in terms of results characterize a true contract of enterprise.

– The know-how, specificity and technicality of the service provider must be related to the service provided.

– The provider's remuneration must be fixed at a flat rate in the contract and the calculation of this flat rate must not be based on units of work such as the number of employees made available or the number of hours worked. This fixed price obliges the client and the service provider to define an objective and concrete and measurable results.

– Concerning the provision of means to perform the service, there may be a suspicion of improper subcontracting if these means are lent to the employee by the client.

– The employees provided must be exclusively supervised and directed by their employer to avoid any link of subordination between the employee and the client, although coordination of the activity by the client is accepted for the proper conduct of the mission. The authority, supervision and managerial monitoring of employees must be clearly under the responsibility of the service provider. The presence of a manager from the service provider at the client's premises and the meetings, interviews and training of employees organized by the service provider clarify the real subordination of employees.

Box 7.2. *The risk of improper subcontracting*[6]

7.2.1.2. *Enhancing the value of the offer through profitability*

This second tactic consists of getting clients to broaden their financial vision of the offer beyond the price of the service alone. This approach can be defensive or offensive.

The defensive approach essentially consists of getting clients to take into account all the costs associated with a service and a service relationship, in order to promote transparent comparisons with competitors. The price of the service is not always the most significant cost borne by clients. Two concepts enable to have a clearer vision of these additional costs, which are often hidden costs: the TCO and switching costs.

The TCO (total cost of ownership) makes it possible to know all the costs – direct and indirect – generated by the acquisition and use of a product or service (Shank and Govindarajan 1992). It is a tool for negotiation, comparison and decision support. It is relevant both for customers in their purchasing strategy and for service providers in their commercial and negotiation approach. Widely used in the field of products, it is more timidly deployed in service activities, notably because of the difficulty in identifying and assessing all the costs associated with a service, particularly indirect costs. The vehicle fleet management market, for example, has made good use of this

---

6 www.legifrance.gouv.fr/affichCodeArticle.do?idArticle=LEGIARTI000006904839&cidTexte =LEGITEXT000006072050&dateTexte=20080501 [Accessed on October 28, 2019]; www. juritravail.com/Actualite/etre-en-conformite/Id/144751 [Accessed on October 28, 2019]; www. decision-achats.fr/Decision-Achats/Article/Comment-eviter-le-delit-de-marchandage--42071-1.htm [Accessed on October 28, 2019]; https://travail-emploi.gouv.fr/droit-du-travail/lutte-contre-le-travail-illegal-10802/article/les-sanctions-liees-au-travail-illegal [Accessed on October 28, 2019]; www.saisirprudhommes.com/fiches-prudhommes/delit-de-marchandage [Accessed October 28, 2019]; www.journaldunet.fr/management/guide-du-management/1200089-delit-de-marchandage-un-risque-pour-les-prestataires-de-service/ [Accessed October 28, 2019].

tool in order to obtain a precise view of the total cost of managing a vehicle (see Box 7.3).

For a long time, fleet buyers made their choices based on a few criteria around price, brand and technical characteristics. With the generalization of long-term leasing contracts, the notion of usage cost has become more relevant than that of purchase cost. The cost of use has continued to grow and is now part of a complex Total Cost of Ownership (TCO). The global TCO is the combination of three specific TCOs:

– The vehicle TCO. To the purchase price of the vehicle are added the financial costs associated with the purchase or the long-term leasing contract, the consumption and maintenance of the vehicle, the tax and social charges on the benefits in kind, and the resale value. It accounts for about 75% of the total TCO.

– The driver TCO. This TCO takes into account the impact of driver behavior on consumption, maintenance and accidents. It is estimated at 20% of total TCO.

– The fleet TCO. It reflects the administrative and management costs of the fleet. It accounts for the remaining 5% of the overall TCO.

The TCM (Total Cost of Mobility) is the latest TCO to be taken into account. As the total cost of mobility, TCM covers all the employee's trips beyond those made with their vehicle. It allows for the integration of a large number of costs (train tickets, parking, cabs, etc.) in order to truly approach the cost of an employee's mobility.

Box 7.3. *Total cost of ownership applied to fleet management*[7]

It is often on the demand and customer side that initiatives to model such global indicators come from. Purchasing and financial directors, concerned with ever greater cost control, are very attentive to these tools. Service providers can rely on such tools to position their offer in a more objective and real way in relation to that of its competitors, who may be better placed on the price of the service but less efficient on indirect costs.

---

7 Arval Mobility Observatory (2020). Le concept de TCO [Online]. Available at: https://mobility-observatory.arval.fr/le-concept-de-tco [Accessed February 10, 2020].

	Strong relevance	Medium to low relevance
Purchase TCO	–	– RFP cost: MH[8] to create and manage the RFP. – Cost reporting: MH to be collected and report information in a table. – Cost negotiation: MH to negotiate the various terms and conditions. – Supplier maintenance cost: MH to manage the contractual relationship with the provider. – Referencing cost: MH for the registration of the provider in the company's IS.
Finance TCO	– Cash cost: cost of capital cost of capital related to any deposit and payment terms granted. – Invoice cost: MH for invoice processing.	– Deposit cost: MH for down payment processing.
Organization and logistics TCO	– Cost of the venue: price charged by the host venue. – Cost of transportation: cost of all transportation. – Agency fees: cost of the agency for the organization of the event. – Speaker cost: fees for speakers at the meeting. – Provider's staff: MH of the provider's staff on site.	– Cost to find a place: MH to search for a venue for the event. – Cost of managing participants: MH for registration and follow-up. – Marketing/communication costs: for the marketing and communication of the event. – Insurance: cost of insurance. – Site personnel costs: cost of client's personnel on site. – Pre-night/post-night: cost of the reserved rooms. – Compliance/security control: MH for verification and control. – Cost of time to locate: MH to visit and choose.

Table 7.1. *Total cost of ownership in business tourism*

The French branch of GBTA (Global Business Travel Association), the international business tourism trade association, formed a working group to develop a financial modeling tool for meetings. The working group used the

---

8 Man hour(s).

Total Cost of Ownership (TCO) methodology to understand the different costs associated with this specific business tourism service. Three sets of TCOs were identified: the TCO for purchasing includes costs related to the purchasing process, the TCO for finance includes costs related to the financial management of the purchase and order, and the TCO for organization and logistics includes the direct costs related to the organization of the meeting or event. Not all of these costs are equally relevant or important[9] (see Table 7.1).

We understand how relevant such a division is for the client as well as for the service provider:

– What are the most significant costs?

– For which costs is it better placed than its competitors?

– What are the costs that its offer manages to cancel?

– What costs can the provider take on?

The notion of switching cost (Klemperer 1995) may also be relevant in defending against a low-cost competitor, since by definition these costs erect a competitive barrier. The switching cost is the cost to the client of changing providers. Transaction costs, discussed in Chapter 3, are considered a type of switching cost. This switching cost is particularly important in B2B services, since relationship, trust, learning and commitment are some of the values that the customer will have to rebuild with the new provider. For example, the client who starts a new relationship with a low-cost international provider will be exposed to a cultural cost related to the creation and maintenance of the relationship, and more concretely may have to integrate time differences in the delivery of the service.

A more offensive approach, linked to the profitability of the offer, would consist of service providers getting their client to consider the service more as an investment, by demonstrating the impact of the service on the client's turnover, results or efficiency. We have already mentioned, for example, the impact of the quality of the maintenance service on the propensity of tenants to pay their rent to the social landlord. In this case, managers must be able to

9 Martre, F., Meimoun, S., Poillerat, C., Estrabeau, C., Strezyk, V., Hernandez, M., Morice, N., Jakubowski, B., Salau, I., Fabron, A., Lebel, S. (2015). Total Cost of Ownership (TCO). GBTA [Online]. Available at: https://hub.gbta.org/groups/reviews/item/20/11/2318?_ga=2.26870 8465.1405840315.1580217553-1319470725.1580217553 [Accessed on February 12, 2020].

demonstrate to their client that their offer secures these different performance levers better than their competitors.

7.2.2. *Strategies for enriching the offer*

This second set of strategies leads providers to rework their offer in more depth than the previous strategies. These strategies can be considered in a second phase, if the strategies of presenting the offer have proved insufficient.

7.2.2.1. *Bringing additional value to the customer*

The customer-perceived value of an offering is a specific concept in marketing that is presented as the result of a comparison between the costs and benefits associated with that offering (de Baynast *et al.* 2017, p. 7). Value differs from the objective quality of an offering in that it is perceived by the customer. If the customer fails to perceive elements that contribute to the performance or quality of the offering, then they will not contribute to the perceived value. The perceived benefits go beyond the performance of the service and the technical quality of the result. They include all the advantages that clients can derive from an offer and from their relationship with service providers, such as the latter' purchasing experience, or more emotional benefits as discussed in Chapter 5. Similarly, costs go beyond the price of the service and reflect all the induced costs of purchasing and delivering the service, as discussed in section 7.2.1.2. There are two ways to create value: by increasing benefits relative to costs and by decreasing costs relative to benefits.

In the context of the commoditization of the offer, managers must focus their efforts on the indirect non-financial costs and on the non-functional benefits, since the direct financial costs and functional benefits have either already been largely worked out, or put the low-cost competitor in a dominant position. In the case of a B2B service, these non-functional benefits and indirect non-financial costs must be extended to the perception of all the members of the buying center, and must also take into account the service delivery phase beyond the purchasing process. The various members of the buying center do not have the same perception of these benefits and costs – the user will naturally be sensitive to the benefits linked to the delivery of the service, and it is likely that a decision-maker will have a broader vision of the purchase and will be concerned by certain more social or environmental externalities.

7.2.2.2. Proposing a solution offer to the customer

If providers manage to broaden their offer beyond the basic offer proposed by their competitors, they succeed in extracting themselves from the dominant competitive field and thus avoid commoditization.

The solution offering is an approach that fits into this logic. Widely implemented in the field of B2B products, it initially recommended enriching the offer by combining products and services in order to provide the customer with a global solution (Tuli *et al.* 2007).

Managers must move away from a vision centered on their service to a customer logic that integrates their offer into the customer's own value creation process. It is possible to approach any service as a contributor to the customer's value creation, adhering to the following stages:

– First, the service directly or indirectly applies to a particular tangible or intangible asset of the client. Identifying that asset enables thinking about a service that actually affects that asset in the client's particular context. It is a common negotiation tactic for service providers to emphasize their knowledge of the client's specific asset. For example, an industrial warehouse cleaning operation must take into account the precise composition of the products formerly stored, as certain components, like solvents in particular, present risks of explosion. Service providers will then adapt their service, the products and the equipment used to the client's warehouse.

– Then by extending the asset to the process in which it is inserted, the service is placed in the context of this process. Daytime cleaning of offices, in the presence of employees and during the client's activity, does not have the same stakes as nighttime cleaning, which will take place without interference with the client's activity process.

– Finally, at an even more global level, the aim is to identify the company's activity linked to the previous processes and assets in order to be able to provide the client with a truly global solution for this activity. The logistics sector illustrates this orientation towards a global and integrated offer of the client's supply chain (see Box 7.4).

In simple terms, logistics concerns the physical flow of goods from the producer to the consumer, combined with the necessary information flows.

Many players are involved in these logistics processes: the shipper, the carrier, the forwarding agent, the planner, the platform and warehouse marketer and, more broadly, the logistics service provider. All these players contribute to the efficiency of the supply chain. This multiplicity of players raises issues of management, coordination and responsibility. For the customer in particular, this complexity in the management of its *supply chain* justifies the use of a global service provider who would not simply take charge of one part of its supply chain (transport, storage, etc.) but the whole. This is a single contact person who takes overall responsibility for all of the customer's logistics flows. This global service provider is called a Fourth Party Logistics Provider (4PL), in charge of managing, controlling, coordinating and optimizing the first three levels of logistics:

– 1PL, the loader;

– 2PL, the transport operator;

– 3PL, the logistics provider.

The 4PL is either a 3PL that has increased its offer to go up a notch in the solution provided to its customer, or management consulting firms or specialized in supply chain, or IT companies.

Thus, the 4PL offers its customer a global solution for the management of one of its key activities that creates significant value: the management of its global supply chain.

Box 7.4. *The 4PL provider, the global logistics solution*[10]

10 Ministère de l'Environnement, de l'Énergie et de la Mer (2016). La logistique [Online]. Available at: www.ecologiquesolidaire.gouv.fr/sites/default/files/logistique%20tour%20d%27 horizon.pdf [Accessed on February 20, 2020].

Formalizing Your Offer

8.1. Positioning the offer

Positioning is a concept and an approach that is well established and clearly defined in the marketing literature. Managers must seize it, both as an element of management of their team, and as a lever of their commercial and operational performance.

8.1.1. *The notion of positioning*

At the heart of the strategic approach to marketing, positioning makes it possible for an offer to be given a clear, distinct and privileged place in the mind of the customer, so that it is preferred over competing offers[1]. It is a strategic choice that the company makes, different from the image which is the set of representations that the customer associates with the company, the offer or the brand.

8.1.1.1. *The importance of positioning*

Positioning is in a way the structuring element of the marketing approach by ensuring the relevance and integration of the various marketing choices and actions. By systematically referring to its positioning to verify the coherence of each marketing decision taken, the company increases its readability on the market and thereby strengthens its competitive position. If

---

1 The notion of positioning was introduced in the early 1970s by two advertisers, Al Ries and Jack Trout, who wanted to go beyond the mere creation of an image to structure the offer around a strong concept perceived by the customer (Ries and Trout 1972).

the company does not take part in defining its positioning, it runs the risk of letting the market decide its identity for it, or worse, perhaps, that the market has no clear idea of what the company does.

Positioning has a double impact on the customer. First, a strong and clear positioning enables customers to better formulate their expectations by having a more precise idea of what the company offers and what it does not. Secondly, positioning plays an important role in customers' decision to buy. Finally, by highlighting the major points of differentiation, positioning helps us to protect against the commoditization of the offer.

8.1.1.2. *The two dimensions of positioning*

The positioning of an offer is based on two dimensions: identification and differentiation.

Identification consists of deciding on the category or reference universe in which the company wants its offer to be classified. The category or reference universe is a more precise and less broad delimitation than the market. In the consulting market, for example, it is possible to distinguish four different categories: strategy consulting, framework consulting, deployment consulting and steering[2]. Each category refers to a specific competitive set. By choosing the category to which it belongs, the company also chooses its competitors. The identification makes it possible for the company to clarify its offer and clients to know which of their expectations can be met. The categories are more or less predefined, leaving more or less freedom to the company to decide on its category. Fitting into a predefined category has the advantage of being anchored in a category that is known and recognized by the target customer, but the disadvantage of being in direct competition with other players. Conversely, creating a new market category puts the company in a market free of any competition, but exposes it to being difficult to identify and understand by its target. Entrepreneurs and start-ups are particularly affected by these decisions. Some may be tempted to create a new category by combining existing categories in an original way. Like Welcome to the Jungle, a start-up in the job search engine market offering companies an annual subscription, which also presents itself as a media and software company for recruiters (Loye 2019).

---

2 Categories proposed by Consult'in France and included in décisions-achats.fr: www. decision-achats.fr/Thematique/category-management-1229/Breves/Acheteurs-comment-choisiez-vous-vos-societes-conseil-316356.htm [Accessed on October 29, 2019].

The second dimension of positioning, differentiation, is built around the distinctive characteristics that the company wants the customer to attribute to its offer. To choose these points of differentiation, we must take into account the customer's expectations, competitors' offers and the company's capabilities. From points of differentiation linked to performance or technical aspects of the offer, to more symbolic or relational elements, via the brand's image, the sources of differentiation are almost infinite. They combine market knowledge and the marketer's imagination.

8.1.2. *The manager and positioning*

By placing positioning at the heart of the strategic stage of the marketing process, managers may feel little concerned by this issue. Moreover, the notion of positioning is derived from advertising and may seem out of step with the reality of B2B. Strategy, marketing and advertising are not the best ways to get managers to take an interest in positioning. However, an appropriation of this notion declined on their perimeter would enable managers, on the one hand, to widen their competitive vision, on the other hand, to articulate a clear discourse on their offer, and finally to ensure the global coherence of their decisions and actions.

8.1.2.1. *Broadening the competitive vision*

One of the two dimensions of positioning is the identification of the category or the competitive universe of the offer. This competitive analysis must be carried out by managers on their perimeter. The specific competitors in a given area are not always the same as those identified by the company at a global level. The analysis of the competitive universe cannot be limited to taking into account easily identifiable direct competitors who are part of managers' daily environment. Competitors are not only those who offer the same service, but also all those who meet the customer's needs with other services or perhaps even with products. This broader vision allows avoiding what Theodore Levitt called marketing myopia, that is, focusing solely on competitors who do the same job or provide the same service (Levitt 1960). Limiting ourselves to our direct competitors is also limiting ourselves in our analysis of the market and the customer. It means confirming our skills and know-how without anticipating the necessary developments, the inevitable changes that will have to be undertaken to react to new forms of competition. We are truly aligned with a customer orientation, starting from the customer's need and not from the service we deliver, and defining our competition based on this need.

8.1.2.2. *Articulating a clear discourse*

By stating the competitive reference universe and the points of differentiation of the offer, managers build a clear vision of their reality. They can easily state it and share it. This constructed vision of their offer enables managers to articulate a clear discourse that they can effectively disseminate both internally and externally.

Internally, managers can use this discourse to bring their team together. A common discourse, centered on the main differentiating elements of the offer compared to the relevant competitors in the area, avoids the fragmentation inherent in the interpretations and perceptions of each individual about the offer and the market. A strong discourse can then become a real narrative that unites the team, and a tool of attraction for the recruitment and integration of new employees. Nevertheless, the vision can evolve and it will evolve all the better if it starts from a precise framework. The common discourse is not in contradiction with a regular re-evaluation by managers and their team, both of the elements of differentiation and of the competitive universe.

A clear and unique message, supported by a strong narrative, can then be broadcast externally, primarily to the customer. Managers and their team transmit the same vision to the various client contacts, both during the purchase and the service implementation phases. In long-term relationships with the customer involving multiple people, the consistency of the discourse can only reinforce its impact.

8.1.2.3. *Ensuring consistency*

From an instrumental perspective, positioning makes it possible for us to judge and evaluate actions and decisions relating to the offer, such as those relating to price. A good action or a good decision must, therefore, be consistent with the positioning. Positioning then enables managers to control, arbitrate and justify choices, whether they are their own or those of their team. A convergence of actions and decisions is automatically established. There may even be a natural self-censorship on the part of the actors not to take actions and decisions that would be in contradiction with the positioning.

8.2. Design of the service offer

In most B2B situations, managers have real autonomy and responsibility for the formalization of the offer they are proposing to a particular client. This formalization takes place at different levels depending on the situation, from the specific offer – designed to respond to a particular call for tenders – to the pre-formatted offer adapted from some of its components. This formalization will be all the more effective if it is consistent with the positioning that defines the general framework of the offer.

8.2.1. *Structure of the service offer*

In order to build the best service offer, it is necessary to first integrate the specificity of the structure around a core service and peripheral services.

8.2.1.1. *Core service and peripheral services*

Any service provider, even the simplest one, does not limit itself to offering a single service but actually offers the customer a package of services. A chauffeur-driven car rental provider does not simply offer a ride. It also offers the possibility to book in advance and to receive a personalized quote. Some provide passengers with a connected tablet, phone chargers, newspapers and drinks; or inform their direct customer of the pick-up. To reduce the complexity of this often vast and heterogeneous set of services offered, it has been proposed to distinguish two categories of service: core service and peripheral service (Eiglier and Langeard 1987, pp. 82–83).

The core service is the main reason why the client approaches the provider. Cleaning of premises is the core service of a cleaning company, transportation of a logistics provider and training of a training organization. It is the core service that defines the company's business and anchors it in a reference market.

Peripheral services are generally numerous and enrich the core service by meeting the customer's complementary expectations while remaining linked to the core service. Warehousing, inventory management and handling are the peripheral services of the core service of a logistics provider. If the peripheral service alone does not justify the activity of the service provider, it is nonetheless essential as it responds to several logics: operational, competitive and financial. The operational logic of the peripheral service is illustrated by the services that the provider is obliged to offer in order to be able to provide the core service. The technical audit of an installation is most of the time necessary in order to propose a maintenance or repair service. Complex environmental performance studies, audits and analyses are also necessary to arrive at recommendations and enable the client to choose a solution for the environmental efficiency of the client organization building that is truly the core service. The competitive logic approaches the peripheral service as an opportunity to differentiate from the competition and to bring a unique added value to the client. The cleaning of a building site after intervention is always appreciated by the customer. Finally, the financial logic consists of pricing the peripheral service, or at least in making a financial profit, even without directly displaying a price in an all-inclusive approach to the offer, for example. The various studies and audits mentioned above can be directly or indirectly invoiced to the client.

8.2.1.2. *Multi-business reality in B2B services*

There is a second level in the richness of a service offering that can be found in almost all providers that have acquired a certain size. These service providers do not limit their service offer to a single core service but expand it around several basic services that are as many different businesses. For example, cleaning companies are expanding their range of services to include handling, inventory management and archive filing, which are still emerging activities mainly developed by large- and medium-sized companies in the sector, but which account for 7% of the sector's total revenue[3]. These new core services often respond to an explicit or latent demand from customers (to simplify the purchasing process, to have a single point of contact, to obtain gains in rationality, etc.) and enable the service provider to move away from the traditional services. These new core services often respond to an explicit or latent demand from clients (simplify the purchasing process, have a single contact, obtain rationality gains, etc.) and enable the service provider to move away from commoditization of its offer and find an additional source of revenue characterized by an often more comfortable profitability.

Major service groups, such as Veolia, Suez and Sodexo, are trying to develop comprehensive offerings to meet different customer expectations with the richest possible offer. This multi-business offer will only become

---

3 Gouttebroze, B. (2017). Panorama des familles d'achat dans les services généraux [Online]. www.decision-achats.fr/Thematique/environnement-travail-1231/Dossiers/panorama-familles-achats-dans-services-generaux-314575/proprete-314581.htm [Accessed on November 2, 2019].

truly strategic if it can offer the customer increased value. Managers may be somewhat shaken by these new approaches, which force them to integrate businesses in which they are not necessarily specialists. Once the sales phase is over, the issue is to overcome silos in the offer implementation phase. If the cleaning team reports a broken door handle to the maintenance team, for example, the quality of the overall service will be directly and positively affected. The role of a local manager is, therefore, essential to transmit this culture of overcoming silos.

This trend, which can be found in many sectors, is characteristic of the multiservice sector, which consists precisely of offering a set of services to the client in an integrated manner (see Box 8.1).

The concept of multiservice was first developed in the 1960s in the United States and England under the term Facilities Management (commonly referred to as FM). In a literal translation, FM indicates outsourcing by a client company of the management of its facilities. The term was hijacked in France in the 1980s to indicate the outsourcing of corporate IT operations. Today, these operations are referred to as outsourcing, but there is still no consensus on the term Facilities Management.

A distinction must be made between multiservice and multi-technical services. Multiservice includes activities such as catering, reception, cleaning, security and green space management, while multi-technical services are more technical in nature, such as the operation and maintenance of a building from a technical point of view (heating, air conditioning, plumbing, electricity, etc.), right through to the management of its energy and environmental efficiency. The range of services that can be offered in a multiservice contract seems to be infinite, which is reflected in the new generic concept of work environment professions.

While the economic dimension of multiservice, namely cost reduction and optimization, remains essential, the service and customer dimension must not be overlooked. Indeed, multi-technical players can sometimes be criticized for being too technical and lacking in customer orientation: entering a meeting room without knocking, climbing on the table to change a light bulb and leaving without apologizing can be technically very efficient but lack a certain courtesy!

Box 8.1. *Multiservice[4]*

---

4 SYPEMI (Syndicat professionnel des entreprises de multiservice immobilier) (2019). L'essentiel [Online]. Available at: www.sypemi.com [Accessed on November 2, 2019].

8.2.2. *Service innovation*

In terms of offerings, B2B is the domain of adaptation and personalization in order to satisfy a customer whose specificities are often too strong to be satisfied with a standard service. The marketing as well as the delivery of a service offer always include an element of innovation.

8.2.2.1. *Challenges of service innovation*

For a long time, management literature has been mainly interested in product innovation. However, innovation in services has always existed, out of competitive, strategic or economic necessity. For some years now, the service sector has been a recognized contributor to innovation, taking advantage of new technologies to develop new service concepts (collaborative platforms, digitalized services, dematerialization of the offer, etc.) and by relying on new market uses. Service innovation is particularly dynamic in the B2B sector, driven by strong customer demand: 78% of companies expect their service providers to accelerate their pace of innovation[5]. Companies must, therefore, succeed in offering their customers new services, especially since innovation makes it possible for them to differentiate themselves from the competition and thus avoid commoditization, solidify their positioning and contribute to their financial performance.

Research in economics on service innovation has demonstrated the need for a specific framework of analysis to approach service innovation and has notably emphasized that innovation in services is not so much produced within research and development departments but comes more broadly from the market and the field, confronted with specific issues during a particular service (Gallouj 1994; Gadrey and Gallouj 1998). On the other hand, if in the field of industrial innovation, it is classic to oppose product innovation and process innovation, in services, because of co-production, this distinction is less effective (Jallat 1994; Abramovici and Bancel-Charensol 2004).

The specificities of innovation in services thus give managers and their team a central role, whether in detecting sources of innovation as close to the ground as possible, or in implementing an innovation that will be all the

---

5 Result from a study of a sample of over 2,000 B2B customers (Salesforce Research 2019).

more successful if it has been tested and deployed in close contact with the market.

8.2.2.2. *Levels of innovation in the service offer*

Service innovation is not limited to disruptive offers that totally bring new services to the market. The manager can be an actor in service innovation by considering three progressive levels of innovation that create value: naming the service offer, enriching peripheral services and adding core services.

A service that is not named has very little chance of being visible to the customer and, therefore, of being valuable. Giving a name to each component of a service means revealing, to the customer and the market, services that they did not identify and, therefore, did not believe existed. While the notion of a catalog of offers is widely accepted and deployed for products, it is less practiced in the field of services. Naming each of the components of its offer forces managers to first identify them themselves, then to share with their team the actual service offer. While core services are generally very well identified and named, this is less true for peripheral services. Identifying peripheral services is a complex process for several reasons. It may be difficult to accept that a service traditionally considered to be inherent to the provider's business can be presented as an offer. For example, for a provider used to cleaning up a job site when leaving, this will be a "natural" thing to do and will not represent a real service in their eyes. It is also difficult for both teams and clients to consider that an offer that is not paid for is still a service. Finally, some elements of value that the service provider provides to its client are not even identified as such. This is what is commonly called hidden services. Service companies, and probably especially B2B service companies, are rich in hidden services. Few service providers, for example, consider their billing as a peripheral service. However, an invoice provides customers with information that enables them to analyze their consumption and produce summary information.

Enriching the peripheral service offer can obviously involve developing new peripheral services and also improving existing peripheral services. Improving an existing peripheral service consists of increasing its content with more innovative features and moving it from a simple operational logic to a competitive and then financial logic (see Box 8.2).

EDF is developing a range of "invoice-related services" (according to the terminology used by the company) for its business customers, such as electronic invoicing flows and grouped invoicing.

EDF's SuiviConso is one of these services directly linked to billing. It has been developed from the elements that the company uses to generate a bill. SuiviConso is presented as a help offered to the customer to better control its energy consumption. The service is clearly named (SuiviConso) and the benefits for the customer are just as clear.

By accessing their customer area, professionals can track their energy expenses on one or more sites and instantly identify consumption peaks or deviations and thus identify sources of energy savings. The tool is particularly well designed from a visual point of view. It is practical because it allows for easily exporting data and customized tables to analyze and share information. It is also efficient since the customer can be notified by email when energy consumption reaches an alert level.

EDF's innovation here concerns the use of the data that the company possesses for billing purposes. This is indeed an innovation because it creates value for the customer. From a purely operational peripheral service, the invoice is now part of a competitive logic (customer satisfaction and competitive differentiation) and financial logic (the customer takes out a subscription).

Box 8.2. *Enriching a peripheral service*[6]

Finally, innovation by increasing the number of core services consists of developing new services that are autonomous from an existing core service and then become new core services. These new core services can be developed *ex nihilo*, but they can also be peripheral services that, as they gain in significance and relevance in the eyes of the customer, are promoted to core service. The example of multiservice developed above illustrates the enrichment of the service offer by the addition of new core services.

8.2.2.3. *Co-creation and co-construction*

Co-creation is the participation of the customer in the process of developing a new offering (Prahalad and Ramaswamy 2000). In this

---

6 EDF (2016). Découvrez le SuiviConso, un service d'EDF Entreprises [Online]. Available at: www.youtube.com/watch?v=RczgzeAxmX8   [Accessed   on   November   10,   2019]; www.edf.fr/entreprises/contrat-et-facture/services-around-the-bill/the-services-around-the-bill [Accessed on November 10, 2019].

approach, the customer is not only asked to react to ideas for new services, but is also fully involved in the generation of ideas for new services and in their development. This involvement of the customer in the innovation process has many positive effects: development of new services that are truly in line with market expectations; reduction of the failure rate of new services; acceleration of the time-to-market; and strengthening of the relationship, trust and proximity with the customer. Co-creation makes it possible to get around a difficulty specific to services. While knowledge of the customers' needs is an essential element in innovation, customers themselves often have difficulty expressing their needs and formulating their expectations when faced with an immaterial offer. This co-creation, which is based on exchange, dialogue and questioning, can overcome this difficulty.

In B2B, the co-construction of the offer is a strong reality because the demand as well as the offer are never completely formalized. During the numerous interactions between the client and the service provider, the offer is often discussed, redefined and refined. The offer is a potential to be constructed by both the provider and the client (Cova and Salle 1999, p. 198). Co-construction essentially concerns the formation of an offer that potentially exists within the service provider. The client accompanies the service provider in the formalization and specification of the offer in order to specify a service that is perfectly in line with its reality and its environment.

Co-creation thus goes further than co-construction. It is situated upstream of co-construction, with the objective of generating new ideas and service concepts. However, co-creation can build on the existence of this practice of co-construction, because these moments in the relationship when the offer is built together can be conducive to ideas for new services. The interweaving of co-construction and co-creation reveals a great potential for innovation in B2B services. All the more so as the whole team can be involved in these processes as each one can be in contact with a particular member of the buying center or a target within the client organization.

Co-creation and co-construction both support and reinforce customer orientation. First of all, it is the knowledge of the client and the trust of each partner in the relationship that enable us to move towards these advanced forms of collaboration, but it is also an opportunity for the service provider to better know, understand and decipher its client's constraints and its business. Finally, it seems relevant to integrate different stakeholders belonging to a common ecosystem into these approaches (Maman *et al.* 2009).

Innovation in a number of B2B service sectors has been marked over the last 10 years by a shift in focus from the decision-maker to the user. This is what has happened in particular in the catering sector, as well as for facility management professions in general: reception, cleaning, technical management of buildings, etc. For a long time, companies were only interested in the customer who made the decision or paid for the service, and too often forgot about the user of the service. In a way, we have moved from B2B to B2C2B, whose main objective is to improve the user's experience.

This reorientation is primarily linked to decision-makers and buyers themselves, who are increasingly interested in the well-being, quality of life and satisfaction of their employees, who are the users of the service. The voice of the employees is becoming increasingly heard, especially via social networks, as they are able to make their claims to the service provider and to the customer who makes the decision. As soon as users speak up and compare their experiences with particularly successful B2C players, they force their company's service providers to be more innovative. The user now expects these different service providers to deliver an experience worthy of the name.

Faced with this reality, the role of on-site managers is changing. They are no longer just the contact persons for the purchasing director or the human resources director, but become the day-to-day contact persons for the service users. Thus, managers acquire an incredible legitimacy in innovation, by being at the heart of the user experience. R&D managers are not really able to understand what makes the quality of the experience for particular users, who are all different, depending on their cultural, business or geographical environment. Innovation will, therefore, be born from observations and feedback that managers will organize with their team. The inverted pyramid or bottom-up models make sense for innovation in these environments. It is by being confronted with a particular problem within their scope, or by identifying a development opportunity, that managers will lead their teams into an innovation process. The role of innovation departments will, therefore, be to facilitate and make way for smoother project management rather than to initiate it.

Once managers have identified a source of innovation with their team, the project process should not be perceived as an obstacle or an insurmountable step. Managers who really want to be innovative must be curious. Curiosity is a real duty for the manager. They must regularly train themselves in new practices and new tools, particularly those linked to agile innovation methods (design thinking, for example). More and more training courses are available remotely, and white papers are also freely available. Managers today can easily find out what design thinking means and what it can bring them. They must also involve their teams in this curiosity, and implement collective intelligence with them, in order to be the driving force behind the transformation and the stimulation of innovation in their company.

Box 8.3. *Testimony of Éric Texier (Founder of BeNova and eeVee Partner – ex-VP Innovation Sodexo Group)*

8.3. Plasticity of the service offer

Plasticity is characterized by malleability, deformability, flexibility or even modifiability. It is also a capacity to take a specific form under a constraint, as the material does under the hand of the worker or the craftsperson. Thus, plasticity becomes synonymous with adaptability, adaptation to change and receptivity to novelty and to the environment.

To speak of the plasticity of the service offer is to recognize its ability to adapt to different markets and clients. It also means giving managers and their team the ability to shape the offer in a more or less radical way, as a craftsperson would do with Earth. Finally, it means giving the customer a place in this possible process of transformation, or more simply of adaptation of the offer. This plasticity is specific to the service offer because of its characteristics (intangibility makes the offer more easily malleable) and its structure (the natural richness of the service offer allows for it to be shaped in many directions). It is particularly strong in a B2B context, because the necessary proximity between the client and the service provider, and the reality of a co-constructed offer, allows for maximum adaptability of the offer.

8.3.1. *Levels of plasticity*

The plasticity of the offer will enable the service provider to adapt its service to its client. The segment remains the main unit of reference from which the offer will be adapted: a specific service offer per segment. But even within a segment, it is necessary to maintain a certain plasticity of the offer in order to continue to adapt it to the specific expectations of particular clients.

8.3.1.1. *Overall plasticity of the offer*

The first level of plasticity is the overall composition of the offer around core and peripheral services. The provider first chooses the core service(s) that will be included in the offer. This choice may be imposed by clients, who exactly know what they want, but it is most often the result of an exchange between providers and their clients. This choice is never totally fixed during the purchase negotiation, because customers can ask their provider for additional services during the delivery of the business, and the provider can be the force of proposal in this direction. Depending on the client, the offer will be more or less extensive depending on the number of core services included. This is what can be observed in multiservice, where some deals are limited to a few core services, while other richer deals include a large number of services. As for the peripheral services specific to each core service, while some are unquestionably necessary, others can be removed from certain cases for economic reasons in particular, while still others can be added to meet specific customer requirements. A hotline or a customer service can be peripheral services offered in markets or to customers with a high economic contribution. Working on the plasticity of our offer also consists of making certain services more salient than others, in order to align the attractiveness of the offer with the profile of the segment or the client.

8.3.1.2. *Plasticity of service attributes*

An offer is defined from its attributes. The attributes are the characteristics, the properties of an offer. They can be objective or symbolic. They play an essential role from the customers' point of view because they make it possible for them to identify and evaluate an offer as well as to perceive its differences compared to competing offers. A car is defined by its brand, color, dimensions, fuel consumption, speed, price and all other attributes that give the necessary information about the product. The attributes of a service specify the way it is performed. For example, for a maintenance operation on a customer site, we will specify the service according to its price, the intervention time, the tools used and the number of people involved. Each service, whether core or peripheral, is characterized by a set of attributes.

The plasticity of the service attributes can be worked on two dimensions: acting on the presence of the attribute or acting on its level.

Among the attributes of an offer, we can distinguish those that are inseparable from those that can be removed without affecting the offer. If price and brand are generally inseparable attributes, the non-contractual guarantee is a dissociable attribute. The provider can then choose to include or not include the dissociable attributes for a given customer in a specific buying situation. An extended non-contractual warranty on a repair service may be exclusively offered in one market or for a customer with a high financial contribution.

The level of an attribute indicates the degree to which the attribute is offered (see Box 8.4). The non-contractual warranty may be for a shorter or longer period of time, and a hotline may be available 24 hours a day, seven days a week, or just during the week in a reduced time slot from 10:00 am to 6:00 pm

---

Booking.com is an online booking platform for accommodation, travel and various activities. The site has two user profiles: partners who offer deals and consumers who buy them. The company is, therefore, both on the B2B and B2C. Customer service is at the heart of the strategy: more than 6,000 full-time employees receive calls from both user targets 24/7. The language in which employees will be able to express themselves is a major issue since only 13.9% of B2B users speak English, while 46.8% speak 5 languages other than English and 39.3% speak 36 other languages. With this in mind, Booking.com has taken the step of offering a truly multilingual customer service. While most companies offer customer service in only a few languages, Booking.com answers its customers in 42 languages to cover all languages spoken by customers! All employees are fluent in English and one other language, many speak three or four languages and some speak up to seven or eight languages.

Availability and language are two major attributes of a customer service. Booking.com has chosen to take these two attributes to an exceptionally high level.

Box 8.4. *Multilingual customer service*[7]

Managers must identify the attributes that are really important to clients. While clients will more easily forgive a provider's poor performance on

---

7 Huston, D. (2016). Priceline's CEO on creating an in-house multilingual customer service operation. *Harvard Business Review*, 94(4), 37–40.

attributes that are less important to them, they will be very demanding on the attributes that are most important to them.

8.3.2. *Presentation of the service offer*

Once the content of the offer has been decided and its plasticity approached, there is one last decision to be made: the way in which it will be presented to customers and marketed. Should it be presented as a whole in the form of a unique package, or on the contrary, is it preferable to present the offer to clients through its various components? An *à la carte* offer or a full package?

8.3.2.1. *The notion of bundling*

Bundling is a term for a marketing and sales practice that consists of combining several products or services within a single offer. Several translations exist: linked offer, bundled offer, offer package, service package, etc. This practice is particularly common in the field of services. It is supposed to offer clients certain advantages. The advantage may be monetary if the tied offer is offered at a price lower than the sum of the prices of each service that makes up the offer. The benefit is non-monetary if the integration of several elements within the same offer provides additional value to the customer. The linked offer simplifies the purchasing process; it enables clients to have a single contact, and the provider can put for the argument that the integration of the offer will bring efficiency, quality and performance. In the field of consulting, for example, concerning digital transformation, the winning offers are often from firms that manage to combine services on strategic and organizational support as well as on technological deployment and cybersecurity issues. The firm must then demonstrate to clients its ability to offer all these different dimensions linked to digital transformation and to carry them out in the most integrated process possible.

From the providers' point of view, the tied offer makes it possible for them to increase their presence at the customer's site, and by reducing the heterogeneity of the demand, opens up perspectives for greater efficiency.

8.3.2.2. *Limits of bundling*

However, the customer may have some reservations about the tied offer. In particular, they may find the offer lacking in transparency and prefer to have a clear view of each component of the offer. This feeling of lack of transparency may be reflected in their assessment of the price: they may feel that they are paying too much for what they get, or that they are paying for services that they do not really need and that they did not choose. The client may also feel that there is a risk in having a single provider responsible for a wide range of services. They may fear a certain dependence and anticipate a wait-and-see attitude on the part of the provider.

Finally, while customers are attracted to the tied offer because of its potential for value and integration, service providers must be able to deliver on these promises. The tied offer strategy should not be a mere display but should provide additional value that can be identified by customers. In order for this global presentation of the tied offer to be positively perceived by clients, service providers benefit by making the breakdown of the offer around its main dimensions transparent, so that clients can accept it without too much reluctance.

Taking Care of One Commercial Action

9.1. Commercial proposal

Whether it is a highly formalized consultation, such as a call for tenders, especially a public call for tenders, or a more informal consultation, a written document is often requested. If this written proposal is retained by the prospect, the service provider will then have the opportunity in many cases to present it orally.

9.1.1. *Documents and materials*

Many documents and written materials are attached to a commercial proposal. They are to be understood as tangible elements that will help the customer to understand the offer and to materialize it. They are, therefore, opportunities for the service provider to enhance its offer.

9.1.1.1. *Tangible elements of the service*

Documents and materials are not limited to the written report sent on the day of submission of the offer. There are also e-mails, letters, brochures and videos sent before or after the submission of the offer. These different documents and materials are not always sent by the same person, the same team, or often by the same department. It is important to ensure that there is a certain consistency between these various elements. Consistency in content, of course, and also in form. This coherence will give a more solid and constructed image of the service and the provider. These different elements embody, in a way, for customers the service they cannot see. The perception that clients will have of these documents, the impression that they will leave on the latter, will contribute to the image and the idea that clients will have of the offer and the provider. They will also circulate within the client organization, passing from hand to hand, from department to department. If they do not end up in a physical or virtual wastebasket too quickly, they will lie around on a desk and may even be kept in a file and brought out again at a later date, perhaps for another consultation.

It is in this dynamic that all of these documents and materials must be designed as tangible elements of the service for the client.

9.1.1.2. *Potential for increasing the value of the offer*

Since it is not possible to physically present a service, offer it for trial, and demonstrate it all of the documents and materials used to present the offer will enable customers to better understand the offer. They must be attractive while being serious. They must inspire confidence and make clients want to go further with the service provider.

The commercial proposal sent to the prospect is the essential element of this approach. Within the framework of a call for tenders, and even more so for a public call for tenders, the content and organization of the commercial proposal are predetermined, and the service provider must in a way fill in predefined boxes. If a framework is not set, it will be up to the provider to build it.

The commercial proposal, quite different from a quotation which is limited to a few pages and a pricing proposal, is a written document that includes a technical part, a financial part, and a contractual and legal part. It will often be read by several people in the customer's organization, with technical, financial or more generalist profiles, taking different roles in the buying center as decision-maker, buyer or user. The challenge of the commercial proposal is to deliver a relevant and readable message for each reader in a single document. Not everyone will be looking for the same information, will read the same parts, and will not devote the same amount of time or attention to reading the document[1].

---

[1] Thierry Craye, in a practical book, gave advice on writing the sales proposal (Craye 2016, pp. 138–168).

9.1.2. *Oral presentation*

Albert Mehrabian, a professor of psychology at the University of California, conducted two studies in 1967 that were to revolutionize oral communication (Mehrabian and Ferris 1967; Mehrabian and Wiener 1967). The researcher's objective was to establish the share of verbal, vocal and visual in oral communication. This is commonly referred to today as the 3-V rule. This rule breaks down the impact of an oral communication in the following way:

– 7% for verbal (words used and their meaning);

– 38% for the voice (the voice, its intonation and its volume);

– 55% for the visual (facial expression, body language and attitude).

Even though Mehrabian's research has been discussed and criticized, especially regarding the accuracy of the percentages and the methodology of the studies, the importance of non-verbal communication is almost never questioned[2]. Non-verbal is undoubtedly the major asset of all good communicators. The more powerful the non-verbal part, the more effective the message will be. Without neglecting the verbal part, which must remain the foundation of a good speech, and especially in B2B situations, we must pay strong and real attention to the non-verbal part if one wants one's speech to have the expected impact. The congruence between non-verbal and verbal parts is the real key to successful speaking in a professional environment. The non-verbal part must not weaken the verbal part, as would be the case if a competent verbal was carried by a non-verbal part lacking in confidence.

Preparation is essential. It starts with knowing one audience in order to adapt one's speech as finely as possible to the profiles and expectations of the people who will be listening. It is also important to practice and not hesitate to rehearse one's presentation. Since it is often a team that presents, the understanding between the team members and the synergy felt will also be key elements of the speech.

9.1.2.1. *Verbal part*

Verbal communication is the foundation of all oral communication. If it is not solid, the speech will not hold. Verbal communication is built from

---

2 For example, a recent study showed that investors attached more importance to body language than to words during entrepreneurial *pitches* (Clarke *et al.* 2019).

words, their syntax and expression, which are structured into a speech. It can be supported by a medium like projected slides.

Words should be chosen so that the vocabulary is appropriate for the audience. Parasitic words (e.g. uh, here and so) must be avoided. Sentences, preferably short, should be kept simple so that they are easily understood.

The stronger the speech, the more logical and coherent its structure. It is important to avoid going off in all directions without a common thread, having too many arguments, wanting to say too much and going over the allotted time. Announcing the structure at the beginning and respecting it is the best way for the speaker to feel comfortable in his or her speech, to keep the audience's attention more easily and, therefore, to increase his or her capacity to convince them. The structure of the speech must highlight the strong arguments of the presentation. They must be clearly identifiable by the audience and must, therefore, be repeated and reformulated throughout the speech. The beginning and the end are the two strongest moments of the speech. The beginning, often called the hook, will immediately capture the attention or disappoint, and therefore strongly influence the apprehension of the audience. The end is the last image, the last word, like a final note.

Finally, a speech comes alive and becomes lively thanks to anecdotes, little stories, what is called story telling. One have to find the right mix, appropriate to the audience and the subject matter, the main thing being to feel comfortable with the exercise.

9.1.2.2. *Non-verbal part*

The importance of non-verbal communication is linked to the conscious and unconscious impact it has on an audience. Non-verbal signals are often interpreted unconsciously by an interlocutor and these signals will be used to translate the state of mind, the intentions or the personality of the speaker[3]. The non-verbal dimension of speaking makes it both an art and a set of techniques. The vocal and the visual parts are the two dimensions of non-verbal communication.

---

3 A new discipline, synergology, has appeared in order to understand the human from its body language. The official website of synergology can be found at the following address: www.synergologie.org [Accessed on November 13, 2019].

The voice carries our words and ideas. It is not only a communication tool but also a vector of emotions. Seductive, persuasive, sometimes intimidating, it has the power to reassure and also to worry or to inflame for better or for worse. The voice reveals and can betray energy, sincerity and involvement. We must learn to know and recognize our voice through its timbre (low or high), its flow (the speed at which we speak), its volume (the sound level) and its intonation (the melody of the voice). If the timbre cannot be modified, it is necessary to learn to regulate its flow, its volume and its intonation. The sound level must be adapted to the context. A low sound level will often tend to discredit the speaker. The flow and intonation must be instrumentalized in order to keep the audience's attention and bring the speech to life. Diction must be clear. Silence must find its place in the speech. It is often the most convincing word.

The visual dimension of non-verbal is the one that has the most impact on speaking according to Mehrabian's studies. It is our body language and is built on four pillars:

– Posture: the general position of the body can give an image of domination and aggressiveness or, on the contrary, of withdrawal and inferiority. It is necessary to find a balanced posture, sitting or standing, which puts the speaker in a constructive and balanced face-to-face relationship with his or her interlocutor. The posture must remain free and avoid giving the feeling of being locked in.

– Gestures: hands should accompany the speech by illustrating it, emphasizing key points and reinforcing the message. They give relief to a speech. They should not betray nervousness but give the impression of being controlled.

– Gaze: it must be sustained, directed towards the speaker. If the audience is composed of several people, without being a large assembly, it is essential to look at each person and avoid focusing on only one of them.

– Face and smile: the face can easily betray tension and anxiety. We should try to keep an open face. A smile is often the best way to establish contact with the other person. So let us remember to smile!

9.2. Commercial negotiation

Negotiation is one of the last steps in the purchasing process before the final contracting phase. Many steps have been taken and it is the negotiation that will allow for deciding between the two or three providers still in the running.

The objective of this section is not to reiterate the principles of negotiation in general and commercial negotiation in particular[4], as this would be far too ambitious. It is a much more modest attempt to highlight the elements that help to keep the negotiation aligned with the customer orientation.

9.2.1. *Preparing for the negotiation*

Experts often repeat that a negotiation is largely won in the preparation phase[5]. Customer orientation is an essential part of the negotiation process, as it focuses on knowing and understanding the customer, which will enable managers to determine their position in the negotiation with greater relevance.

9.2.1.1. *Understanding the context of the negotiation*

At this stage of the buying process, a significant investment has already been made to know customers. This knowledge was necessary to define an offer and formulate the commercial proposal delivered to customers. However, since the offer was made, time has passed, events have occurred and customers have probably advanced their approach. The offers submitted by the competitors, the analyses and the exchanges, which took place within the buying center, could only lead customers to evolve. In particular, they have further improved their level of knowledge and expertise on the service, and the various competing proposals give them a solid basis for analysis and comparison. It would be a mistake to prepare for the negotiation by relying solely on the knowledge of clients acquired before responding to the

---

4 The book by Laurent Combalbert and Marwan Méry offers a comprehensive overview of negotiation in all its forms (Combalbert and Méry 2019). As for commercial negotiation, it is the subject of numerous books (Viau *et al.* 2015; Leroux and Chouraqui 2016).

5 "A good negotiation is divided into 70% preparation and 30% informed improvisation" (Combalbert and Méry 2019, p. 21).

consultation. An update of customer knowledge is necessary. It is a matter of reconsidering the customer's position and precisely that of the various members of the buying center. A few simple questions make it possible for us to get to know customers better:

– Have new events occurred in the analysis of the pipeline?

– Has the buying center evolved? Have some players left the buying center, others joined it?

– Have the expectations of the various members of the buying center changed?

These new questions are delicate because they can call into question truths established before the response to the call for tenders. We must be willing to question or at least consider again past analyses and perceptions. Cognitive biases that lead to false hypotheses or bad analyses are particularly dangerous at this stage. A negotiation situation must be analyzed from the client's point of view. The challenge is to understand the buyer's true motivations, which are not always clearly formulated or, if they are said, can sometimes serve as a screen for hidden issues.

9.2.1.2. *Defining one's position*

It is also in this preparation phase that managers must decide on the position they will hold during the negotiation. They should think about the strategy they will be able to deploy during the negotiation and the tactics the prospect will tend to lead them towards.

The negotiation strategy will be based on the objectives and limits or conditions that we choose to set. The objectives that managers set must be consistent with their business proposal and knowledge of the client. The objectives must be ambitious but remain realistic, that is, leave room for a possible agreement with the client.

The limits or conditions that are placed on the negotiation must clearly formulate the famous diplomatic red line that will not be crossed. It can be expressed in terms of price, deadlines, technical requirements, and also in terms of ethics and values. One must be prepared to say no and know precisely when the negotiation will have to be broken off.

Combalbert and Méry distinguished three negotiation strategies according to the outcomes generated and the ethical dimension (Combalbert and Méry 2019, pp. 246–253):

– competition, where each party sets the goal of winning over the other, maximizes results but the ethical dimension is weak;

– cooperation, where each party agrees to share the gain obtained with the other, has a strong ethical dimension but generates fewer results than competition;

– coopetition, which in the context of negotiation is defined as the transition to a logic of cooperation after having engaged in a logic of competition. It allows for maximizing results and ethics simultaneously.

Negotiation tactics are often dictated by the client who proposes a global negotiation on the whole contract or prefers to bring the supplier progressively on each point of the proposal.

9.2.2. Negotiating

To keep the customer orientation at the heart of the negotiation, managers must develop their listening skills and mobilize their emotional intelligence.

9.2.2.1. Listening

In his latest letter to shareholders, Serge Kampf, founder of Cap Gemini, placed listening at the heart of his vision: "One factor of stability is that we have always placed the client at the heart of our thinking and our actions. Our fundamental principle is to take the time to listen to them"[6].

Listening is a key attribute of customer orientation and it is too often forgotten during sales negotiations. We often think we are in a listening situation when we really are not:

– Listening is not analyzing. To be in a true listening posture, we must not try to analyze or judge at the same time what the interlocutor says.

---

6 Capgemini (2014). Lettre de Serge Kampf. In *Rapport Annuel 2014*, CapGemini (ed.) [Online]. Available at: www.capgemini.com/fr-fr/wp-content/uploads/sites/2/2017/07/annualreport2014capgemini_7.pdf [Accessed on October 14, 2019].

Listening and analysis should not be done simultaneously. First one listen, then one analyze in order to avoid as much as possible any bias of interpretation or judgment that would lead to a bad analysis.

– Listening is not preparing one's answer. If, when listening to one's interlocutor, one is already preparing one's answer or objection, one will lose information, and thus alter the quality of the feedback one will produce.

– Listening is not anticipating the words of the other person. Even though one know or think one know what the other person is going to say, the time spent listening is a source of satisfaction for the person expressing himself or herself.

– Listening is to make oneself totally available to the other person. The risk of not being available to the other person is to bring everything back to oneself, one's experience, one's framework of analysis, and one's mental categories and beliefs. This availability makes it easier to accept several interpretations of reality and opens the way to a more constructive and creative exchange.

Uncertainty, stress, haste and lack of self-confidence are some of the parasites of listening. They are often found in negotiation situations. One must, therefore, be particularly vigilant in maintaining one's attention. To reactivate listening, it is advisable to ask open-ended questions and to rephrase what has been said. This listening will not only be appreciated by one's interlocutors but will also allow one to be more agile in the negotiation.

9.2.2.2. Emotional intelligence

It is difficult not to accept the role that emotion plays in any negotiation. Emotional intelligence, popularized by Goleman in his 1995 book, is now considered an essential managerial skill.

It reflects the ability to perceive, understand and manage one's emotions and those of others. It also appears as a key skill in any negotiation process. Understanding and managing one's own emotions as well as those of one's interlocutors allow for a calmer and more constructive negotiation, in the sense of a true customer orientation.

The emotional intelligence model is structured around five competencies (Goleman 2014, pp. 523–525):

– Self-awareness: knowing one's own inner states, preferences, resources and intuitions.

– Self-control: knowing how to manage one's inner states, impulses and resources.

– Motivation: the emotional tendencies that help us achieve our goals.

– Empathy: awareness of the feelings, needs and concerns of others.

– Social skills: inducing favorable responses in others.

Anne[7] had had a fairly modest service contract with a community for several years. In January, she learned that the client intended to move towards a contract with a much broader scope of services. In April, the call for applications was published, giving potential candidates one month to respond. The call for applications was essentially a first administrative step in the bidding process. The client had chosen to use a global public performance contract for a period of 15 years and for an amount of 10,500 k€. Given the size of the project, companies were forming consortia composed of service providers with complementary technical backgrounds. In June, three groups of companies were selected and received the initial consultation document indicating the client's expectations, mainly concerning technical, economic and legal aspects. The bid was due on September 9 at 5 pm.

The group led by Anne was called for a presentation on October 17. Two weeks before the presentation, the client gave the group a dialogue sheet containing about 60 questions related to the submitted offer. These questions would be used as a basis for the discussion during the presentation. The client asked the group to limit the number of participants to eight people and provided a precise agenda. The presentation was scheduled from 9 am to 6 pm and was organized around alternating presentation and discussion phases. During the presentation phases, the client indicated that they would not interrupt the speakers and that they will ask questions during the discussion phase. The day included three presentation phases of 1.5 hours each, structured around the client's three

7 For confidentiality reasons, the real identity of the manager as well as those of his employer and client is masked.

main issues. Each of the three presentations would be followed by a discussion with the client lasting a similar amount of time.

Anne's group was intensely involved in the preparation of the defense. First, the questions were dealt with. Then, it was necessary to decide who would participate in the defense. Each of the partners of the group would be represented. It was decided that the legal director of the consortium's representative would not be present but would be available by phone. A cybersecurity expert would also be available if the client had any specific questions. Everyone was fine-tuning their speeches and slides were being carefully prepared. Three presentations of 1.5 hours each required serious preparation. It was decided to open the presentation with a video. The communication departments of the various partners were mobilized to carry out the editing. As this preparation was mainly done remotely, it was essential that the team meet the day before for final adjustments, for a general rehearsal, and also to activate a collective energy that could well be important in front of the client. The team met in a hotel seminar room for a day of work, which ended with a friendly dinner. Everyone stayed overnight at the hotel to leave together the next morning.

The presentation took place precisely as indicated in the preparatory document sent by the client. When Anne and her partners from the group entered the examination room, they discovered a committee composed of 12 people, most of whom they did not know. The chairman of the committee, the director general of services, let each member of the committee introduce themselves. The purchasing director, the technical director and the assistant to principal were obviously present. Experts, collaborating with the client on specific points of the offer, complete the committee. The client was very particular about the time allowed for presentations. Before the end of the allotted time, the chairman of the committee systematically indicates that there were only 30 seconds left. During the exchange phases, specific points were discussed: some points were non-negotiable, others were accepted by the client, and yet others had to be reconsidered by the client who would provide a clear answer later. For example, the group asked for additional site visits. The client accepted and indicated that specific days of visit would be communicated to them. The difficulty of the presentation consisted of being, at the same time, concentrated on the quality of the answers given to the customer and mobilized on a very great capacity of listening in order to capture the deep expectations of the customer.

According to Anne, the presentation went well overall, but she was aware that an additional level would have to be reached to enable the group to win the tender. At the end of this presentation, the client would send the candidates a final consultation file modified according to all the exchanges the client had with the different groups. This final consultation file would obviously not be fundamentally different from the initial consultation file; it would not impose a solution but would orientate more precisely on the commitments. During the presentation, the client indicated that he would send this final file at the beginning of November and that the groups would have one month to respond. He also indicated that there would be no new defense.

Box 9.1. *Testimony of an operations manager*

Delivering the Service

Introduction to Part 4

The service is not performed in a factory under the supervision of a production manager. It is managers, surrounded by their team, who collaborate with their client to deliver the service.

Understanding the fundamentals of customer orientation in B2B services (Part 1), then knowing the customer (Part 2), and finally, shaping the offer (Part 3), makes it possible for managers to approach this final stage of their mission with both confidence and enthusiasm. Confidence combined with a mastery of the issues and an enthusiasm drawn from the anticipation of the challenges identified: freeing up the human element, managing service operations and marketing the tangible.

The human element is at the heart of the service. B2B densifies the human relationship. Liberating the human element in B2B services means making a tireless commitment to ensuring that people remain the measure of all performance. Performance by and for people. Understanding, once again, the men and women of the client who meet the men and women of the service provider. The challenge for the manager is immense but exciting: to involve the client and mobilize the team.

Operations management focuses on the production process and applies equally to a product or a service. Operational excellence is the objective of operations management. The search for this excellence must, on the one hand, take into account the specificities of the production of a service, and also integrate the customer orientation. The role of the manager is to harmonize operational efficiency and customer orientation within their territory.

While the core of the service offer is by definition immaterial, many tangible elements accompany it. Premises, equipment, vehicles and documentation are some of the elements used by the service provider and inherent to the service. These tangibles are not simply accessories to the service, but carry real stakes for the service provider in general, and for the manager in particular. Marketing tangibles means recognizing their importance in the eyes of the client.

Unlocking Human Potential

10.1. Associating the client

Today, customers are recognized as having an active role in their consumption, in their relationships with suppliers and service providers, and more broadly in the economy. The customer no longer just has to choose, buy and consume, but is also an actor through co-production, co-creation or co-design. The line between production and consumption is becoming blurred, as is the distinction between producer and consumer. The neologism *prosumer* has even been created to describe this new reality (Ritzer and Jurgenson 2010). These developments have been widely discussed in the B2C field. While customer activism refers to a specific reality in B2C, it remains a fact that the very nature of the service implies customer participation regardless of the field of application.

10.1.1. *Principles of client participation in the service*

10.1.1.1. *Reality*

Customers' participation in the service is a direct consequence of its production process. The customer is an element of the service model and is the co-producer of the service[1]. This is the essential specificity of service management: customers are not mere consumers of the service, and they are also its producer. The discovery of this reality of a customer as an

---

1 The co-production of service, a consequence of servuction, is presented in Chapter 2.

"economic agent participating" in the production of the service is very old and goes back to the very first efforts to understand services[2]. Participation refers to the information that clients must give or receive, the actions that they must perform, and the efforts that they must make in order to obtain the service (Bitner *et al.* 1997). Allowing the provider access to a site, providing the necessary authorizations if the site is particularly risky, giving the provider the information needed to intervene, and providing facilities are all information, actions and efforts on the part of the client in order for the provider to intervene and carry out its mission.

The literature takes into account three dimensions to better approach this participation. These three dimensions remain relevant in a B2B context:

– The level (Bitner *et al.* 1997). Customer involvement can be low (freight transport), moderate (website maintenance) or high (training).

– The nature (Eiglier and Langeard 1987, p. 40). The client's participation can be physical by performing physical tasks or actions, intellectual when the client must receive, process and give information, or affective when emotions or feelings are involved. All three types of participation can occur in the same service. For example, for a team building service to be fully successful, the three natures of participation must be mobilized.

– The object (Eiglier and Langeard 1987, p. 39). The customer participates in specifying, performing or controlling the service. During the purchasing process, the customer's participation applies to the specification of the service, whereas during the service realization phase, these three objects of participation may be mixed.

10.1.1.2. *Issues*

Customer participation in the service impacts provider productivity and customer satisfaction.

---

2 Eric Langeard considered Victor R. Fuchs to be the first author to highlight the participation of the client in the realization of the service. He quoted an extract from his book *The Service Economy*, published in 1968 by Columbia University Press, New York: "One lesson we learn from our study of productivity in services is the important role of the consumer as an economic agent actively participating in the process of making the service [...] productivity in the automobile industry is not affected by the prudence or recklessness of the end user of the car or by his degree of intelligence" (Langeard 1987, p. 32).

Since by participating in the service the client becomes a production agent, a part-time employee, productivity is automatically affected. The client's participation, if it is in line with the provider's expectations, will contribute positively to the service process; however, if the client does not assume its role or assumes it incorrectly, it will harm the provider's organization and business. If the client has not prepared the access authorizations on the day of the service, the team will not be able to perform the service as planned. At best, there will be a delay in the start of the service, at worst a postponement. The service provider will not only suffer a financial loss evaluated in hours not worked, but will also have to face a demobilization of the team and will have to reorganize its schedule.

From the client's point of view, this participation may be experienced as a burdensome constraint or, on the contrary, it may be appreciated, offering savings in time or money, providing greater comfort in the relationship with the service provider and in consumption, making it possible for the client to control and personalize the service, or simply providing pleasure. It can be a source of satisfaction.

Because of this double challenge – operational and marketing – participation must be anticipated, managed and controlled by the provider in order to find the right balance between productivity and satisfaction.

10.1.2. *A more complex reality in B2B*

10.1.2.1. *Moments*

In a B2B context, three key moments of customer participation can be distinguished: before the commercial negotiation, during the commercial negotiation and during the realization of the service.

Upstream of the commercial negotiation, the purchasing process is an essential step in the service relationship. In the best case, it leads to a negotiation. The purchasing process and the negotiation are the first two moments during which the client participates in the specification of the service. The more complex, intangible and innovative the service, the less standardized and predefined it is, giving the customer an actual opportunity to contribute to the definition, formalization and specification of the service. This participation is first of all contractual through the specifications, the consultation or the invitation to tender. These are the first spaces that the client grants itself in order to be able to state its requirements to its provider. This participation of the client in the formalization of the provider's offer will continue in a non-contractual way throughout the purchasing process. During meetings and work sessions, and after gathering various information, the client will give indications; deliver analyses, perceptions and feelings; and specify expectations, which will be for the service provider as many sources of necessary adaptations of its offer. During the purchasing process, the client is fully capable of influencing both the intrinsic characteristics of the service and its implementation process. For example, it will specify the service provider's staff the client organization wants to work with, the equipment used for the intervention and even the organization of the intervention.

The negotiation is a moment of intense encounter between the service provider and the client. During the negotiation, the client will remain very active and will try to obtain the last adjustments often in terms of deadlines, prices or payment conditions. At this stage, the participation is essentially intellectual and the object is the specification: the client suggests, proposes, requests, demands new services, complementary services or simply adaptations of the proposed services. The affective dimension of the participation is also to be considered since it has been previously recognized that emotion has its place in a B2B relationship. The negotiation phase tends to exacerbate this affective dimension.

During the realization of the service, the client's participation will intensify, as it will give its provider the information and means necessary to prepare and carry out the service and it will be in charge of missions and tasks essential to the preparation and realization of the service.

Finally, for certain services, the presence and validation of the customer are essential to mark the end of the service. The reception of a work site by the customer, which is materialized by the signature of a receipt, contractually signifies the end of the work site and opens the final stage of the payment balance.

10.1.2.2. Participants

In a B2B environment, the customer is not reduced to a single individual but to a multiplicity of people. Thus, when we talk about customer participation, the challenge is also to identify all the people in the customer's organization who are likely to participate in the service at the three different moments described in the previous section.

During the first two moments, the purchasing process and the negotiation, it is the members of the buying center who will be involved in the service. The different members of the buying center will have different forms of participation. It is interesting at this stage to go back to the analysis of the buying center in order to anticipate the probable participation of each member. The buyer will be in his or her role in trying to orient the provider's offer. A member qualified as enthusiastic at the end of the buying center analysis will follow his or her logic if he or she gives the provider major information. However, the hostile member may take actions that could negatively impact the provider's position.

During service delivery, the third moment of client participation, the targets of the service will participate. Targets were defined in Chapter 6 as all the people who come into contact with the service provider during the service delivery phase. Three types of targets were distinguished: the beneficiary, the facilitator and the observer. The participation of the beneficiary is close to the reality of the client's participation in B2C. The facilitator's participation is used to prepare the service or to carry it out in a direct or indirect way. The facilitator transmits information, performs tasks and provides material or human resources. The facilitator can block the service and prevent it from taking place. In the previous example of the building site access not being issued on time, it was the facilitator's participation that was faulty. The observer by definition has a weaker participation since he or she does not take part in the service; however, it is important to keep in mind his or her potential role in monitoring and evaluating the service and the provider.

10.1.3. *The manager orchestrates the client's participation*

This B2B customer participation appears to be dispersed among multiple actors and stretched throughout the service relationship. The manager's involvement is then expected to manage this customer participation as well as possible. In accordance with the customer orientation, the manager must orchestrate this participation in order to find the right resonance between performance and productivity, on the one hand, and customer satisfaction, on the other hand.

10.1.3.1. *Decrypting*

Although the notion of customer participation was initially developed in the B2C context, we have just seen that it also applies to B2B. Taking into account the impact of participation on productivity, researchers encourage companies, on the one hand, to educate customers to participate and, on the other hand, to offer them compensation. We are in a global perspective where the company would direct the participation of customers with the mission of educating them and the duty of rewarding them. This underlying hypothesis of a company in a position of domination[3] must be reconsidered in a B2B framework in which a relationship of dependence on the service provider, which can go as far as submission and modifies the approach to customer participation.

During the purchasing process and during the negotiation, by accepting the client's demands which may put it in difficulty, the service provider is in a position of dependence and submission. In order to win a consultation, it may have to accept, under pressure from the client, to modify its service by making commitments that could prove difficult to respect during the realization. The client's participation concerns the specification of the service in order to best satisfy its own interests, which may be in contradiction with those of the service provider. It is then up to the manager to control this participation. The injunction is certainly more tenable if the manager's responsibility covers the commercial and the operational or delivery aspects. Tensions are commonly observed between a sales team that has not been able to control the client's participation during the specification of the service, and an operational team that finds itself in difficulty in performing the negotiated service.

During the service delivery phase, the client may be eager to control the service and influence it to suit its own interests. For example, the client may ask the staff to do a little more, to stay a little longer, or to perform a small

---

3 The French legislator has understood the risks of this relationship, by officially creating in 1993 the French consumer code to which B2C is subject, while B2B is subject to the French commercial code. The essential function of the consumer code is to protect and defend consumers against abuse of weakness of which they could be victims.

task that was not foreseen in the contract. It is also a question of dependency when considering the facilitator's involvement. The provider is dependent on the facilitator to prepare, start, perform or conclude a service. This dependence is all the more difficult to manage, since unlike the beneficiary, the facilitator has no personal incentive to ensure that the service runs smoothly. The occupant of an unheated office will do everything possible to facilitate a rapid intervention by the service provider, but the building manager may be less zealous in scheduling the intervention as soon as possible! There may also be extreme situations where the facilitator's interest is in impeding the service. In an organizational context, the involvement of certain targets is likely to lead to power issues.

The manager is rarely face-to-face with the client to manage participation in the service of different targets. The team must, therefore, be made aware of this reality and of its drifts, and trained to take charge of the client's participation.

10.1.3.2. Accompanying

Accompanying consists of creating the right conditions for the client to participate. The challenge is to find the necessary resources to bring the client as much as possible towards an effective participation. Co-creation and co-construction approaches are the means to positively support customer participation in the purchasing phase. In the implementation phase, it is necessary to obtain the participation of the different targets of the client (see Box 10.1).

Engie Cofely, which became Engie Solutions on January 1, 2020, is a major player in the energy transition and offers service solutions to improve the energy and environmental performance of its customers, companies and local authorities.

The company is committed to sustainable development and wishes to support its customers' CSR strategy by providing them with concrete solutions. Energy represents a significant item in the budget of a company or a community. To improve the energy performance of a building, Engie Cofely has a strong conviction that it is necessary to combine the intelligence of tools (new technologies, Big Data, Internet of Things) and the intelligence of people. By mobilizing and involving all the stakeholders in a building, Engie Cofely is able to fully realize its promise. Beyond simply raising awareness and providing information, the company has implemented solutions that accompany and support the customer's participation in this energy performance challenge:

– A customer extranet that enables the building manager (the main user of the service) to access a dashboard indicating the main monitoring and consumption indicators from which he or she can trigger action plans to achieve energy savings.

– An intranet deployed at the client's site that enables any employee (the beneficiary of the service) to request, for example, a reduction in the temperature of his or her office if he or she feels it is too hot.

– Physical ecoboards (display panels installed in the common areas of a building such as the lobby) or virtual (web platform) that provide continuous information on the level of consumption of a site and suggest daily eco-actions in order to promote eco-citizen behavior.

– A web platform adapted to the client's context and reality, communicating the results of building users who have put eco-actions into practice. This feedback is a form of recognition and reward for the client's commitment and participation. The platform is also used for gaming operations and the organization of fun or educational internal challenges. For example, Roannais Agglomération, which has deployed this solution in several of its facilities, organizes educational workshops for children who use the swimming pool, based on an application developed by Engie-Cofely: a series of questions is asked to the children like in the Rotor the Beaver quiz with questions like "What is the first source of electricity?"

– E-community managers are identified among the client's employees and supported in order to maintain the mobilization of the building's occupants over time.

Box 10.1. *Supporting targets to achieve participation[4]*

Support becomes more difficult in a framework of dependence and submission, with targets that complicate the provider's action. The manager must try to identify the causes of this obstruction and to evaluate whether or not they are voluntary. Explaining, reassuring and being transparent are often enough to defuse such conflictual situations. It is also necessary to

4 www.engie-cofely.fr [Accessed on November 27, 2019]; www.engie-cofely.fr/savoir-faire/performance-energetics/ [Accessed on November 27, 2019]; www.engie-cofely.fr/references/roannais-agglomeration-loire/ [Accessed on November 27, 2019].

commit to simplifying the customer's task in order to facilitate his or her adhesion.

Finally, these difficult situations should not mask the reality of an often-positive participation from the client and the various targets of the service. A warm welcome from the service provider's employees on site, an efficient administrative follow-up of the service order, an enthusiastic collaboration from the client's teams, or even the client's presence at the service provider's side in complicated moments, are all opportunities for the service provider to show its gratitude to its client for its contribution to the successful completion of the service.

10.1.3.3. *Checking*

The client's participation creates a potential risk that the service will go astray because of the client. This risk is obvious in the case of the client who hinders the good progress of the service, but it can also be present, even for a positive participation.

It is, therefore, essential that the service provider takes a position of control over the client's participation, first to ensure that the service is carried out in accordance with the offer, and also to protect itself against any possible conflict with the client. Any delay or drift in a service that is linked to a failure in the client's participation must be quickly identified by the service provider and clearly communicated to the client. Participation must be formalized, traced and shared with the client in order to avoid or anticipate any conflict. From the e-mail to the registered letter, passing by various intermediate statements of the situation of the service, the service provider must protect itself against the deviations of result that would not only be its responsibility.

Valtus defines itself as a *premium* interim management consulting firm, integrating a transformation and change implementation dimension. A company calls upon an interim manager in a delicate period such as during a merger-acquisition, a restructuring, the sudden departure of a manager or to implement an ambitious company project. The interim manager can be positioned in the general management, functional or operational departments.

In the most complex situations, interim managers may have up to four different clients to interact with:

– the interim management consulting firm that entrusts them with the mission;

– the client who introduced the firm to the president of the company, like an investment fund;

– the president of the company that pays the firm for the service;

– the various stakeholders of the company with whom interim managers will have to carry out mission.

These multiple interactions necessarily generate tensions both in the mission and for the interim manager. What interfaces should be put in place with whom? How can we work in complete transparency with these different players? On the one hand, it is the role of the firm to support interim managers in the specific environment of their assignment. On the other hand, interim managers must manage to overcome these tensions by putting themselves in a position of genuine service to the company, and not to a particular stakeholder. The client is, thus, the company, as the common good of all its stakeholders, management, shareholders and employees. This position is obviously not easy to maintain, since there are necessarily relationships of power and influence, within which interim managers can be used. However, such a posture enables them to establish their legitimacy and to attest to his or her integrity. Interim managers must, therefore, have enhanced skills, well beyond technical, business and sectoral expertise. Relational finesse will enable them to manage the complexity of multiple interfaces. Soft skills such as adaptability, listening skills, humility, pugnacity and resilience will be essential to successfully complete the mission, involving all stakeholders. At the beginning of the mission, interim managers will have to mobilize a wide range of skills, mixing soft and hard skills, in order to create trust as soon as possible. During the mission, they will have to articulate a double capacity to learn and to transmit. Initially, they will learn from the company in order to best carry out their mission. Then, they will have to mobilize the collective energies and reveal the potential of each person, whether it is at the level of the direct teams for which they are responsible or of the management team, in order to transmit the value of the mission beyond its end.

The client, through its multiple identities, is at the heart of the mission. It is, therefore, up to the interim manager to integrate a customer orientation, by putting the various stakeholder services of the company into motion as harmoniously as possible.

Box 10.2. *Testimony of Bertrand Falcotet (Partner, Valtus)*

10.2. Mobilizing the team

The team, that is, managers' collaborators, completes the human dimension of the service on the provider's side. This team must be approached by managers with a broad and open vision because it is not limited to their direct collaborators. The service in a B2B environment often leads this team to evolve in a specific context. Managers will have to put the customer orientation at the heart of their leadership.

10.2.1. *A team in a service situation*

Researchers and practitioners of service management have been particularly interested by human resources issues. The analysis of the reality of service employees leads to a profound break with traditional approaches. Like all staff, service employees have missions to perform and in particular a value to produce. But, unlike production staff, and because of the involvement of the customer, they carry out their work in the presence of and with the customer. It is this reality that the notion of front line employees, specific to service activities, illustrates: employees in contact with the customer in order to provide the service.

10.2.1.1. *Challenges of front line employees*

This front line employee is confused in the customer's mind with the service, the company and the brand. They materialize the service that the customer cannot see, are the ambassadors of the service provider during the relationship with the customer, and the latter relies on them to form an idea of the brand and build an image of it. These phenomena will be all the stronger if the staff is visible and present during the service relationship. Even for highly automated services or in the context of the new digital economy, if the core of the service is carried out without staff, on the contrary, these services often go through very important deployment, adjustment and control phases in B2B, during which the employees are very present and very involved in the relationship with the customer.

Front line employees are the real driving force of customer orientation. They are responsible for satisfying both their company and their customers. This dual obligation can become a paradoxical injunction, especially when the company's need for efficiency clashes with customer satisfaction. It is then often the responsibility of each employee to find the ridge between the company's constraints and the customer's expectations in each service situation, which is always unique. Employees must constantly avoid the two precipices that are the withdrawal into their company associated with an indifference towards their customer that can go as far as contempt, on the one hand, and a submission to the customer to the detriment of the interests of their company, on the other hand.

Finally, the front line employees must assume several roles. Beyond their operational role, their behavior, their speech, and their attitude will be perceived by the customer and may become a source of satisfaction or dissatisfaction. This more relational role of the staff consists of encouraging the establishment of an appropriate relationship with the customer. A third role, which may seem less systematic but which is important for customer orientation, is the commercial role. This commercial dimension of the front line employee's mission can be precisely formalized when, for example, they are asked to offer additional services. However, this dimension is often discrete, indirect, almost invisible, and in line with the statements so often heard in companies: "Our drivers are our best salespeople! Our technicians are our best salespeople! Our consultants are our best salespeople!"

The management of front line employees must, therefore, take these specificities into account. The literature has very early intuited the importance of staff satisfaction and its link with customer satisfaction (Berry 1981). In the early 1990s, a team from Harvard Business School, focusing on the challenges of service management, began to analyze the key success factors of successful service companies. In 1994, the researchers affiliated with the team proposed a global model that positioned employee satisfaction as an antecedent to customer satisfaction (Heskett et al. 1994). This link between staff satisfaction and customer satisfaction is now a widely accepted key success factor in companies[5]. Some go so far as to advise taking care of employees before customers (Nayar 2010), while others advocate a balance between caring for employees and caring for customers. This is the concept of symmetry of attentions® initially developed within the Accor group in the early 2000s, which is now a registered trademark of the Service Academy and "posits that the quality of the

---

[5] A recent longitudinal study found that an improvement in employee satisfaction significantly increases customer satisfaction and symmetrically, a deterioration in employee satisfaction leads to a significant decrease in customer satisfaction (Wolter et al. 2019).

relationship between a company and its customers is symmetrical to the relationship of this company with all of its employees"[6].

The quality of management, therefore, has an indirect impact on customer satisfaction and loyalty.

10.2.1.2. *Front line employees with a B2B environment*

While in B2C, the front line employees generally welcome the customer in their company, in B2B the staff is most often required to travel to the customer's premises. They may just stay a while, as in the case of a delivery driver who goes from one customer to the next, or they may stay a little longer, from a few hours to a few days for a technical intervention, up to a long-term assignment where the staff will be relocated to the customer's premises for several months or years, as in the case of a receptionist, for example. Box 10.3 shows the employee's point of view on the reality of working on a client site.

Working on site means working on other people's premises

"When you arrive, you're clueless". One is quickly assigned to one or another of the various team leaders. Then, one goes straight to one's workstation with little or no information about the company and its risks. Even finding the bathroom is problematic. The same is true for the infirmary. One have no knowledge of the place, no information about the nature of the work. It is word of mouth that lets one to learn the codes and get your bearings.

Box 10.3. *Feedback from an employee on a client assignment[7]*

By being at the client's location, the staff no longer has any privacy. There is no backstage at the customer's, everything is on the customer's stage. If the cashier, the teacher and the waiter have, in their company, their office or their cabinet, spaces that are reserved for them where they can extract themselves from the gaze and the contact of the customer; the staff at the customer's has no such spaces. They take their breaks at the client's premises and most of the time with the client. They must therefore, even

---

6 www.symetriedesattentions.com. [Accessed on November 30, 2019].

7 Gauthier, T. (2017). Le service sur site : les enjeux du management. Mémoire MSc 2 Management et Marketing des Services, IAE Aix-Marseille, Aix Marseille Université, pp. 9–10.

during these breaks, respect the culture, rules and practices of their client. Because even during these breaks, the behavior of the staff will be observed, consciously or not by the client, and will contribute to the evaluation of the provider.

The staff posted to the client site is a nomadic staff. The term "professional nomadism" is used to describe the reality of working outside the company. This nomadism creates a physical distance with the company, the manager and colleagues as well as a more psychological distance that is mainly a feeling (Williams *et al.* 2014). The physical distance is an obstacle to proximity and direct exchange with one's manager and close colleagues, and more broadly with all the employees of one's company. This physical distance between managers and their collaborators has an impact on their communication and mutual understanding (Torrès 2003), and it makes it more difficult to exchange complex information and communicate tacit knowledge (Grossetti 2001). Bourdieu's work reveals that physical proximity strengthens social ties and contributes to the creation of a distinctive social capital that encourages mutual aid and solidarity (Bourdieu 1979). Unquestionably, the socialization of nomadic staff will be more difficult to create and maintain. These nomadic staff may be tempted to socialize more within their client's company. Perhaps they will prefer to participate in a meal with their client's employees rather than with their company's colleagues.

How can one manage one's employees from a distance? Can remote management and local management be reconciled? Remote management is undeniably fraught with risks: a weakening of the sense of belonging, a weakening of the collective, a decrease in informal communication. Managers must identify which of their various missions are really compromised by distance. While the definition of objectives and rules can be shared at a distance, on the contrary, listening, moral support and the strengthening of personal relationships cannot be done at a distance. Despite the distance, it is up to managers to create a climate of proximity.

> Didier[8] has been in charge of an operation, works and maintenance contract on an industrial site for three years. He spends about 80% of his time on his client's site. He manages a team of about 30 people, most of whom he has recruited and who have

---

8 For confidentiality reasons, the real identity of the manager as well as those of his employer and client is masked.

taken up their posts directly on the client's site. Didier and his team are physically present on the client's site and occupy premises that are exclusively reserved for them.

The main challenge when immersed in the client's business is to maintain a sense of belonging to the employer. The very perception of who the real employer is can be disturbed. The danger is then to do everything the client asks without even bothering to sell the service: the power, influence and charisma of the client are such that some employees perform services without even billing them. Didier has often had conflicts with some of his team members who recognized that they had performed services for free for the client, in order to please the client organization, without finding this abnormal. On the contrary, they were surprised when their manager pointed this out to them. This is a trap that young managers and employees often fall into, as they get caught up in the customer's attention and find it difficult to maintain a healthy relationship. The very first challenge for an on-site manager is to strongly unite the team around the company so as not to let the customer take over the entity. The team must clearly identify its manager as its one and only superior. In this daily proximity that one experiences on site, the customer has a natural tendency to interfere. The client even took the liberty of pressuring Didier one day to pay exceptional bonuses to people in his team who tended to give in easily to his demands. On a lighter note, the client is quite comfortable making judgments about Didier's management style.

The manager must, therefore, succeed in connecting his team to the company so that they feel integrated, even though they have little direct contact with their employer. By integrating into their work, the tools, methods and resources deployed by headquarters, employees realize that their company supports them in their daily work at the customer's. Seminars, training sessions and even individual interviews are additional ways for the manager to remind team members that they belong to the company. It is up to the manager to work on this sense of belonging on a daily basis. This is not always easy, as there is no proven miracle recipe to apply. It is a managerial process that takes time but it is imperative to do it. It is a kind of value that must be shared with the team. The manager must also set an example. Embodying a manager who defends the interests of the company more naturally encourages the team to adopt this posture.

Nevertheless, the advantages of being an autonomous manager on the client's site should not be overlooked. The freedom and independence offered by the situation can be appreciable depending on the profile and personality of the manager.

Box 10.4. *Testimony of a client site manager*

10.2.2. *An expanded team*

10.2.2.1. *Outlines*

The service team is made up of all the people who will participate in the delivery of the service. These are the service actors who will meet the targets of the service at the customer's site and perform the service with them.

These actors fall into three categories:

– actors who are under the hierarchical responsibility of the manager. They make up the direct team;

– actors who belong to the service provider company but who are not under the hierarchical responsibility of the manager. They are hierarchically attached to other departments, other entities of the company. For example, upstream, the marketing and communication department can help managers prepare the documents and media to present their offer, and downstream, the accounting and financial department will be in charge of sending and monitoring the invoice. We can speak of an indirect team;

– actors who are not employees of the service provider but belong to other companies, as is the case when subcontractors or co-contractors are used. They form a third team, the external team.

It is this extended team that will be in charge of providing the service to the client. The client will tend to identify it as the provider's team and more precisely as the manager's team, without systematically distinguishing between these three different entities. Managers have a hierarchical responsibility over their direct team only. Customer orientation leads managers to extend their managerial responsibility beyond their sole hierarchical responsibility.

In service management, it is customary to distinguish between the back office and the front office, the former being invisible to the customer while the latter is in contact with the customer[9]. This distinction is tending to fade in B2B in favor of a *continuum* reflecting the intensity of the interaction between the target and the actor. Back office staff can move to the front office because of the proximity between customer and provider. For example, the billing department is a key player in any service. In B2B, the

9 This distinction between the back office and the front office is clearly represented in the servicing model reproduced in Chapter 2 in Figure 2.1.

billing department is often required to interact directly with the customer without any dispute: a missing data on one side or the other, or a piece of information or a clarification communicated by one or the other. The hierarchy or the functional departments, which are often defined as back office, are very regularly exposed in B2B and become at some point actors in contact with a customer target.

In the specific context of intellectual services, the notion of contact personnel applies to generally higher hierarchical levels: the brilliant creative in an advertising agency, the charismatic partner in a consulting firm, the wealthy trader in an investment firm or the influential lawyer in an investment bank is emblematic employees of the service provider whose contact is expected by the client.

Bob Easton, President and CEO of Accenture Australia and New Zealand, put it plainly[10]:

> I've been with Accenture for 20 years, on the front lines delivering services to our largest clients. People think of "frontline service workers" as employees at a call center or at an airline desk. I'm a senior executive, and I'm definitely a frontline service worker.

10.2.2.2. Promoting horizontality

The actors responsible for customer satisfaction are not all under the hierarchical authority of the manager. Departments, teams, employees and partners – who sometimes very distant from a cultural, technical and business point of view – are jointly responsible for the realization and performance of the service. Managers must establish and maintain a relationship with all these players in order to provide the customer with the overall satisfaction expected.

Alongside vertical relationships with reporting lines, managers are also responsible for horizontal relationships without reporting lines. While there is consensus on the importance of these horizontal relationships for creating customer value, these relationships are known to be difficult to create and maintain (Casciaro *et al.* 2019). These horizontal relationships allow for a collaborative approach and the creation of collective intelligence. They

---

10 Anonymous (2018). Sorry is not enough. *Harvard Business Review*, 96(1), 20–22.

contribute to breaking down the famous silos in the company and must find reasons to exist to go beyond the initial phase of getting to know a client. A few in the company today question their legitimacy, but how many employees really devote time and energy to them? The process often fails because of a lack of practice and a lack of pragmatic implementation. Once again, managers are in an ideal situation to become the entrepreneur of these horizontal relationships. Since the performance of the service depends on the quality of these relationships, there is an urgent need to implement a collaborative approach between the departments and teams involved in customer satisfaction.

The meeting, exchange and sharing must be done naturally around actual problems related to the satisfaction of the customer:

– pooling of views, perceptions and information on the client and its expectations;

– analysis of service failures and proposal of corrective actions;

– identification of service targets at the client's site;

– dissemination of the role and contribution of each actor to the service, so that everyone has a global vision of the service that his or her company delivers;

– celebration of successes and recognition of the importance of the "other", the "other team", in service performance and customer satisfaction.

It is up to managers to set an example of this collaborative approach so that it can spread more naturally to their team.

10.2.3. *Customer-oriented leadership*

Customer-oriented leadership is built on management that is consistent with the principles of customer orientation. It draws its legitimacy from the now widely accepted reality of a strong and positive relationship between management quality and customer satisfaction and loyalty. There are many management styles that can be relevant in different contexts. In the context that interests us here, management can only be embodied in customer-oriented leadership. Such leadership translates into an attention that managers must pay to their teams as well as to themselves.

10.2.3.1. *Taking care of one's teams*

As discussed earlier in section 10.2.1.1, frontline employees in an extended team have a complex and often difficult posture. There is a risk that the team will perceive client orientation as an additional issue, and that its implementation will be met with reluctance and resistance. Customer orientation must be perceived by the team as a source of fulfillment and well-being at work, and in no way as a burden or a difficulty. This is not utopian, but a simple pragmatic principle. If the service actors satisfy the customer in pain, frustration or resentment, customer orientation will not be tenable. Respecting the first three milestones of customer orientation presented in this book will naturally help avoid these pitfalls: understanding and sharing with one's team the specificities of the service and B2B dimensions of one's environment, getting to know one's customer and valuing one's offer. This work, this reflection, and these upstream exchanges enable managers and their team to approach the realization of the offer with a feeling of greater control, a source of solid confidence in their ability to deploy customer orientation.

The principles of customer orientation are excellent anchors for the manager's leadership:

– listening to customers is at the heart of customer orientation: put listening to one's colleague at the heart of one's leadership and adopt a coaching posture (Ibarra and Scoular 2019);

– customer orientation thrives on a balanced relationship based on trust: putting the employee relationship at the heart of one's leadership and building quality and authentic relationships (Meyronin *et al.* 2019);

– emotion plays an important role in customer relations: put emotion back at the heart of one's leadership by encouraging the emergence of positive emotions within one's team (Barsade and O'Neill 2016).

10.2.3.2. *Taking care of oneself*

To acknowledge that managers are engaged on many fronts is an understatement. Managers must take care of the customer, their employees and their teams. They are asked to be exemplary and to encourage the development of their employees. The challenge is all the more delicate as managers in B2B environments have often been promoted because of their technical excellence without really having been supported in their managerial potential. Taking a step back, distancing oneself, and introspection then quickly become essential to cope with overactivity and excessive demands. Managers must also think about themselves. Because if the relationship is at the heart of a customer-oriented leadership, the relationship with the other is first built in a relationship with oneself. Managers must take time to work on this relationship with themselves. If doing it "for themselves" bothers them, they must convince themselves that they are also doing it for their employees. To unleash the potential of their employees, they must first reinforce and solidify their own potential around their know-how as well as their interpersonal skills. Training is an essential lever for the development of managers. Beyond the transmission of knowledge and practices, it is also an opportunity to take a break from the daily routine. Managers must be able to recharge their batteries through contact with new knowledge as well as through interaction and exchange with trainers and participants.

Finally, in technical environments, managers often have difficulty becoming aware of, expressing and controlling their emotions. Their training, their personal orientation and their career path have often dissuaded them from doing so. This is perhaps managers' biggest challenge: integrating their emotions into their leadership. In trying to define the contours of an emotionally intelligent company, Daniel Goleman emphasized the need for each employee to know how to manage his or her emotions and allow himself or herself to express them. He illustrated his point with the example of a Canadian gas refinery (Goleman 2014, p. 868):

> We had a spate of workplace accidents at this site, some of them fatal. A consultant called in to help out told me. I found that in the macho culture of the petrochemical industry, guys never expressed their feelings. If someone came to work with a hangover, was worried about a sick child, or upset about an argument with his wife, his co-workers never asked him how he was doing that day or if he was feeling well enough to concentrate on his work. As a result, the guy was inattentive and sometimes caused an accident.

11

Managing Service Operations

11.1. Operational efficiency

The way a company manages its operations defines its operational efficiency. Operational efficiency is an issue for any company, whether it is an industrial or service company. This challenge is all the more urgent as the competitive environment intensifies and the company's competitiveness needs to be strengthened. In services, operations and processes have specificities that must guide the choices and actions of the service provider in improving its operational efficiency.

11.1.1. *Operational effectiveness framework*

11.1.1.1. *Purpose*

When reading through corporate reports, operational efficiency is a recurring theme in the presentation of goals and strategies. Operational efficiency is seen as a key factor in solid, profitable and responsible corporate growth. The link between operational and financial performance is widely emphasized to justify the focus on operational efficiency strategies and approaches. Efficiency is used as a powerful lever for business competitiveness, which is all the more powerful in a turbulent competitive environment.

Operational efficiency aims to improve all the processes of the company that lead to the product or service, that is, the operational execution. It is the performance in terms of productivity, quality of the offer and cost reduction that the company aims to increase through the implementation of an operational efficiency process. It is its value creation that the company seeks to maximize by eliminating the roots of inefficiency and waste. Lean management[1] or the Six Sigma[2] method is often associated with operational efficiency approaches. Lean management is a tool that contributes to improving operational efficiency by relying on just-in-time practices, problem solving and employee involvement. The Six Sigma method relies on the analysis of multiple indicators to reduce defects and costs. The processes targeted by the operational efficiency approach are diverse and numerous. They concern the methods and actions deployed, the resources used, the technologies mobilized and the tasks performed. Operational efficiency must be approached by the company as a continuous improvement of its processes and set excellence as the ultimate goal. This operational excellence then becomes a state of mind which, to be real in the company, must be shared by all employees.

11.1.1.2. *Implementation*

The implementation of an operational efficiency approach starts with the analysis and knowledge of the processes that the company deploys to deliver its product or service. These processes must then be compared with the objectives set. A process is hardly good or bad in absolute terms. It must be evaluated in relation to set objectives: quality of the offer, costs incurred, benefits obtained and so on. Operational efficiency is not systematically associated with cost reduction and can have other objectives than just financial savings. For example, better-trained staff will perform better and thus contribute to greater operational efficiency. But to have a better-trained workforce, the company must invest in appropriate training programs and move away from a short-term cost reduction objective.

Once the processes have been identified and the objectives have been set, the company can establish its indicators for operational efficiency. This involves setting indicators that are known and shared within the company. Measurement, control and monitoring are the basic tools for implementing operational efficiency. Using these indicators, it becomes easier to identify processes that are unproductive, wasteful or inefficient with respect to the

---

1 Lean management methods were imported from Japanese factories and the Toyota production system.

2 The Six Sigma method developed in the 1980s at Motorola refers to the Greek letter for the standard deviation of a distribution, that is, the dispersion around the mean. The method aims to reduce the difference between a part leaving a production line and the expected standard.

objectives set. For example, by breaking down employees' tasks, it can be seen that only a small proportion of their time is actually spent on productive tasks, and that most of it is wasted on unproductive tasks: moving around, waiting, checking and filling out administrative documents. Box 11.1 provides an illustration of this approach.

Operational efficiency is one of the four pillars of Sodexo's strategic plan, *Focus on Growth*. The Group intends to improve its operational efficiency by optimizing the management of food and labor costs and by simplifying the organization. In its Foodservices activity, for example, Sodexo is seeking to improve efficiency and productivity while providing a better quality of life in the workplace by innovating around new technologies in the kitchens.

Starting in 2018, Sodexo implemented a common performance management system for all of the Group's activities named STEP, for *Sodexo Targets for Enhanced Performance*. The ambition of STEP is to:

– identify underperformance;

– understand the causes;

– implement corrective actions.

In its 2018–2019 universal registration document, Sodexo congratulated itself on having "entered a new phase of growth thanks to renewed operational discipline", which notably enabled it to improve operational productivity at its sites and achieve its operating margin target.

A continuous improvement initiative called I PROMISE illustrates this new operational discipline. I PROMISE aims to identify non-value-added activities in order to free up time to truly innovate and create value. Teams are directly involved and share their best practices. Deployed at more than 1000 sites by the end of 2019, the initiative has, for example, freed up 1.5 hours per week to focus on creating value for the customer.

Box 11.1. *Operational efficiency as a strategic focus*[3]

---

3 Sodexo (2019). Document d'enregistrement universel 2018–2019 [Online]. Available at: https:// sodexo.publispeak.com/document-enregistrement-universel-2018-2019/article/C2/ [Accessed on February 13, 2020]; Sodexo (2018). Document de référence 2017–2018 [Online]. Available at: www.sodexo.com/files/live/sites/sdxcom-global/files/PDF/Finance/Sodexo-Document-Reference-2017-2018.pdf [Accessed on February 13, 2020].

11.1.2. *Specificities of operational efficiency in services*

11.1.2.1. *A contributing client*

The client is part of the process, the co-producer of the process as elaborated in Chapter 10. The client, depending on the type of service, is more or less at the heart of the process. The production of the service does not take place away from the client and out of sight. The client is present at the production of the service and is a stakeholder. Imagine a customer walking through the production line of a factory and witnessing all the operations, processes, and tasks carried out on the line, and taking control of a particular workstation. This is what happens in the delivery of a service; the customer takes part in a more or less important part of the service production process and participates in it to a greater or lesser extent. The production of the service takes place not only in the presence of the customer but also with his or her contribution. The operational efficiency of service processes must, therefore, take into account this double specificity; the customer must appreciate the process as a spectator and be comfortable with it as an actor. If in a traditional industrial context, the company is the only one able to contribute to and control the operational efficiency of its processes, in the service context, it must share this prerogative with the customer. The customer becomes an actor and potentially a contributor to operational efficiency. The service provider must integrate its customer into its operational efficiency plan.

11.1.2.2. *Process variability*

Service is recognized as being heterogeneous by nature. The human factor is largely responsible for this heterogeneity; depending on the client and the personnel who interact in the process, the service will be more or less different. The timing of the service is also a considerable factor of heterogeneity. This heterogeneity of the result is, thus, the result of the heterogeneity of the processes. It is particularly difficult in services to obtain a perfect consistency of the different processes involved in the realization of the service. The human dimension of service production, the simultaneity of production and consumption and the sensitivity of the service to its environment make it difficult to reproduce identical processes that have been defined upstream. Operational excellence is obviously an objective and a culture that the service can share with the product. Operational efficiency is a strategy that is as relevant in the industrial as in the service sectors. However, the service provider will have to integrate, in its reflections and action plans, this difficulty to completely standardize and control upstream its various processes. For example, while it is possible in the industrial sector to implement a quality control system that avoids putting a defective product or series on the market as a result of a deviant process, this is not possible in the service sector, at least not with the same degree of rigor. To remedy these deviations from the norm, the service sector has developed the concept of service recovery or incident recovery. This is a post-production and, therefore, post-consumption control in which the service provider tries to recover its error from its client, using various practices ranging from apologies to financial compensation.

Operational excellence and operational efficiency in services must deal with this potential variability of processes.

11.2. Manager's responsibility for customer-oriented operations

Operational excellence cannot be pursued without the collaboration of managers. Managers must, therefore, ensure that operational efficiency within their scope remains in harmony with their customer orientation.

11.2.1. *Operations and quality of service*

It is through the process that the service is realized and that quality is delivered. The customer's expectations remain the frame of reference for the process. Moreover, the service process is deployed around a back office and a front office. The quality of the service will then also be the result of a good coordination between back office and front office.

11.2.1.1. *Alignment with customer expectations*

Operational efficiency, its approaches and tools are not by nature contrary to customer orientation. The Six Sigma method, in particular, starts from the measurement of the customer's expectations and then moves on to the identification and resolution of production problems.

And yet, it is not uncommon to observe processes that do not take into account customer expectations. Once the principles have been discussed and the methods explained, the temptation can be great to revert to automatisms, reflexes or habits that produce processes that are out of step with the customer. The process then often sacrifices customer orientation in favor of an internal orientation. The only thing that is sought is to achieve internal objectives, cost, simplification or comfort, without balancing them with the customer's expectations. Customer-oriented processes can even be hijacked, especially by employees, not always consciously. Constant vigilance is required to maintain this customer orientation of processes.

11.2.1.2. *Coordination between back office and front office*

Service production models distinguish between back office and front office operations. This distinction leads to different approaches to operational excellence. While customer orientation must remain the guiding principle for both back and front office processes, it is expressed somewhat differently.

The back office customer is internal; it is the front office. The objective of the back office process is then to accompany the front office as well as possible. In B2C, the front office has been widely discussed in the context of the network. The service company is considered to be a network company, that is, it is made up of several units in a given territory where the customer can obtain its service (a hotel, a bank, a supermarket, etc.). This concept of network is just as real in B2B but manifests itself in a different way, since the most common rule is a staff that goes to the customer rather than a customer that goes to the service provider. The provider's front office is, therefore, carried out at the customer's premises. This reality places additional constraints on processes and their efficiency. Without much difference with B2C, a failing back office can quickly ruin both operational efficiency and service quality. Moreover, in B2B, front office processes must be able to fit into the customer's environment. For example, should the organization of breaks be aligned with those of the customer or on the contrary be at odds with the constraints of the service and the customer's request? Technical interventions at the customer's site during holidays, weekends, nights or vacation periods can allow for a more serene intervention of the service provider and a comfort and productivity gain for the customer since there is no stop or disruption of his activity, but what is the impact on the cost of the service?

For a better coordination of the back office and the front office, the processes must keep a certain flexibility to adapt to the specificity of the customer. It is managers who are in the best position to regulate this flexibility within their perimeter and for their client.

11.2.2. *Operations and service experience*

The experience economy is now well-established in our societies (Pine and Gilmore 1999). While this experience economy first largely penetrated the consumer world, the B2B world must now redouble its efforts to convert to it. User experience and user interface are the new grails. We saw in Chapter 2 that service can be defined as an experience for the customer. This experience is formed from observations, actions and interactions that create emotions and feelings. Processes are the main supports of this experience. These processes are also the daily life of the service personnel, and they also become the support for the employee experience. The service experience appears to be a combination of the customer experience and the employee experience, as we cannot be truly separated from the other. The true customer-oriented process thus becomes the process that manages to enhance both the customer experience and the employee experience.

11.2.2.1. *Customer experience*

From the customer's point of view, the right process is the one that the customer appreciates and that enhances or improves their experience with their provider. Managers and their team can ask themselves a few simple questions in order to better approach the process from a customer experience perspective:

– Does our process simplify our customer's experience with our service?

– Does our process save our client time or at least not waste any?

– Does our process provide our customer with satisfaction, surprise and pleasure?

– Are the different steps of our process essential?

The first watchword must be simplification and seamlessness, because this is what customers are increasingly experiencing in the various experiences they have on a daily basis with companies such as Apple, Amazon or Airbnb. In these questionings, the field team in contact with the customer is valuable because it is likely to activate a culture of continuous improvement by remaining attentive to the alignment of processes with the experience expected by the customer.

The customer experience is the result of everything the customer experiences when in contact with the service provider. The customer journey is now a tool widely used by companies to better understand this customer experience. The customer journey traces, in a chronological way and from the customer's point of view, all the stages of a service relationship. The tool is starting to be deployed in B2B and is perfectly suited to better understand the processes from the customer's point of view[4].

11.2.2.2. Employee experience

A company that transforms its customer experience, but forgets to also focus on the experience of its employees, may well not reap the benefits of its investments. As we saw earlier, employee satisfaction comes before customer satisfaction. It is just as illusory to try to satisfy customers without taking care of employees as it is to enrich the customer experience without focusing on the employee experience. The customer experience is largely dependent on the processes, tools and skills used by employees.

The employee experience must mirror the customer experience: simplifying life, making tasks easier, organizing a rewarding and safe working environment, and supporting employees in their development of skills. Simplifying processes, in particular, is also a source of efficiency and satisfaction for employees (see Box 11.2).

This employee experience is the result of the company's culture, its strategies, actions and resources. The global policy of the provider in terms of recruitment and retention has an undeniable impact on this employee experience. Nevertheless, managers have real leeway to give their own impetus to the employee experience of their team. It is enough to observe the behavior of various managers in the same company, and to listen to their respective employees, to realize that the teams evolve in different work environments that create heterogeneous employee experiences. Managers must be attentive to the experience of their extended team members and seek

4 An example of customer journey improvement for a professional distribution company is developed on the SETEC IS website: www.is.setec.fr.www.is.setec.fr/parcours-client [Accessed on February 7, 2020].

the right balance between the customer's experience and that of their employees.

The *dabbawalla* are the meal delivery people based in Mumbai, India. Since 1890, they have been picking up between 130,000 and 200,000 home-cooked meal baskets every day, taking them to the client's office, and returning them empty to their homes the same day. The error rate (i.e. a meal basket that would not reach the right person) is extremely low. The manager announces 1 error in 16 million transactions!

One of the key success factors of the *dabbawalla* organization is the simplicity of the processes. To know where to put the lunch basket, a few visual indications on the lid are enough:

– in the center, a number written in large and bold indicates the district in which the lunch Box must be delivered;

– on the edges of the lid, a few characters, including a number that indicates the identity of the delivery person in charge of the lunchbox, an alphabetical code of 2 or 3 letters for the office building and a number for the floor;

– a combination of colors and shapes to indicate the place of origin of the lunch Box.

Box 11.2. *Simplified service processes*[5]

11.2.3. *Operations and profitability*

As elaborated in the first part of this chapter, operational effectiveness also involves an analysis of efficiency and productivity, and aims to track down sources of waste and inefficiency. In this sense, service activities have long tended to standardize processes and incorporate technology. It is up to managers to question the limits of standardization and technology in the context of customer orientation. Here again, it is up to managers to find the right balance between standardization and technology, on the one hand, and customer orientation, on the other hand.

---

5 TEDx Talks (2011). TEDxSSN - Dr. Pawan Agrawal - Mumbai Dabbawalas [Online]. Available at: www.youtube.com/watch?v=N25inoCea24 [Accessed on February 7, 2020]; Thomke, S. (2012). Mumbai's model of service excellence. *Harvard Business Review*, 90 (11), 121–126.

11.2.3.1. *Process standardization*

Standardization approaches have generally been less natural and more discussed in services than in industry. While standardization is recognized for its impact on service quality and operational efficiency, the virtues of personalization for customer satisfaction are equally recognized. Because of their scope and proximity to the customer, managers are particularly well placed to reconcile standardization and personalization.

The service provider, driven to be more competitive and committed to efficiency strategies, will inevitably be led to standardize certain processes and, therefore, part of its service operations. In order not to lose customer orientation, especially at critical moments in the service relationship, managers will inevitably be led to counterbalance this standardization programmed "from above" with a personalization spontaneously cultivated in the uniqueness of a customer relationship.

11.2.3.2. *Technologies and the process*

Unquestionably, technologies enable companies to find new sources of productivity and efficiency. While improving processes, technologies can also offer customers an enhanced experience. Robotization, digitalization and artificial intelligence are the technologies that allow for rethinking processes for more efficiency and potentially for more customer satisfaction.

But as for standardization, managers will be the guarantors of a good balance between human beings and technology, so that the customer, as well as the employee, does not have the feeling that technology replaces humans but that it helps them in accordance with what some already call the bionic enterprise[6].

The CEGID group is the leading French publisher of management solutions. The group develops and deploys solutions and software for the public and private sectors in the areas of finance, taxation, payroll and talent management, sales management, business management and production management.

Traveling consultants are usually assigned to the customer's premises for missions of varying duration, in order to support them in the deployment and use of their software solutions. After developing distance-learning courses, then integrating

---

6 Referred to by Rich Lesser, CEO of BCG, in an interview with *Les Échos* (Barroux *et al.* 2020).

digital-learning approaches, the group wanted to go further by transforming the consultant's job in depth. By changing an essential point in the process, a new model was devised: the consultant would no longer travel to the customer's premises, but a pool of sedentary consultants, covering a very wide range of expertise, would be made available to customers in return for a subscription. Despite this change in process, we remain a service provider and not a support provider.

The customer quickly saw the benefits of this new model:

– Instead of having a consultant on an episodic basis for a few days, the client has a permanent team of about 40 consultants.

– No matter how skilled a consultant is, he or she cannot be an expert on all the functionalities of a software solution. The customer who subscribes to this new service keeps a dedicated contact person while benefiting from the specific expertise of the entire team.

– While the price of the consultant is usually established by the day, we can with this model go towards micro-services, and call a consultant for one hour only on a precise point.

– The hazards related to the consultant's travel (a transport strike, a missed plane, a health problem, etc.) are in check.

In addition to increased customer satisfaction, this new offering model brings direct financial benefits to the company, while letting it to move towards better management of its human resources.

From a financial perspective, the benefits of the model are twofold:

– The service is sold as a three-year subscription with tacit renewal, which allows for recurring revenues and a stabilized financial model.

– The model offers the opportunity of a complementary sales channel. Through monthly meetings between customers and their dedicated contacts, new offers can be presented and if a need is detected, the sales team can quickly take over. In practice, the mobile consultant does not have time for these presentations.

Human resource management is improved for several reasons:

– The turnover of consultants is significantly reduced. An itinerant consultant generally wishes to settle down after two to three years and then to leave the company. The sedentarization of the position normalizes the life of the consultant and encourages him or her to stay longer in the company.

– New employees are integrated more quickly. The team of experienced consultants in one place trains new employees more quickly and effectively, reducing the risk of resignation.

– This group of sedentary consultants acts as a kind of nursery, preparing the consultants, who will be brought to be itinerant, to the business and to the customers. The first interventions can be done remotely. The consultant gains confidence by being supported by the rest of the team, which allows him or her to prepare for the next assignment with the client in the best possible conditions.

This service reorganization offers the company a sustainable business model, the employee an enriched experience and the customer increased satisfaction.

Box 11.3. *Testimony of Jérôme Ricard (Product Marketing Manager HCM Solutions, CEGID)*[7]

---

7 The testimony relates to a previous mission for which CEGID's management committee asked Jérôme Ricard to design and deploy a new offer.

Marketing the Tangibles

12.1. Tangible elements of the service

Valarie A. Zeithaml and Mary Jo Bitner provide a broad definition of the tangible elements of service:

> The environment in which the service is delivered and where the firm and customer interact, and any tangible components that facilitate performance or communication of the service (Zeithaml and Bitner 1996, p. 26).

This definition implies a great variety of tangible elements and refers to a double function of these elements.

12.1.1. *Nature of tangible elements*

12.1.1.1. *Two realities*

The definition of the tangible elements of the service makes it possible to distinguish two key dimensions: a place, the one in which the service takes place, and the various tangible elements necessary for the realization or the communication of the service.

Beyond the place, such as a building, an agency, an office or a meeting room, we will find a heterogeneous set of tangible elements ranging from equipment to vehicles, including documents or the website. All these tangible elements are not necessarily contained in the place of service. Several realities of tangibles in B2B can be found:

– A hotel that receives both B2C and B2B customers in the same place. We are close to the issues traditionally discussed in the literature and addressed by B2C companies on the importance of location in customer evaluation and satisfaction.

– A digital service company that creates a website for a client. The notion of physical location is not really relevant in this case, except for the meetings between the client and the service provider that can take place in the premises of one or the other. On the contrary, the tangibles will be really important for the customer: website of the provider, documents and preparatory models, exchanged *mails* and so on.

– A catering company that provides the service at the client's premises. The company restaurant is in a way a third place, neither completely at the client's nor completely at the service provider's, but it is a place that will be essential in the client's feelings. The tangibles are also essential in this context: the food, the staging of the dishes, the equipment and crockery used and so on.

– A company that performs on-site maintenance services performs the service in a location that is completely owned by the customer.

These tangible elements are also distinguished according to managers' control over them. Some tangibles, such as a building or premises, are generally beyond managers' scope of responsibility, while others, such as intervention equipment, depend on their investment choices.

12.1.1.2. *Tangibles at the customer's premises in B2B*

The tangible elements of the service have mainly been dealt with in the context of a customer going to the service provider to obtain a service, which is the usual B2C context. There are certainly service activities in B2B where this is the case: the example of the hotel in the previous section as well as car rental, distribution for professionals or the coworking company.

It appears, as previously discussed in Chapter 10 where it was noted that employees travel to the client's location to perform the service, that in the case of many B2B services, the tangible elements are located at the client's location. In this case, three realities can be distinguished:

– The service provider's employees arrive at the client's premises with their own tangible elements to perform the service. A landscaping company, for example, performs its service using its own equipment. The main issue here is to ensure that the service provider's equipment will be able to function properly in the client's environment. The difficulty that the service provider may encounter in connecting its equipment to an electrical outlet, for example, will delay or complicate the service. It is not the client who must appropriate the tangible elements of the provider, but the provider that must integrate its tangible elements into the client's environment.

– The service provider's employees use the tangible elements provided by the client to perform the service. In the case of an engineering service with on-site personnel, the client provides the collaborator with a desk, a computer and software. The challenge here is a little more complex, since the collaborator must appropriate the vast majority of the tools required to perform the service.

– The place where the service is provided belongs to the client. This is the case in the two previous examples of the maintenance of green spaces and an engineering service on the client's premises. The traditional perspective of studying the place of service as a place that welcomes the client, in which it must feel good and have a satisfactory experience, is completely reversed; in B2B, the place of service becomes a place that welcomes the service provider, in which it must perform the service.

From the managers' point of view, the well-being of their employees takes on a new complexity: this well-being must be ensured outside the company, in a physical and social environment belonging to the client.

12.1.2. *Dual function of tangible elements*

It has been said that the tangible elements of the service constitute both a factory and a showcase. As a factory, the tangible elements take on an operational function, and as a showcase they take on a marketing function.

12.1.2.1. *Operational function*

The operational function of the tangible elements of the service indicates their essential role in the production and realization of the service. Most services require materials, equipment and a location. Even a service with a high intellectual and intangible content, like consulting for example, needs a minimum of tangible elements to perform the service.

Because of the co-production of the service, these tangible elements will be used by both the provider and the client. When all or part of the service is performed at the customer's site, the factory becomes mobile or outsourced. The operational function of the tangible elements is made more complex. These tangible elements are used in an environment that does not depend on the service provider. Their operational function must, therefore, be adapted to the specific environment of the customer.

Finally, this operational dimension of the tangibles is part of operational efficiency. In some sectors, these tangibles represent major investments that must be controlled and valued (see Box 12.1).

Public works companies (Bouygues Construction, Eiffage, Vinci, etc.) use numerous machines and equipment to build bridges, airports, buildings, parking lots, and other industrial sites. Excavators, bulldozers, cranes and dumpers are all assets that depreciate and are usually amortized over eight years. However, they are not all used full time, as some specific equipment may only be used 30% of the time. Within the same company, it can be observed that an agency or a team may have to refuse a contract due to a lack of equipment, while another agency or another team has this equipment and it is not used.

To remedy these sources of inefficiency, the start-up Sharemat, created in 2017, offers to track all of a company's equipment in real time on a web platform with their location, number of hours of use and maintenance information. If the company wishes, it can also rely on its platform to rent its equipment during non-use times.

Box 12.1. *Management of the Machine Pool*[1]

12.1.2.2. *Marketing function*

The tangible elements of the service speak to the customer because they are visible. They indicate a quality, an image and contribute strongly to their experience. They have a communication function and more broadly a marketing function, because they have the potential to contribute to customer satisfaction. The tangible elements of the service not only help customers set their expectations, but also influence their perception of performance. This marketing function of tangibles is all the more important when customers are

---

1 https://sharemat.fr [Accessed on February 8, 2020]; Guimard, E. (2019). Le matériel de travaux publics en mode réseau. *Les Échos* [Online]. Available at: https://business. lesechos.fr/entrepreneurs/financing-your-growth/0601904638404-sharemat-met-le-materiel-de-travaux-publics-en-mode-collaboratif-332019.php [Accessed on September 30, 2019].

unfamiliar with the provider or have difficulty evaluating the service. In these situations, clients tend to use tangibles as signals or indicators (see Box 12.2).

The presentations and written reports that consultants give their client are tangible elements inherent to this kind of services.

Hergert Smith Freehills, an international law firm, used design to enhance its client documents. A task force was set up to prepare simpler, clearer and more attractive document templates for clients. The presentation of legal audits in particular was reviewed by mixing text and computer graphics to make them more accessible to the client.

Box 12.2. *The design of customer documentation*[2]

Personal protective equipment (PPE) such as helmets, gloves or safety shoes must follow a triple logic:

– From an operational point of view, PPE is intended to protect the user. PPE is clearly defined by the French Labor Code (Article R.233-83-3) as "a device or means intended to be worn or held by a person in order to protect him or her against one or more risks likely to threaten his or her health and safety"[3].

– From a marketing point of view, PPE is often seen by the customer (intervention, repair and on-site work). It then becomes an indicator of image and professionalism. Despite the high price of this equipment, some service providers also choose to equip their temporary workers and subcontractors with their own PPE, often marked with the company's logo.

– From a user's point of view, PPE must be comfortable and aesthetic so that it is easily worn and sometimes even enjoyed.

Box 12.3. *Personal protective equipment*

---

2 www.herbertsmithfreehills.com [Accessed on February 8, 2020]; Iweins, D. (2019). Comment Herbert Smith Freehills se convertit au design. *Les Échos Executives* [Online]. Available at: https://business.lesechos.fr/directions-juridiques/droit-des-affaires/contrats-et-clauses/0602009354005-how-herbert-smith-freehills-converts-to-design-332361.php [Accessed on October 14, 2019].

3 www.legifrance.gouv.fr/affichCodeArticle.do?idArticle=LEGIARTI000018511366&cidTexte=LEGITEXT000006072050&dateTexte=19960818 [Accessed on February 8, 2020].

Managers obviously do not control all the tangible elements that customers evaluate. Nevertheless, concerning the tangible elements that managers can control, they must ensure their marketing impact. They can thus make their team aware of the importance of these tangibles for clients, or include an image variable in their investment choices, beyond the operational variable alone. Personal protective equipment is a particularly good example of the different challenges of tangibles (see Box 12.3).

12.2. Challenges of tangibles

12.2.1. *The human being in a physical environment*

It is recognized that the physical environment of a service has an impact on the satisfaction of the customer and on the image of the company (Aubert-Gamet 1996).

12.2.1.1. *Stimulus–response model*

The stimulus–response relationship stems from the behaviorist approach, which defines an individual's behavior as a response to a *stimulus*. This historical reference model has been enriched by other approaches that notably give actors agency over their environment, but today it still remains a theoretical reference for analyzing the behavior of actors within a space and notably a service location (Zeithaml *et al.* 2017, p. 294). The main hypothesis is that the characteristics of the physical environment of the service will affect both the customer and the staff, and that they will behave in it according to internal processes that are specific to them (Bitner 1992). These behaviors, which are formed in reaction to the environment, may only concern the individual in particular, such as prolonging his or her presence in the place, or may have an influence on the social interactions between the staff and the customer in particular. In B2C, many studies have been conducted to show the impact of the attributes of a physical environment (space design, music, warmth, smell, etc.) on customers and their behavior (purchase rate, path, time spent, etc.). The model also recognizes the importance of the physical environment of the service on the well-being and behavior of employees. An adequate workspace – with appropriate temperature, air quality and lighting – not only contributes to employee comfort and satisfaction, but also affects productivity and efficiency at work, as well as social interactions between employees and with the customer. This last point becomes particularly relevant in a B2B context where the place of service is often the customer's premises.

12.2.1.2. Manager's responsibility

As previously mentioned, managers are not responsible for all the tangibles. In the same way, in the case where their team intervenes at the customer's premises, managers have limited power of action on the physical environment of the service realization. Nevertheless, managers must keep in mind the impact of the physical environment on their employees and find ways to best support them in this environment, which is, before being the place of the service, the customer's environment. The challenge is also to get the client to welcome the service provider in order to provide the best conditions for the intervention. Managers must often educate the client.

12.2.2. Tangible element of the service brand

The brand is a name or symbol affixed to an offer. It is primarily used to identify and recognize a particular offer and to differentiate it from the competition. It is also a means of expression and affirmation for the customer (Kapferer 1991).

Companies then seek to build strong brands to attract and retain customers while charging higher prices.

The strong brand becomes a solid financial asset for the company, which gives it maximum financial value. A strong brand, that is, a brand that cumulates high awareness and a positive and favorable image (Keller 1993), is, however, not easy to build and maintain, and only a few actually manage to do so. While branding strategies were initially a concern for B2C firms, B2B firms, particularly in services, are now equally concerned with these issues (see Box 12.4).

12.2.2.1. Service brand challenges

In services, a strong brand also has the task of making a service that is by nature intangible and heterogeneous more understandable. The brand must inspire confidence in clients, even though they naturally perceive a risk in committing to a service provider. It is more difficult for clients to identify the benefits of the offer and the brand can help them to do so.

The service brand goes beyond the offer and is associated in customers' mind with all the experiences, processes and interactions they have had with the brand. It makes it possible for the customer to "better visualize the invisible" (Berry 2000). It is then necessary to recognize that the tangible elements of the service will contribute to defining in clients' mind the idea that they have of the brand of their provider.

On January 1, 2020, the Engie group launched a new brand: Engie Solutions. This new brand is an umbrella brand replacing the brands Engie Cofely, Engie Axima, Engie Ineo and Engie Réseaux. Engie Solutions is presented globally as a accelerator of the zero-carbon transition in direct link with the mission of the Engie group. The new brand is positioned as a player in energy performance to help its customers improve the performance of their plants, the comfort of their buildings and the attractiveness of their territories. It emphasizes the proximity with its customers and the advantage of a single contact for a global support of the customer in favor of its energy performance[4].

The tangibles will be for the customer one of the essential elements of this new brand: uniforms, vehicles, commercial documents, email signatures, signage and so on.

The question then arises as to how this new brand will be applied in the field by agencies, teams and clients' sites. How will the head office support this change of brand and how will managers relay this change? How enthusiastically will the teams embrace it? For Engie Cofely, for example, depending on the attachment to the Cofely brand, the transition to the Engie Solutions brand will be more or less easy.

The service brand is, therefore, not only a matter of strategy and a corporate decision, but also an implementation issue for which managers and teams are the main actors.

Box 12.4. *Rebranding*

---

4 www.lesechos.fr/industrie-services/energie-environnement/engie-reorganise-ses-services-energetiques-en-france-1134841 [Accessed on February 12, 2020]; www.engie-cofely.fr/actualites/engie-cofely-devient-engie-solutions/ [Accessed on February 12, 2020]; https://marseille.latribune.fr/entreprises-finance/2019-10-29/ce-nouveau-modele-que-wilfrid-petrie-deploie-pour-engie-831934.html [Accessed on February 12, 2020]; www.engie-solutions.com/fr [Accessed on February 12, 2020].

12.2.2.2. *Manager's responsibility*

In services, it is managers who bring the brand to life on the ground. Of course, it is not managers who decide on the brand strategy, but since the service experience in general and the tangibles in particular contribute to the brand image, they and their team are the ones who bring it to life for the customers. A van with the provider's logo on it that is damaged on the side of the road sends signals to passing motorists. Dirty and damaged work clothes also send messages to the client's various targets who pass the service provider. Such negative signals are unfortunately very effective in damaging or destroying a brand image, despite the often very heavy investments made by the company to build and maintain it.

Managers must be vigilant about the proper use of tangibles bearing the company's brand, both in space (e.g. harmonization of communication media used by the extended team) and in time (e.g. harmonization of tangibles used during the purchasing process and during the realization of the service). They must convey the message to their teams that the brand can support their work and their efforts in the field, with the customer. The brand reassures, gives credibility and engages customers. It is, therefore, relevant for field teams to rely on the brand and to make the best possible use of it. For managers, the brand is also a tool for recruiting, building loyalty and motivating employees.

Conclusion

While customer orientation is often presented as a global orientation of the company, drawn as a vision or thought of as an intention by the governing bodies of an organization, this book leads us to realize the responsibility of the manager.

Managers' primary mission is to implement this strategic objective of a customer-oriented company within their own area. Beyond that, in B2B service environments, managers are required to become the creators of this customer orientation. On the one hand, they must promote it to their teams in order to obtain their indispensable support, and on the other hand, they must renew it on a daily basis within their ecosystem. In this sense, customer orientation gives managers an essential position.

Managers are largely defined by reference to the meaning of "managing" in its most common translations, to direct, or maneuver. Managers are, thus, an employee who manages, directs, coordinates, organizes and who is invested with power and responsibility. If we dig a little deeper into the etymology of the word manager, we find, in connection with an Italian root *maneggiare*, the Latin root *manus*, "hand". The hand is the organ of touch and grip, the most active sense. The hand also symbolizes action in one of its meanings (to put one's hand to work). The intuition of the importance of managers' handshake, proposed in the very first pages of this book, converges with this short lexicological analysis!

Action is, therefore, a founding mission of managers' function. Managers must be or become a person of action. In this sense, it is legitimate to ask managers not to limit themselves to being the simple disseminator of customer orientation and also its most valiant actor. Action is to be distinguished from the permanent agitation feared by so many managers. It is distinguished by the thoughtfulness that must guide it. Action must be decided on the basis of an intention. It is this intention that gives meaning to the action, rather than its actual consequences, which can sometimes be far from the intention. Customer orientation, being the search for a balance between the creation of value for the customer, and the creation of value for the company, becomes an intention that carries a meaning shared by the different stakeholders. This distinction between the intention and the consequences of the action should encourage managers to be bold and innovative. The possible failure of an action, one that does not lead to the expected result, should not call into question the meaning of the intention. On the contrary, any action, subject to the hazards of its deployment, should encourage managers to show humility and resilience. In an organizational context, the action must also be explained and prepared (we talk about an action plan). Managers' action will be reinforced by this necessity: to justify their actions to their hierarchy, and to rally their team around the action in order to make it a real collective project. Customer orientation becomes a solid framework for the managers' action.

Action cannot really be undertaken without freedom. Managerial freedom is not to be sought in the absence of constraints, which would be futile, but in a capacity to act within these constraints, and sometimes even thanks to these constraints. However, managers must be careful not to confuse the necessary organizational constraints with their own fears, inhibitions or beliefs. From these constraints, managers must free themselves, by maintaining their curiosity, their attention and their questioning. Managers are never as free in their actions as when they manage to understand their meaning and context. Customer orientation, by giving meaning to the managerial action, reinforces managers' freedom.

Finally, knowledge is the best source and guide for managers' freedom of action. To truly act in a complex world, managers must acquire knowledge in areas that are often different from their initial training. To be truly customer-oriented, managers must also maintain, often on their own, new skills, especially in soft skills, and keep themselves regularly informed of emerging practices, which are continuously feeding the field of management.

Customer orientation, by giving meaning to managers' action, by reinforcing their freedom, and by encouraging them to maintain his knowledge, regenerates the managerial mission. Customer orientation thus gathers the necessary elements to maintain, and sometimes regain, the vital energy essential to any manager.

References

Abramovici, M. and Bancel-Charensol, L. (2004). How to take the customers into consideration. *The Service Industries Journal*, 24(1), 56–78.

Adner, R. (2016). Ecosystem as structure: An actionable construct for strategy. *Journal of Strategy*, 43(1), 39–58.

Akrout, H. and Akrout, W. (2011). La Confiance en B2B : vers une approche dynamique et intégrative. *Recherche et applications en marketing*, 26(1), 59–80.

Ancelin-Bourguignon, A. (2018). La dynamique des doubles contraintes dans les organisations : propositions pour limiter leur caractère toxique. *Revue française de gestion*, 270(1), 143–157.

Anderson, M. and Sullivan, M. (1993). The antecedents and consequences of customer satisfaction for firms. *Marketing Science*, 12(2), 125–143.

Anderson, E. and Weitz, B.A. (1989). Determinants of continuity in conventional industrial channel dyads. *Marketing Science*, 8(4), 310–323.

Assens, C. and Ensminger, J. (2015). Une typologie des écosystèmes d'affaires : de la confiance territoriale aux plateformes sur Internet. *Vie & Sciences de l'entreprise,* 200(2), 77–98.

Aubert-Gamet, V. (1996). Le design d'environnement commercial dans les services : appropriation et détournement par le client. Management Science PhD Thesis, Université de droit, d'économie et des sciences d'Aix-Marseille III, Institut d'administration des entreprises, Aix-en-Provence.

de Bandt, J. (1995). *Services aux entreprises*. Economica, Paris.

Barabel, M. and Meier, O. (2015). *Manageor*. Dunod, Paris.

Barroux, D., Boudet, A., Jasor, M. (2020). Pour le patron du BCG, "la mondialisation ne s'arrête pas, mais elle évolue". *Les Échos* [Online]. Available at: www.lesechos.fr/industrie-services/services-conseils/pour-le-patron-du-bcg-la-mondialisation-ne-sarrete-pas-mais-elle-evolue-1169929 [Accessed 7 February 2020].

Barsade, S. and O'Neill, O.A. (2016). Manage your emotional culture. *Harvard Business Review*, 94(1), 58–66.

Bauer, R.A. (1960). Consumer behavior as risk taking. In *Dynamic Marketing for a Changing World, Proceedings of the 43rd American Marketing Association Conference*, Hancock, R.S. (ed.). American Marketing Association, Chicago.

de Baynast, A., Lendrevie, J., Levy, J. (2017). *Mercator*. Dunod, Paris.

Bell, D. (1973). *The Coming of Post Industrial Society*. Basic Books, New York.

Berry, L.L. (1981). The employee as customer. *Journal of Retail Banking*, 16(3), 108–116.

Berry, L.L. (2000). Cultivating service brand equity. *Journal of the Academy of Marketing Science*, 28, 128–137.

Bitner, M.J. (1992). Service scapes: The impact of physical surroundings on customer and employees. *Journal of Marketing*, 56(2), 57–71.

Bitner, M.J., Faranda, W.T., Hubbert, A.R., Zeithaml, V.A. (1997). Customer contributions and roles in service delivery. *International Journal of Service Management*, 8(3), 193–205.

Bonin, G. and Jean, S. (2010). La pratique de l'orientation client – le cas Findus. *Décisions Marketing*, 59, 67–70.

Booms, B.H. and Bitner, M.J. (1981). Marketing strategies and organizational structures for service firms. In *Marketing of Services*, Donnelly, J.H. and Georges, W.R. (eds). American Marketing Association, Chicago.

Bourdieu, P. (1979). *La Distinction. Critique sociale du jugement*. Éditions de Minuit, Paris.

Burns, J. (1978). *Leadership*. Harper & Row, New York.

Capgemini Research Institute (2018). The secret to winning customers' hearts with artificial intelligence. *Cap Gemini* [Online]. Available at: www.capgemini.com/wp-content/uploads/2018/07/AI-in-CX-Report_Digital.pdf [Accessed 27 August 2019].

Casciaro, T., Edmondson, A.C., Jang, S. (2019). Cross silo leadership. *Harvard Business Review*, 97(3), 130–139.

Clarke, S., Cornelissen, J.P., Healey, M. (2019). Actions speak louder than words: How figurative language and gesturing in entrepreneurial pitches influences investment judgments. *Academy of Management Journal*, 62(2), 335–360.

Cohen, D. (2018). *Il faut dire que les temps ont changé...* Albin Michel, Paris.

Combalbert, L. and Méry, M. (2019). *Negociator*. Dunod, Paris.

Courtecuisse, M. (2018). Le consulting 4.0 – vers une intelligence augmentée. *Les Échos* [Online]. Available at: www.lesechos.fr/2018/01/le-consulting-40-vers-une-intelligence-augmentee-1118242 [Accessed 2 January 2018].

Cova, B. and Salle, R. (1999). *Le marketing d'affaires*. Dunod, Paris.

Craye, T. (2016). *Les fiches outils – focus des appels d'offres*. Eyrolles, Paris.

Daidj, N. (2011). Les écosystèmes d'affaires : une nouvelle forme d'organisation en réseau. *Management & Avenir*, 46, 105–130.

Damasio, A. (2003). *Spinoza avait raison*. Odile Jacob, Paris.

Davenport, T.H. (2005). The coming commoditization of processes. *Harvard Business Review*, 83(6), 100–108.

Davidson, R. (2018). *Les Profils émotionnels*. Les Arènes, Paris.

Day, G.S. (1994). The capabilities of market-driven organizations. *Journal of Marketing*, 58(4), 37–52.

Deshpandé, R. and Webster, F.E. (1989). Organizational culture and marketing: Defining the research agenda. *Journal of Marketing*, 53(1), 3–15.

Deshpandé, R., Farley, J.U., Webster, F.J. (1993). Corporate culture, customer orientation and innovativeness in Japanese firms: A quadrad analysis. *Journal of Marketing*, 57(1), 23–37.

Dupont-Calbo, J. (2020). L'ère des "cost-killers" aux achats dans les entreprises semble être révolue. *Les Échos* [Online]. Available at: www.lesechos.fr/industrie-services/services-conseils/lere-des-cost-killers-aux-achats-dans-les-entreprises-semble-revolue-1160707 [Accessed 7 January 2020].

Dwyer, F.R., Schurr, P.H., Oh, S. (1987). Developing buyer-seller relationships. *Journal of Marketing*, 51(2), 11–27.

Eiglier, P. (2004). *Marketing et stratégies des services*. Economica, Paris.

Eiglier, P. and Langeard, E. (1987). *Servuction, le marketing des services*. McGraw-Hill, Paris.

Esslimani, B. (2012). L'orientation marché : une composante de la culture d'entreprise au service des attitudes au travail. *Questions de management*, 1, 25–36.

Fornell, C., Mithas, S., Morgeson, F.V., Krishnan, M.S. (2006). Customer satisfaction and stock prices: High returns, low risk. *Journal of Marketing*, 70(1), 3–14.

Fourastié, J. (1949). *Le grand espoir du XXᵉ siècle*. Presses universitaires de France, Paris.

Frachet, S. and Mercaillou, L. (2019). Les garagistes de l'aérien bénéficient de vents porteurs. *Les Échos* [Online]. Available at: www.lesechos.fr/pme-regions/centre-val-de-loire/les-garagistes-de-laerien-beneficient-de-vents-porteurs-1146579 [Accessed 8 November 2019].

France Stratégie-DARES (2015). Les métiers en 2022. Rapport du groupe Prospective des métiers et qualifications, 114 [Online]. Available at: www.strategie.gouv.fr/sites/strategie.gouv.fr/files/atoms/files/fs_rapport_metiers_en_2022_27042015_final.pdf [Accessed 2 September 2019].

Frydlinger, D., Hart, O., Vitasek, K. (2019). A new approach to contracts. *Harvard Business Review*, 97(5), 116–125.

Gadrey, J. (1992). *L'économie des services*. La Découverte, Paris.

Gadrey, J. (2003). *Socio-économie des services*. La Découverte, Paris.

Gadrey, J. and Gallouj, F. (1998). The provider-customer interface in business and professional services. *The Service Industries Journal*, 18(2), 1–15.

Gallouj, F. (1994). *Économie de l'innovation dans les services*. L'Harmattan, Paris.

Goderis, J.P. (1998). Barrier marketing: From customer satisfaction to customer loyalty. *CEMS Business Review*, 2(4), 285–294.

Goleman, D. (2014). *L'intelligence émotionnelle*. J'ai lu, Paris.

Gotteland, D. (2019). Quel leadership pour implémenter et développer une culture d'orientation marché ? *Décisions Marketing*, 94, 53–70.

Granovetter, M. (1985), Economic action and social structure: The problem of embeddedness. *American Journal of Sociology*, 91(3), 481–510.

Greenstein, S. (2004). The paradox of commodities. *IEEE Micro*, 24(2), 73–75.

Grönross, C. (1999). Le marketing des services : consommation et marketing de processus. *Revue française du marketing*, 197, 9–20.

Grossetti, M. (2001). Les effets de proximité spatiale dans les relations entre organisations : une question d'encastrements. *Espace et Société*, 101, 203–219.

Gruca, T. and Rego, L.L. (2005). Customer satisfaction, cash flow, and shareholder value. *Journal of Marketing*, 69(3), 115–30.

Guibert, N. (1999). La confiance en marketing : fondements et applications. *Recherche et applications en marketing*, 14(1), 1–19.

Gupta, S. and Zeithaml, V. (2006). Customer metrics and their impact on financial performance. *Marketing Science*, 25(6), 687–717.

Häkansson, H. (1982). *International Marketing and Purchasing of Industrial Goods: An Interaction Approach*. John Wiley, Hoboken.

Hartline, M.D., Maxham, J.G., McKee, D.O. (2000). Corridors of influence in the dissemination of customer-oriented strategy to customer contact service employees. *Journal of Marketing*, 64(2), 35–50.

Hausladen, I. and Zipf, T. (2018). Competitive differentiation versus commoditization: The role of big data in the European payments industry. *Journal of Payments Strategy & Systems*, 12(3), 266–282.

Heskett, J.L., Jones, T.O., Loveman, G.W., Sasser, W.E., Schlesinger, L.A. (1994). Putting the service profit chain to work. *Harvard Business Review*, 72(2), 164–170.

Hirschman, E.C. and Holbrook, M.B. (1982). Hedonic consumption: Emerging concepts, methods and propositions. *Journal of Marketing*, 46(3), 92–101.

Holmes, A. (2008). *Commoditization and the Strategic Response*. Gower Publishing, Abingdon.

Homburg, C., Koschate, N., Hoyer, W.D. (2006). The role of cognition and affect in the formation of customer satisfaction: A dynamic perspective. *Journal of Marketing*, 70(3), 21–31.

Ibarra, H. and Scoular, A. (2019). The leader as coach. *Harvard Business Review*, 97(6), 111–119.

INSEE (2018a). Les entreprises en France. INSEE Références, 75 [Online]. Available at: www.insee.fr/fr/statistiques/3639594 [Accessed 2 September 2019].

INSEE (2018b). Les entreprises en France. INSEE Références, 74–75 [Online]. Available at: www.insee.fr/fr/statistiques/3639594 [Accessed 2 September 2019].

INSEE (2018c). Les entreprises en France. INSEE Références, 55 [Online]. Available at: www.insee.fr/fr/statistiques/3639594 [Accessed 2 September 2019].

INSEE (2018d). Les entreprises en France. INSEE Références, 130 [Online]. Available at: www.insee.fr/fr/statistiques/3639594 [Accessed 2 September 2019].

INSEE (2019a). L'économie française – comptes et dossiers [Online]. Available at: www.insee.fr/fr/statistiques/4180914 [Accessed 2 September 2019].

INSEE (2019b). Les services marchands échappent au ralentissement de l'activité en 2018. INSEE Première, 1762 [Online]. Available at: www.insee.fr/fr/ statistiques/4183162 [Accessed 26 August 2019].

Jallat, F. (1994). Innovation dans les services : les facteurs de succès. *Décisions Marketing*, 2, 23–29.

Julienne, E. and Banikema, A. (2017). Vendre à court terme et construire une relation à long terme : les principes d'influence au secours de la vente orientée client. *Décisions Marketing*, 88, 89–104.

Kahneman, D. (2011). *Système 1 /Système 2, les deux vitesses de la pensée*. Flammarion, Paris.

Kankam-Kwarteng, C., Donkor, J., Acheampong, S. (2019). Measuring performance of SME's service firms. *Journal of Management Research*, 19(2), 103–119.

Kapferer, J.N. (1991). *Les marques : capital de l'entreprise*. Éditions d'Organisation, Paris.

Keller, K.L. (1993). Conceptualizing, measuring and managing customer-based brand equity. *Journal of Marketing*, 57(1), 1–22.

Kennedy, K.N., Goolsby, J.R., Arnould, J. (2003). Implementing a customer orientation: Extension of theory and application. *Journal of Marketing*, 67(4), 67–81.

Kirka, A.H., Jayachandran, S., Bearden, W.O. (2005). Market orientation: A meta-analytic review and assessment of its antecedents and impact on performance. *Journal of Marketing*, 69(2), 24–41.

Klemperer, P. (1995). Competition when consumers have switching costs: An overview with applications to industrial organization, macroeconomics and international trade. *Review of Economic Studies*, 62(4), 515–539.

Kohli, A.K. and Jaworski, B.J. (1990). Market orientation: The construct, research propositions, and managerial implications. *Journal of Marketing*, 54(2), 1–18.

Kraljic, P. (1983). Purchasing must become supply management. *Harvard Business Review*, 61(5), 109–117.

Kucera, D. and Roncolato, L. (2016). Dynamique industrie-services et développement économique. *Revue internationale du travail*, 155(2), 167–217.

Kumar, N. (2006). Strategies to fight low-cost rivals. *Harvard Business Review*, 84(12), 104–112.

Kumar, V., Venkatesan, R., Leone, R.P. (2011). Is market orientation a source of sustainable competitive advantage or simply the cost of competing? *Journal of Marketing*, 75(1), 16–30.

Lam, S.K., Kraus, F., Ahearne, M. (2010). The diffusion of market orientation throughout the organization: A social learning theory perspective. *Journal of Marketing*, 74(5), 61–79.

Landier, A. and Thesmar, D. (2013). *10 idées qui coulent la France*. Flammarion, Paris.

Langeard, E. (1987). Essai de formulation de trois concepts d'intermédiation pour la gestion et le développement des activités de services à réseau. Management Science PhD Thesis, Université de droit, d'économie et des sciences d'Aix-Marseille, Institut d'administration des entreprises, Aix-en-Provence.

Lauternborn, R. (1990). New marketing Lithany. *Advertising Age*, 26.

Le Cun, Y. (2019). *Quand la machine apprend : la révolution des neurones artificiels et de l'apprentissage profond*. Odile Jacob, Paris.

Leroux, E. and Chouraqui, E. (2016). *Négociation commerciale, de la théorie à la pratique*. Vuibert, Paris.

Levitt, T. (1960). Marketing myopia. *Harvard Business Review*, 38(4), 45–56.

Levitt, T. (1981). Pour vendre vos produits intangibles, matérialisez-les ! *Harvard l'Expansion*, 107–110.

Liao, H. and Subramony, M. (2008). Employee customer orientation in manufacturing organizations: Joint influences of customer proximity and the senior leadership team. *Journal of Applied Psychology*, 93(2), 317–328.

Lovelock, C.H. (1996). *Services Marketing*. Prentice Hall, Upper Saddle River.

Loye, D. (2019). Welcome To The Jungle continue son développement européen. *Les Échos* [Online]. Available at: https://business.lesechos.fr/entrepreneurs/financer-sa-creation/0602126983440-welcome-to-the-jungle-continue-son-developpement-europeen-332679.php [Accessed 29 October 2019].

Maman, C., Jougleux, M., Abramovici, M., Bancel-Charensol, L. (2009). *L'innovation dans les services de proximité : enjeux, cadre d'analyse et premiers résultats*. AIMS, Grenoble.

Matsuno, K. and Mentzer, J.T. (2000). The effects of strategy type on the market orientation – Performance relationship. *Journal of Marketing*, 64(4), 1–16.

Matthyssens, P. and Vandenbempt, K. (2008). Moving from basic offerings to value-added solutions: Strategies, barriers and alignment. *Industrial Marketing Management*, 37(3), 316–328.

Mehrabian, A. and Ferris, S.R. (1967). Inference of attitudes from nonverbal communication in two channels. *Journal of Consulting Psychology*, 31(3), 248–252.

Mehrabian, A. and Wiener, M. (1967). Decoding of inconsistent communications. *Journal of Personality and Social Psychology*, 6(1), 109–114.

Meyronin, B., Grassin, M., Benavent, C. (2019). *Repenser vraiment l'humain au cœur de l'entreprise – le management par le care*. Vuibert, Paris.

Michel, D., Salle, R., Valla, J.P. (1996). *Marketing Industriel*. Economica, Paris.

Mullins, R.R., Ahearne, M., Lam, S.K., Hall, Z.R., Boichuk, J.P. (2014). Know your customer: How salesperson perceptions of customer relationship quality form and influence account profitability. *Journal of Marketing*, 78(6), 38–58.

Narver, J.C. and Slater, S.F. (1990). The effect of market orientation on business profitability. *Journal of Marketing*, 54(4), 20–35.

Narver, J.C., Slater, S.F., MacLachlan, D. (2004). Responsive and proactive market orientation and new-product success. *Journal of Product Innovation Management*, 21, 334–347.

Nayar, V. (2010). *Employees First, Customers Second*. Harvard Business School Press, Boston.

Ngobo, P.V. and Ramaroson, A. (2005). Facteurs déterminants de la relation entre la satisfaction des clients et la performance de l'entreprise. *Décisions Marketing*, 40, 75–84.

Oliver, R.L. (1980). A cognitive model of the antecedents and consequences of satisfaction decisions. *Journal of Marketing Research*, 17(4), 460–469.

Oliver, R.L. (1997). *Satisfaction*. McGraw-Hill, New York.

Oliver, R.L. (1999). Whence consumer loyalty? *Journal of Marketing*, 63(special issue), 33–44.

Oliver, R.L., Varki, S., Rust, R.T. (1997). Customer delight: Foundations, findings, and managerial insight. *Journal of Retailing*, 73(3), 311–336.

Olson, E.G. and Sharma, D. (2008). Beating the commoditization trend: A framework from the electronics industry. *Journal of Business Strategy*, 29(4), 22–28.

Parasuraman, A., Zeithaml, V.A., Berry, L.L. (1985). A conceptual model of service quality and its implication for future research. *Journal of Marketing*, 49(4), 41–50.

Pekovick, S. and Rolland, S. (2012). L'impact de l'orientation client sur la performance des entreprises françaises : étude empirique des effets directs et modérateurs. *Recherche et applications en marketing*, 27(4), 11–38.

Piercy, N.F., Harris, L.C., Lane, N. (2002). Market orientation and retail operatives' expectations. *Journal of Business Research*, 55, 261–273.

Pine, B.J. and Gilmore, J.H. (1999). *The Experience Economy: Work is Theater and Every Business is a Stage*. Harvard Business School Press, Boston.

Poujol, F. and Siadou-Martin, B. (2012). Quand l'orientation client du vendeur conduit au développement de la relation : le rôle modérateur de la propension relationnelle du client. *Gestion 2000*, 29(2), 87–103.

Prahalad, C.K. and Ramaswamy, V. (2000). Co-opting customer competence. *Harvard Business Review*, 78(1), 79–90.

Rauyruen, P. and Miller, K.E. (2007). Relationship quality as a predictor of B2B customer loyalty. *Journal of Business Research*, 60(1), 21–31.

Reichheld, F.F. (1996). *L'effet loyauté*. Dunod, Paris.

Reimann, M., Schilke, O., Thomas, J.S. (2010). Toward an understanding of industry commoditization: Its nature and role in evolving marketing competition. *International Journal of Research in Marketing*, 27(2), 188–197.

Ries, A. and Trout, J. (1972). The positioning era cometh. *Advertising Age*, 24th April.

Ritzer, G. and Jurgenson, N. (2010). Production, consumption, prosumption: The nature of capitalism in the age of the digital "prosumer". *Journal of Consumer Culture*, 10(1), 13–36.

Romero, J. and Yague, M.J. (2015). Relating brand equity and customer equity: An exploratory study. *International Journal of Market Research*, 57(4), 631–652.

Salesforce Research (2019). State of the connected customer [Online]. Available at: www.salesforce.com/company/news-press/stories/2019/06/061219-g/ [Accessed 18 September 2019].

Santi, M. and Nguyen, V. (2012). *Le business model du low cost : comprendre, appliquer et contrecarrer*. Eyrolles, Paris.

Sasser, W.E., Olsen, R.P., Wyckoff, D.D. (1978). *Management of Service Operations: Texts, Cases, and Readings*. Allyn & Bacon, Boston.

Seiders, K., Voss, G., Grewal, D., Godfrey, A. (2005). Do satisfied customers buy more? Examining moderating influences in a retailing context. *Journal of Marketing*, 69(4), 26–43.

Shank, J.K. and Govindarajan, V. (1992). Strategic cost management: The value chain perspective. *Journal of Management Accounting Research*, 4, 179–199.

Slater, S.F. and Narver, J.C. (2000). Intelligence generation and superior customer value. *Journal of the Academy of Marketing Science*, 28(1), 120–127.

Sousa, C.M.P. and Coelho, F. (2013). Exploring the relationship between individual values and the customer orientation of front-line employees. *Journal of Marketing Management*, 29(15–16), 1653–1679.

The Boston Consulting Group (2015). Industry 4.0. The future of productivity and growth in manufacturing industries [Online]. Available at: www.bcg.com/fr/ publications/2015/engineered_products_project_business_industry_4_future_ productivity_growth_manufacturing_industries.aspx [Accessed 10 February 2020].

Toman, N., Adamson, B., Gomez, C. (2017). The new sales imperative. *Harvard Business Review*, 95(2), 117–125.

Torrès, O. (2003). Petitesse des entreprises et grossissement des effets de proximité. *Revue française de gestion*, 144, 119–138.

Touraine, A. (1969). *La société post-industrielle*. Denoël Gonthier, Paris.

Tuli, K., Kohli, A., Bharadwaj, S.G. (2007). Rethinking customer solutions: From product bundles to relational processes. *Journal of Marketing*, 71(3), 1–17.

Turnbull, P.W. and Valla, J.P. (1986). *Strategies for International Industrial Marketing: The Management of Customer Relationships in European Industrial Markets*. Croom Helm Ltd, Routledge, Abingdon-on-Thames.

Turnbull, P.W. and Wilson, D.T. (1989). Developing and protecting profitable customer relationships. *Industrial Marketing Management*, 18(3), 233–238.

Valla, J.P. (1978). Une analyse du comportement de l'acheteur industriel. *Revue française de gestion*, 17, 77–84.

Viau, J., Sassi, H., Pujet, H. (2015). *La négociation commerciale*. Dunod, Paris.

Viot, C. (2018). Ubérisation des services : les clients sont-ils toujours gagnants ? *Vie et sciences de l'entreprise*, 205, 23–47.

Webster, F.E. (1988). Rediscovering the marketing concept. *Business Horizons*, 31, 29–39.

Weick, K.E. (1995). Sensemaking in organizations. *Sociologie du travail*, 38(2), 225–232.

Westbrook, R. (1987). Product/consumption-based affective responses and postpurchase processes. *Journal of Marketing Research*, 24(3), 258–270.

Williams, L.E., Stein, R., Galguera, L. (2014). The distinct affective consequences of psychological distance and construal level. *Journal of Consumer Research*, 40(6), 1123–1138.

Williamson, O.E. (1975). *Markets and Hierarchy*. The Free Press, New York.

Williamson, O.E. (1985). *The Economic Institution of Capitalism*. The Free Press, New York.

Wind, Y. and Cardozo, R.N. (1974). Industrial market segmentation. *Industrial Marketing Management*, 3(3), 153–165.

Wolter, J.S., Bock, D., Mackey, J., Xu, P., Smith, J.S. (2019). Employee satisfaction trajectories and their effect on customer satisfaction. *Journal of the Academy of Marketing Science*, 47(5), 815–836.

Zablah, A.R., Franke, G.R., Brown, T.J. (2012). How and when does customer orientation influence frontline employee job outcomes? A metaanalytic evaluation. *Journal of Marketing*, 76(3), 21–40.

Zeithaml, V.A. and Bitner, M.J. (1996). *Services Marketing*. McGraw-Hill, New York.

Zeithaml, V.A., Bitner, M.J., Gremler, D.D. (2017). *Services Marketing – Integrating Customer Focus Across the Firm*. McGraw-Hill, New York.

Index

Other titles from

in

Innovation, Entrepreneurship and Management

2021

ARCADE Jacques
Strategic Engineering (Innovation and Technology Set – Volume 11)

BÉRANGER Jérôme, RIZOULIÈRES Roland
The Digital Revolution in Health (Health and Innovation Set – Volume 2)

BOBILLIER CHAUMON Marc-Eric
Digital Transformations in the Challenge of Activity and Work:
Understanding and Supporting Technological Changes
(Technological Changes and Human Resources Set – Volume 3)

BUCLET Nicolas
Territorial Ecology and Socio-ecological Transition
(Smart Innovation Set – Volume 34)

LIMA Marcos
Entrepreneurship and Innovation Education: Frameworks and Tools
(Smart Innovation Set – Volume 32)

MACHADO Carolina, DAVIM J. Paulo
Sustainable Management for Managers and Engineers

MAKRIDES Andreas, KARAGRIGORIOU Alex, SKIADAS Christos H.
Data Analysis and Applications 3: Computational, Classification, Financial,
Statistical and Stochastic Methods
(Big Data, Artificial Intelligence and Data Analysis Set – Volume 5)
Data Analysis and Applications 4: Financial Data Analysis and Methods
(Big Data, Artificial Intelligence and Data Analysis Set – Volume 6)

MASSOTTE Pierre, CORSI Patrick
Complex Decision-Making in Economy and Finance

MEUNIER François-Xavier
Dual Innovation Systems: Concepts, Tools and Methods
(Smart Innovation Set – Volume 31)

MICHAUD Thomas
Science Fiction and Innovation Design (Innovation in Engineering and
Technology Set – Volume 6)

MONINO Jean-Louis
Data Control: Major Challenge for the Digital Society
(Smart Innovation Set – Volume 29)

MORLAT Clément
Sustainable Productive System: Eco-development versus Sustainable
Development (Smart Innovation Set – Volume 26)

SAULAIS Pierre, ERMINE Jean-Louis
Knowledge Management in Innovative Companies 2: Understanding and
Deploying a KM Plan within a Learning Organization
(Smart Innovation Set – Volume 27)

2019

AMENDOLA Mario, GAFFARD Jean-Luc
Disorder and Public Concern Around Globalization

BARBAROUX Pierre
Disruptive Technology and Defence Innovation Ecosystems
(Innovation in Engineering and Technology Set – Volume 5)

DOU Henri, JUILLET Alain, CLERC Philippe
Strategic Intelligence for the Future 1: A New Strategic and Operational Approach
Strategic Intelligence for the Future 2: A New Information Function Approach

FRIKHA Azza
Measurement in Marketing: Operationalization of Latent Constructs

FRIMOUSSE Soufyane
Innovation and Agility in the Digital Age
(Human Resources Management Set – Volume 2)

GAY Claudine, SZOSTAK Bérangère L.
Innovation and Creativity in SMEs: Challenges, Evolutions and Prospects
(Smart Innovation Set – Volume 21)

GORIA Stéphane, HUMBERT Pierre, ROUSSEL Benoît
Information, Knowledge and Agile Creativity
(Smart Innovation Set – Volume 22)

HELLER David
Investment Decision-making Using Optional Models
(Economic Growth Set – Volume 2)

HELLER David, DE CHADIRAC Sylvain, HALAOUI Lana, JOUVET Camille
The Emergence of Start-ups
(Economic Growth Set – Volume 1)

HÉRAUD Jean-Alain, KERR Fiona, BURGER-HELMCHEN Thierry
Creative Management of Complex Systems
(Smart Innovation Set – Volume 19)

LATOUCHE Pascal
Open Innovation: Corporate Incubator
(Innovation and Technology Set – Volume 7)

LEHMANN Paul-Jacques
The Future of the Euro Currency

LEIGNEL Jean-Louis, MENAGER Emmanuel, YABLONSKY Serge
Sustainable Enterprise Performance: A Comprehensive Evaluation Method

LIÈVRE Pascal, AUBRY Monique, GAREL Gilles
Management of Extreme Situations: From Polar Expeditions to Exploration-Oriented Organizations

MILLOT Michel
Embarrassment of Product Choices 2: Towards a Society of Well-being

N'GOALA Gilles, PEZ-PÉRARD Virginie, PRIM-ALLAZ Isabelle
Augmented Customer Strategy: CRM in the Digital Age

NIKOLOVA Blagovesta
The RRI Challenge: Responsibilization in a State of Tension with Market Regulation
(Innovation and Responsibility Set – Volume 3)

PELLEGRIN-BOUCHER Estelle, ROY Pierre
Innovation in the Cultural and Creative Industries
(Innovation and Technology Set – Volume 8)

PRIOLON Joël
Financial Markets for Commodities

QUINIOU Matthieu
Blockchain: The Advent of Disintermediation

RAVIX Joël-Thomas, DESCHAMPS Marc
Innovation and Industrial Policies
(Innovation between Risk and Reward Set – Volume 5)

ROGER Alain, VINOT Didier
Skills Management: New Applications, New Questions
(Human Resources Management Set – Volume 1)

SAULAIS Pierre, ERMINE Jean-Louis
Knowledge Management in Innovative Companies 1: Understanding and Deploying a KM Plan within a Learning Organization
(Smart Innovation Set – Volume 23)

SERVAJEAN-HILST Romaric
Co-innovation Dynamics: The Management of Client-Supplier Interactions for Open Innovation
(Smart Innovation Set – Volume 20)

SKIADAS Christos H., BOZEMAN James R.
Data Analysis and Applications 1: Clustering and Regression, Modeling-estimating, Forecasting and Data Mining
(Big Data, Artificial Intelligence and Data Analysis Set – Volume 2)
Data Analysis and Applications 2: Utilization of Results in Europe and Other Topics
(Big Data, Artificial Intelligence and Data Analysis Set – Volume 3)

UZUNIDIS Dimitri
Systemic Innovation: Entrepreneurial Strategies and Market Dynamics

VIGEZZI Michel
World Industrialization: Shared Inventions, Competitive Innovations and Social Dynamics
(Smart Innovation Set – Volume 24)

2018

BURKHARDT Kirsten
Private Equity Firms: Their Role in the Formation of Strategic Alliances

CALLENS Stéphane
Creative Globalization
(Smart Innovation Set – Volume 16)

CASADELLA Vanessa
Innovation Systems in Emerging Economies: MINT – Mexico, Indonesia, Nigeria, Turkey
(Smart Innovation Set – Volume 18)

UZUNIDIS Dimitri, SAULAIS Pierre
*Innovation Engines: Entrepreneurs and Enterprises in a Turbulent World
(Innovation in Engineering and Technology Set – Volume 1)*

2016

BARBAROUX Pierre, ATTOUR Amel, SCHENK Eric
*Knowledge Management and Innovation
(Smart Innovation Set – Volume 6)*

BEN BOUHENI Faten, AMMI Chantal, LEVY Aldo
*Banking Governance, Performance And Risk-Taking: Conventional Banks
Vs Islamic Banks*

BOUTILLIER Sophie, CARRÉ Denis, LEVRATTO Nadine
Entrepreneurial Ecosystems (Smart Innovation Set – Volume 2)

BOUTILLIER Sophie, UZUNIDIS Dimitri
The Entrepreneur (Smart Innovation Set – Volume 8)

BOUVARD Patricia, SUZANNE Hervé
Collective Intelligence Development in Business

GALLAUD Delphine, LAPERCHE Blandine
*Circular Economy, Industrial Ecology and Short Supply Chains
(Smart Innovation Set – Volume 4)*

GUERRIER Claudine
*Security and Privacy in the Digital Era
(Innovation and Technology Set – Volume 1)*

MEGHOUAR Hicham
Corporate Takeover Targets

MONINO Jean-Louis, SEDKAOUI Soraya
*Big Data, Open Data and Data Development
(Smart Innovation Set – Volume 3)*

MOREL Laure, LE ROUX Serge
*Fab Labs: Innovative User
(Smart Innovation Set – Volume 5)*

PICARD Fabienne, TANGUY Corinne
Innovations and Techno-ecological Transition
(Smart Innovation Set – Volume 7)

2015

CASADELLA Vanessa, LIU Zeting, DIMITRI Uzunidis
Innovation Capabilities and Economic Development in Open Economies
(Smart Innovation Set – Volume 1)

CORSI Patrick, MORIN Dominique
Sequencing Apple's DNA

CORSI Patrick, NEAU Erwan
Innovation Capability Maturity Model

FAIVRE-TAVIGNOT Bénédicte
Social Business and Base of the Pyramid

GODÉ Cécile
Team Coordination in Extreme Environments

MAILLARD Pierre
Competitive Quality and Innovation

MASSOTTE Pierre, CORSI Patrick
Operationalizing Sustainability

MASSOTTE Pierre, CORSI Patrick
Sustainability Calling

2014

DUBÉ Jean, LEGROS Diègo
Spatial Econometrics Using Microdata

LESCA Humbert, LESCA Nicolas
Strategic Decisions and Weak Signals

2013

HABART-CORLOSQUET Marine, JANSSEN Jacques, MANCA Raimondo
VaR Methodology for Non-Gaussian Finance

2012

DAL PONT Jean-Pierre
Process Engineering and Industrial Management

MAILLARD Pierre
Competitive Quality Strategies

POMEROL Jean-Charles
Decision-Making and Action

SZYLAR Christian
UCITS Handbook

2011

LESCA Nicolas
Environmental Scanning and Sustainable Development

LESCA Nicolas, LESCA Humbert
Weak Signals for Strategic Intelligence: Anticipation Tool for Managers

MERCIER-LAURENT Eunika
Innovation Ecosystems

2010

SZYLAR Christian
Risk Management under UCITS III/IV

2009

COHEN Corine
Business Intelligence

ZANINETTI Jean-Marc
Sustainable Development in the USA

2008

CORSI Patrick, DULIEU Mike
The Marketing of Technology Intensive Products and Services

DZEVER Sam, JAUSSAUD Jacques, ANDREOSSO Bernadette
Evolving Corporate Structures and Cultures in Asia: Impact of Globalization

2007

AMMI Chantal
Global Consumer Behavior

2006

BOUGHZALA Imed, ERMINE Jean-Louis
Trends in Enterprise Knowledge Management

CORSI Patrick *et al.*
Innovation Engineering: the Power of Intangible Networks

Printed and bound by CPI Group (UK) Ltd, Croydon, CR0 4YY